I0002838

Exam Ref DP-600 Implementing Analytics Solutions Using Microsoft Fabric

Daniil Maslyuk
Johnny Winter
Štěpán Rešl

Exam Ref DP-600 Implementing Analytics Solutions Using Microsoft Fabric

Published with the authorization of Microsoft Corporation by:
Pearson Education, Inc.

Copyright © 2025 by Pearson Education, Inc.

Hoboken, New Jersey

All rights reserved. This publication is protected by copyright, and permission must be obtained from the publisher prior to any prohibited reproduction, storage in a retrieval system, or transmission in any form or by any means, electronic, mechanical, photocopying, recording, or likewise. For information regarding permissions, request forms, and the appropriate contacts within the Pearson Education Global Rights & Permissions Department, please visit www.pearson.com/permissions.

No patent liability is assumed with respect to the use of the information contained herein. Although every precaution has been taken in the preparation of this book, the publisher and author assume no responsibility for errors or omissions. Nor is any liability assumed for damages resulting from the use of the information contained herein.

ISBN-13: 978-0-13-533602-1
ISBN-10: 0-13-533602-3

Library of Congress Control Number: 2024912313

$PrintCode

TRADEMARKS

Microsoft and the trademarks listed at http://www.microsoft.com on the "Trademarks" webpage are trademarks of the Microsoft group of companies. All other marks are property of their respective owners.

WARNING AND DISCLAIMER

Every effort has been made to make this book as complete and as accurate as possible, but no warranty or fitness is implied. The information provided is on an "as is" basis. The author, the publisher, and Microsoft Corporation shall have neither liability nor responsibility to any person or entity with respect to any loss or damages arising from the information contained in this book or from the use of the programs accompanying it.

SPECIAL SALES

For information about buying this title in bulk quantities, or for special sales opportunities (which may include electronic versions; custom cover designs; and content particular to your business, training goals, marketing focus, or branding interests), please contact our corporate sales department at corpsales@pearsoned.com or (800) 382-3419.

For government sales inquiries, please contact governmentsales@pearsoned.com.

For questions about sales outside the U.S., please contact intlcs@pearson.com.

CREDITS

EDITOR-IN-CHIEF
Brett Bartow

EXECUTIVE EDITOR
Loretta Yates

ASSOCIATE EDITOR
Shourav Bose

DEVELOPMENT EDITOR
Songlin Qiu

MANAGING EDITOR
Sandra Schroeder

SENIOR PROJECT EDITOR
Tracey Croom

COPY EDITOR
Linda Laflamme

INDEXER
Timothy Wright

PROOFREADER
Donna E. Mulder

TECHNICAL EDITOR
Nuric Ugarte

EDITORIAL ASSISTANT
Cindy Teeters

COVER DESIGNER
Twist Creative, Seattle

COMPOSITOR
codeMantra

GRAPHICS
codeMantra

FIGURE CREDIT
Figure 2.38 The Apache Software Foundation

Contents at a glance

Contents

Chapter 2   Prepare and serve data   61

Acknowledgments

Daniil Maslyuk

I'd like to acknowledge the team at Pearson who made this book happen, including Loretta Yates, who trusted us to write this book, and Shourav Bose, who managed the project. Songlin, Nuric, and Linda, the editors, made this book a better read. And I'd like to thank my co-authors, Johnny and Štěpán, without whom I wouldn't have been able to write this book.

Johnny Winter

I'd like to thank my co-authors Daniil and Štěpán for their ongoing advice and support, and Daniil in particular for inviting me to join the project. Thanks to our sponsoring editor Shourav for his support and patience. Special thanks to my wife Amanda for being supportive and allowing me the time and space to complete my contributions to the book, which often ate into our spare time. I'd also like to thank my employers, Advancing Analytics, a great bunch of colleagues and, dare I say it, friends. They have supported me in attending Fabric community events, given me the opportunity to get hands on with Fabric and learn the platform end to end, and supported me with my Fabric Analytics Engineer certification.

Štěpán Rešl

I want to acknowledge my friends and colleagues from DataBrothers for their endless support and encouragement in co-authoring this book and for allowing me to share my thoughts and ideas: Adam, Róza, Míra, Janek, and Lukáš. I especially want to thank my brother Matěj, who stood behind me all the time and helped me organize everything in my work schedule so that I could participate in this book. I also would like to thank my co-authors Daniil and Johnny for their support, cheerful mindset, and advice during this whole project.

About the Authors

DANIIL MASLYUK is an independent business intelligence consultant, trainer, and speaker who specializes in Microsoft Power BI. Daniil blogs at xxlbi.com and tweets as @DMaslyuk.

JOHNNY WINTER is a data and analytics consultant who has been working with business intelligence software since 2007, specializing in the Microsoft data platform since 2016. He's a self-confessed business intelligence geek, and in his spare time runs the website and YouTube channel *Greyskull Analytics*, where he likes to nerd out about all things analytics.

ŠTĚPÁN REŠL is a lead technical consultant and a Microsoft MVP in the Data Platform category. As a technical consultant, Štěpán focuses on assisting medium and large organizations in deploying and maintaining their data solutions. He is also a speaker and co-organizer of conferences. In his spare time, he runs a blog called *DataMeerkat*, where he focuses on topics related to data analytics.

Introduction

This book covers all the skills measured in the exam DP-600: Implementing Analytics Solutions Using Microsoft Fabric. In each chapter, you'll find a combination of step-by-step instructional content and related high-level theoretical material. The aim is to show you the settings you need to select and buttons you need to click to carry out the tasks required, as well as to cover key concepts that you need to understand when designing an analytics solution. Ultimately, we cover not only the how, but also the why.

This book covers every major topic area found on the exam, but it does not cover every exam question. Only the Microsoft exam team has access to the exam questions, and Microsoft regularly adds new questions to the exam, making it impossible to cover specific questions. You should consider this book a supplement to your relevant real-world experience and other study materials. If you encounter a topic in this book that you do not feel completely comfortable with, use the "Need more review?" links you'll find in the text to find more information and take the time to research and study the topic.

Organization of this book

This book is organized by the "Skills measured" list published for the exam. The "Skills measured" list is available for each exam on the Microsoft Learn website: *microsoft.com/learn*. Each chapter in this book corresponds to a major topic area in the list, and the technical tasks in each topic area determine a chapter's organization. If an exam covers six major topic areas, for example, the book will contain six chapters.

Preparing for the exam

Microsoft certification exams are a great way to build your resume and let the world know about your level of expertise. Certification exams validate your on-the-job experience and product knowledge. Although there is no substitute for on-the-job experience, preparation through study and hands-on practice can help you prepare for the exam. This book is *not* designed to teach you new skills.

We recommend that you augment your exam preparation plan by using a combination of available study materials and courses. For example, you might use the *Exam Ref* and another study guide for your at-home preparation and take a Microsoft Official Curriculum course for the classroom experience. Choose the combination that you think works best for you. Learn more about available classroom training, online courses, and live events at *microsoft.com/learn*.

Note that this *Exam Ref* is based on publicly available information about the exam and the authors' experience. To safeguard the integrity of the exam, authors do not have access to the live exam.

Microsoft certifications

Microsoft certifications distinguish you by proving your command of a broad set of skills and experience with current Microsoft products and technologies. The exams and corresponding certifications are developed to validate your mastery of critical competencies as you design and develop, or implement and support, solutions with Microsoft products and technologies both on-premises and in the cloud. Certification brings a variety of benefits to the individual and to employers and organizations.

> **MORE INFO   ALL MICROSOFT CERTIFICATIONS**
>
> For information about Microsoft certifications, including a full list of available certifications, go to *microsoft.com/learn*.

Access the exam updates chapter and online references

The final chapter of this book, "Exam DP-600: Implementing Analytics Solutions Using Microsoft Fabric updates," will provide information about changes to content, such as additions of new exam topics, removal of content from the exam objectives, and revised mapping of exam objectives to chapter content. The chapter will be made available from the link below as exam updates are released.

Throughout this book are addresses to webpages that the author has recommended you visit for more information. Some of these links can be very long and painstaking to type, so we've shortened them for you to make them easier to visit. We've also compiled them into a single list that readers of the print edition can refer to while they read.

The URLs are organized by chapter and heading. Every time you come across a URL in the book, find the hyperlink in the list to go directly to the webpage.

Download the Exam Updates chapter and the URL list at *MicrosoftPressStore.com/ERDP600/downloads*.

Errata, updates, & book support

We've made every effort to ensure the accuracy of this book and its companion content. You can access updates to this book—in the form of a list of submitted errata and their related corrections—at:

MicrosoftPressStore.com/ERDP600/errata

If you discover an error that is not already listed, please submit it to us at the same page.

For additional book support and information, please visit *MicrosoftPressStore.com/Support*.

Please note that product support for Microsoft software and hardware is not offered through the previous addresses. For help with Microsoft software or hardware, go to *support.microsoft.com*.

Stay in touch

Let's keep the conversation going! We're on X/Twitter: *twitter.com/MicrosoftPress*.

CHAPTER 1

Plan, implement, and manage a solution for data analytics

The first step on your Microsoft Fabric journey is to set up your Fabric environment. You will need to plan which items your solution will use, the settings you will need to configure, which Fabric tier to buy, and how you will manage development activities and security for your solution.

This chapter will provide comprehensive options for planning and setting up your governance. By using the individual Fabric components each for their purpose, you can achieve not only a functioning ecosystem, but also an overview understanding of the process involved.

Skills covered in this chapter:

- Skill 1.1: Plan a data analytics environment
- Skill 1.2: Implement and manage a data analytics environment
- Skill 1.3: Manage the analytics development lifecycle

Skill 1.1: Plan a data analytics environment

When planning your solution, you first need to identify the necessary items, which will vary depending on your requirements and the skillset of the team delivering them. You will also need to decide which Fabric capacity (or capacities) to purchase.

Understanding your options and planning the settings according to the appropriate groups is a good approach. If you review everything regularly, you can be sure that the settings conform to your organization policies.

This skill covers how to:

- Identify requirements for a solution, including components, features, performance, and capacity stock-keeping units (SKUs)
- Recommend settings in the Fabric admin portal
- Choose a data gateway type
- Create a custom Power BI report theme

Identify requirements for a solution, including components, features, performance, and capacity stock-keeping units (SKUs)

Fabric contains several experiences including Data Factory, Synapse Data Engineering, Synapse Data Warehouse, Synapse Data Science, Power BI and Real-Time Intelligence.

The DP-600 exam focuses on the following subset of items within these experiences:

- Lakehouses
- Data warehouses
- Notebooks
- Dataflows
- Data pipelines
- Semantic models
- Reports

These are the areas and items within Fabric that an analytics engineer is typically concerned with. Don't worry, you're not expected to understand every component inside of every experience!

However, even with this narrower scope, there is not necessarily one right way to do things (though there may be some wrong ways!). The shape of your data analytics solution may vary depending on your requirements and other factors:

- **Data volume**   How much data do you need to onboard to your solution? Dataflows are limited to 50 queries so are suitable for low volumes. Data pipelines can handle a larger volume and offer more flexibility in terms of parameterization and re-use so lend themselves to more scalable metadata driven and automated solutions.

- **Data variety**   For storing data, Fabric leverages the delta file format across all experiences. As a first processing step, however, you may need to land your data in a variety of file formats. Lakehouses are better suited to landing semi-structured and unstructured file types, such as JSON, whereas a data warehouse handles structured data in tables and schemas far better.

- **Data velocity**   How quickly you need to process your data may play a factor in which items you decide to use. Data pipelines and dataflows lend themselves to batch processing, but if you need to stream data in real time, then you might consider event streams (though these are not explicitly covered in the scope of this exam).

- **Data security**   Using a lakehouse or data warehouse as an access point for your data provides differing security features. Data warehouses offer additional features, such as dynamic data masking and object-, column-, and row-level security. Lakehouses have row- and table-level security for the T-SQL endpoint but are less secure if utilizing Spark. Further details of the security considerations when using Spark are discussed later in this chapter under Skill 1.2, in the "Implement data sharing for workspaces, warehouses, and lakehouses" section.

You also need to consider the skillsets of the individuals who will build the solution. Those familiar with Spark and Python will be comfortable with using notebooks for data transformation tasks, whilst those more at home using T-SQL may prefer to use stored procedures with data warehouses. Citizen developers building smaller solutions may prefer dataflows, especially if they are already familiar with using Power Query. None of these are exclusive choices. You can mix and match objects in different parts of your solution.

All of this is without yet considering your Fabric capacity (or capacities, as you may wish to split your workloads over more than one). You will need to purchase capacity from which to operate the workloads for your solution, and choosing the right one (or ones) for your solution requires some thought. For example, the compute power available for each Fabric stock-keeping unit (SKU) is measured in Capacity Unit seconds (CUs). The more compute required, the more CUs you will require. Those compute requirements will be dependent on the volume and cadence of your data loads, the complexity of your transformations, the complexity of semantic model calculations, and the throughput of users querying the semantic model. You may decide that it's worth purchasing more than one capacity to allow you to manage these various workloads separately.

Fabric workloads are provisioned on Fabric SKUs. The Fabric SKUs, also known as F SKUs are billed per second with no commitment, meaning you can pause and resume the capacity as you see fit and pay only for when it is in use. There is also a reserved pricing tier available for F SKUs, which gives a discount if committing to keep the capacity always on.

Table 1-1 lists the available SKUs and their associated CU allocation.

TABLE 1-1 Fabric SKUs

Fabric SKU	CUs
F2	2
F4	4
F8	8
F16	16
F32	32
F64	64
F128	128
F256	256
F512	512
F1024	1024
F2048	2048

The CUs consumption is not a hard limit per SKU. It is based on an average over a 24-hour period, giving you the ability to take advantage of bursting and smoothing. *Bursting* allows you to use additional compute resources to handle spikes in capacity requirements over short periods of time, and *smoothing* then pays back that additional compute consumption when the capacity is less in demand. So, for a given operation an F64 SKU, for example, can use more than 64 CUs, so long as that usage averages out over the day.

Currently, there is no authoritative guide to help you calculate the CUs you will need for your solution. Microsoft recommends experimenting to figure out the best fit. Using the **Microsoft Fabric Capacity Metrics** app is your best means of monitoring your CUs usage to better understand how many CUs are required for operating your solution and whether you might want to consider scaling up or scaling out your Fabric SKU(s).

Beyond the CU requirement, there are other licensing elements worth considering too. F64 SKUs and above include unlimited Power BI licenses for viewing content (you still need a Pro license to publish and edit content) as well as Copilot features.

The final constraint to consider is the budget. SKUs with a higher CU allocation come with increased costs, and whilst everyone would prefer their solutions to operate on the most powerful kit, you must ultimately compromise between the amount of money you are prepared to spend versus the level of performance that is good enough.

> **NEED MORE REVIEW?** **MICROSOFT FABRIC PRICING**
>
> Pricing details for Microsoft Fabric SKUs are available at *azure.microsoft.com/en-us/pricing/details/microsoft-fabric*.

Recommend settings in the Fabric admin portal

To use the Fabric Service, you must first enable it within the admin portal in the **Tenant Settings** section, which you can access with the Fabric admin (historically Power BI admin) permission assigned to the account within Entra ID or using the O365/M365 Admin portal. To access the admin portal, click the **gear** icon (alias Settings) next to your profile icon. This option will be hidden behind the **ellipsis** icon if you have a lower screen resolution or a smaller application window. You will see a sidebar where the **admin portal link** is located in the **Governance and Insights** section. All users can see and use this link, but only users with the aforementioned permissions will also see the Tenant Settings section. The Tenant Settings page is divided into sections for more straightforward navigation.

Individual settings are being updated, and new ones are being added on a regular basis, so it is a good idea to audit and check them regularly (for example, once per month) to ensure that everything is always set according to your organization's policies and requirements.

Fabric settings

The Microsoft Fabric section in the admin portal contains three settings. Shown in Figure 1-1, the **Users can create Fabric items** setting allows you to start creating individual Fabric items within Power BI workspaces. It has four possible states:

- Enabled for all users
- Enabled for a subset of organizations using defined security groups
- Enabled for all users *except* specific security groups
- Prohibited for all users

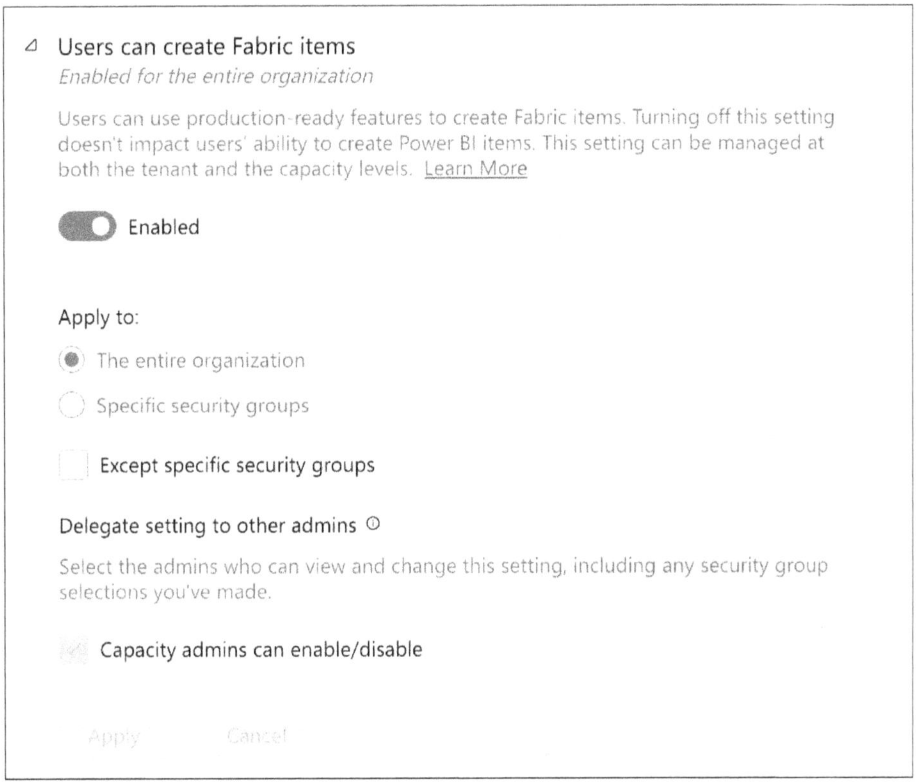

FIGURE 1-1 Expanded view of the User can create Fabric items setting

If this setting is disabled, it does not restrict Power BI users or developers who use purely Power BI Items. This setting also has delegation capacity, which allows it to be subsequently modified within Individual capacities.

As mentioned earlier, the setup allows users or the entire company to use the Data Factory, Data Engineering, Data Science, Data Warehouse, and Real-Time Analytics experiences. To activate the persona's Data Activator and thus enable the creation of Reflex-type items, you can set the **Data Activator** setting in the same way as **User can create Fabric items**.

Finally, the **Users can create Fabric environments to save and apply Spark settings** setting allows users to create environments in which they can set up Spark runtimes, compute resources, and libraries for themselves and their colleagues in each workspace, which should be pre-installed for developing items from a Data Engineering or Data Science experience.

All three settings allow you to unlock individual Fabric options and specify specific options for the respective users. Each item uses an associated capacity, so think about the strategy with which these options will be allocated or whether they will be automatic for all users. Doing so will help you with long-term planning of these capacities.

In the Help and Support settings section, **Users can try Microsoft Fabric paid features** is enabled by default. It allows a subset of users or all of all to activate a trial Fabric capacity for 60 days and use it to test individual Fabric options. If the **Users can create Fabric items** setting is enabled also, users create Fabric items. Any capacity activated as a trial is labeled FT1 and, from a resource's standpoint, is very similar to the paid capacity F64.

Workspace settings

The Workspace settings control whether users can create workspaces, how long workspaces will be kept after deletion for possible restoration, and whether users can reset their My Workspace capacity from the admin's assigned capacity.

In addition, the **Use semantic models across workspaces** setting allows selected developers to use semantic models in other workspaces on which they have Build permission. This applies to creating composite models from different workspaces, placing reports and semantic models in different workspaces, and copying a report to another workspace. The permissions set within the semantic model are respected, so if a user has access to a report but does not have access to its semantic model, they will not be able to view the report's content.

Information Protection settings

The Information Protection section focuses on the possibility of using Microsoft Purview Information Protection Sensitivity Labels within Fabric and Power BI items, as shown in Figure 1-2. Be aware, you cannot create protection labels here; you can only set whether existing labels can be used.

FIGURE 1-2 Information Protection Sensitivity Label applied on a report

The first setting, **Allow users to apply Sensitivity Labels for content**, allows specific users to assign or change protection labels on an item. Keep in mind that all users in the organization can see the labels that have been applied to an item, regardless of whether they are allowed to edit those labels. Any labels applied to an item also apply to any PDF, Excel, or PowerPoint file exported from that item.

Some data sources may already have Information Protection Sensitivity Labels assigned, and if so, it is unnecessary to assign them again; instead, you can use the **Apply Sensitivity Labels from data sources to their data in Power BI** setting to ensure that items inherit the same Sensitivity Labels that are applied to their data source(s). These labels are transferred only for specific supported data sources connected in Import mode. This upstream label is assigned in the Power BI service environment only if this setting is enabled; in Power BI Desktop, this transfer occurs even if this setting is disabled. This transfer can occur only if the user setting up the connection to the given resource has a Pro or Premium Per User license.

Because the Fabric items together form the stream of data from the source through the individual items to the user, the **Automatically apply Sensitivity Labels to the downstream content** setting allows users to set the protection label as close as possible to the source and then let it be propagated to the items in the direction of the data stream. This setting has two modes: *Default* (disabled) and *Admin Enabled* (enabled). Default means that the content author can decide whether the Sensitivity Label they chose should be applied to subordinate items or to only the currently created one. Admin Enabled does not allow the user to decide and automatically assigns the label to follow-up items if possible, but it will never sleep over a tag assigned manually or with a higher weight.

According to internal governance, admin roles within workspaces may need to have the option of overwriting the automatic labels with custom Sensitivity Labels. To do this, enable the **Allow workspace admins to override automatically applied Sensitivity Labels** setting, which, unlike most settings, cannot be set only for specific users. You can turn it on and off, automatically affecting all workspace admins.

For security reasons, admins can also completely prohibit any content bearing the label with protection settings from being able to be shared via links. To do so, enable the **Restrict content with protected labels from being shared via a link with everyone in your organization** setting, which can only be turned off or on for everyone (Figure 1-3).

Export and Sharing settings

Requirements for exporting content to various Excel, MHTML, XML, Word, PowerPoint, and CSV formats are integral to Power BI and, thus, Fabric. Who can perform these individual exports is set within the **Export and Sharing** section. In addition to these options, the section's settings offer the ability to publish reports on the web, copy visuals as images, and print the content of reports and dashboards. For sharing, you'll find settings that allow content to be shared using links integration into Microsoft Teams, as well as options that enable external users to access your environment and possibly, in addition to consuming reports, to participate in the development of individual items or to have a subscription set to your content.

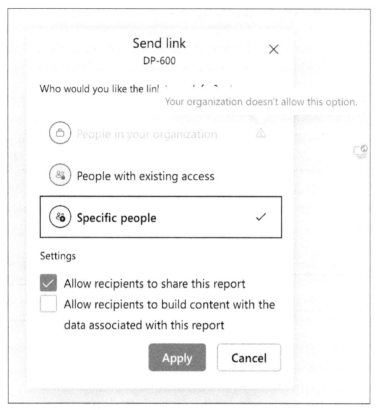

FIGURE 1-3 Disabled wide sharing option

For example, **Allow DirectQuery connections to Power BI semantic models** enables developers to connect to an already existing semantic model and use DirectQuery instead of Live Connection mode. This, in turn, allows users to combine multiple semantic models into one and extend them with additional data and thus create composite models.

Content from Power BI (semantic models, dataflows, reports, applications) and Fabric (lakehouses, warehouses, data pipelines, notebooks, DataFlow Gen2, experiments, and so on) can be endorsed to make it easier to find and increase its visibility. In primary condition, each item is without any endorsement. Assigning content as **Promoted** is possible without any specific admin settings, and users can promote their content in a workspace if they have written permission on a model. Another option for increasing the level of endorsement is **Certification**, which should be an option only for specific users. It should intentionally highlight content that meets internal company guidelines and is ready for broader use. All certified content is shown higher than promoted content. However, the admin must allow certification in this section within the **Certification** settings (Figure 1-4).

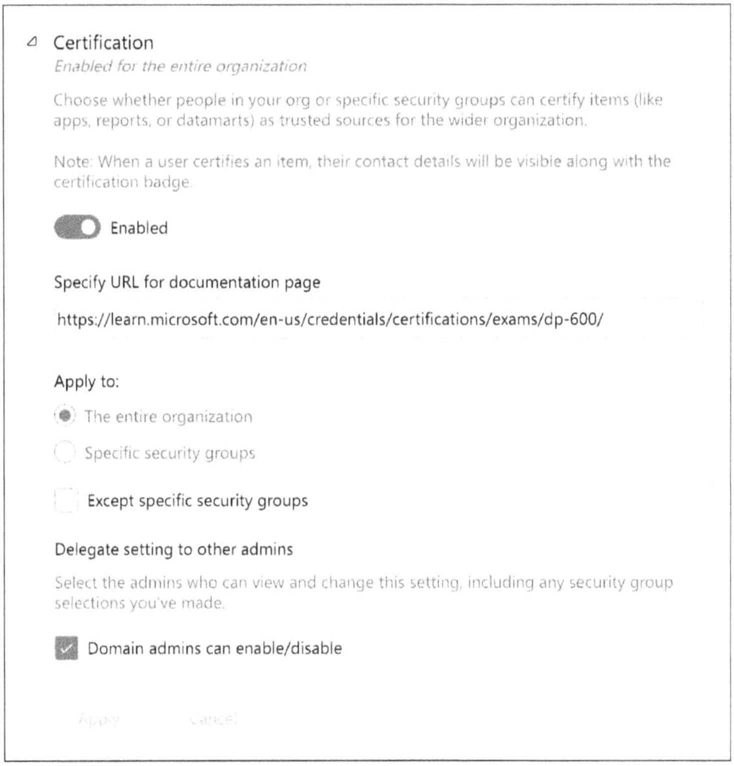

FIGURE 1-4 Expanded view of the Certification settings

When **Certification** is enabled, it is enabled for the entire organization but can be scoped to only some security groups that can set content as certified. This is because certification is a two-step process in most cases. First, users will apply for the certification. Then, someone from a dedicated group might do an eligibility test and, based on that, decide if the content should have a certified label. In the setting, there is an option to enter a link to the documentation page, which can also contain a form requesting certification. A user who does not have authorization to perform certification sees the **Certified** option unavailable in the **Endorsement and discovery** setting and, at the end of the text, a link that sends it to the set address. Figure 1-5 illustrates configuring on endorsement.

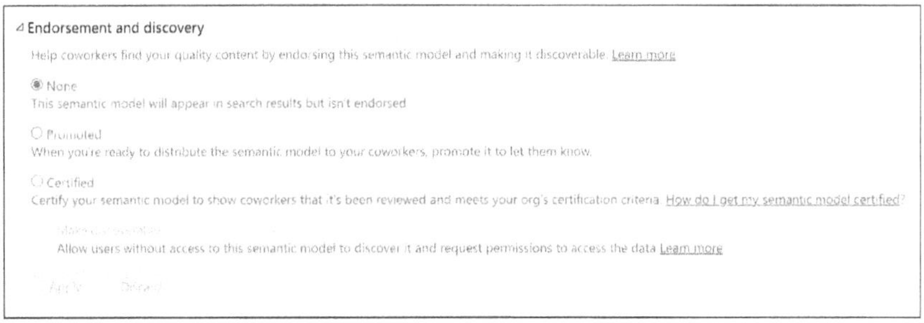

FIGURE 1-5 Endorsement and discovery setting for a semantic model

Endorsement and discovery settings

The Endorsement and discovery section settings allow you to define what type of content can be found within the Browse or OneLake data hub even without direct authorization to the workspace or the semantic model, since discoverability is a capability of the semantic model. Currently, there are four settings:

- **None**   Does not endorse content.
- **Promoted**   Endorses content as promoted.
- **Certified**   Endorses content as certified.
- **Make discoverable**   Specifies whether the given content should be findable.

The **Make discoverable** setting triggers the entire discovery option because it says that selected users, the entire company, or all except selected users have the option to perform a discovery (Figure 1-6).

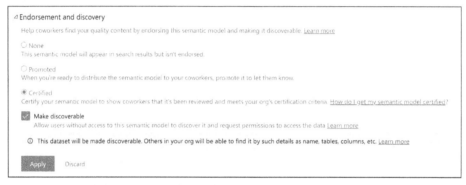

FIGURE 1-6 Enabled discovery option for certified semantic model

Integration settings

The Integration section focuses primarily on connecting Microsoft World with SSO (single sign-on) access and other worlds such as Redshift, Snowflake, or Oracle. There are also settings here that allow you to use the integration between SharePoint and Microsoft Lists together with Power BI, Azure Maps Visual, Map, and filled map visuals, or use the ability to view Power BI files stored in your OneDrive storage and create sharing links from these views. But there are also other settings. For example, the **Allow XMLA endpoints and analyze in Excel with on-premises datasets** option allows selected users to use two significant capabilities: XMLA endpoints and analysis in Excel.

The XMLA protocol is used for communication between client applications and the module that serves workspaces and semantic models, and XMLA endpoints can be used for many purposes, such as modifying semantic sets, lifecycle management, settings, performing updates or backups, and more. In addition, XMLA endpoints can be managed via Capacity settings when the bases in each capacity (capacity per capacity and capacity per user) are set to Read-Only.

If users want to make changes through them, they must adjust this setting to the appropriate capacity and reset it to Read/Write.

> **IMPORTANT**   **XMLA ENDPOINTS ARE CONTROLLED ON THE CAPACITY LEVEL**
>
> You can enable the **Allow XMLA endpoints and analyze in Excel with on-premises datasets** setting for the entire capacity only, not for individuals or groups in capacities. In the same way, the XMLA endpoint can be turned off completely.

The analysis in Excel capability enables you to connect to the semantic model via Live Connection using Excel as a pivot table source, so users can then analyze and verify data stored in the semantic model using Excel and its formulas. It would help to have Build permission within the model you are connecting to. That connection is subject to the set RLS (row-level security) and OLS (object-level security) model rules. Therefore, if users have a higher authorization or Write, then, as with the model itself, neither RLS nor OLS applies to them.

Also in this section, the **Dataset Execute Queries REST API** setting allows authorized users to send DAX queries against semantic models where they have at least Build permission. These queries can be performed using the Power BI REST API under their identity, which respects RLS and OLS. If a user has Write permission (in other words, these forms of security do not apply to that individual), that user can enable the **Impersonate User** parameter and execute DAX queries as a different user. The Dataset Execute Queries REST API setting also allows you to use the **Run a query against a dataset** and **Run a JSON query against a dataset** predefined actions within workflows (historically Power Automate).

When enabled, the **Enable granular access control for all data connections** security setting automatically disconnects all data sources if a user edits an item without proper authorization for all sources. You can turn this setting on and off for the entire organization only.

Semantic models or their data can be imported into OneLake for subsequent enrichment or modification. Still, for this to be possible, the **Semantic models can export data to OneLake**, and the setting must be enabled. After turning this setting on, this export option can be found in the semantic model settings. Still, exporting to OneLake can only be done in Power BI Premium (P) or Fabric (F) capacity, and the user must have model contributor (Read, Write, Explore) permissions. At the same time, the semantic model must be turned on in the **Large Semantic Model Storage Format** setting.

After activating the **Semantic models can export data to OneLake** option within the model, you need to refresh the model to save the data as Delta tables. In addition, users can also store semantic model tables in OneLake. Although **Semantic models can export data to OneLake** applies to the entire organization, you can set **Users can store semantic model tables in OneLake** for a specific user list only. If you turn off the former setting, all models will stop being imported. However, the import will continue if you deactivate the latter setting or remove the user who made this setting from the allowed group. The individual will be able to stop it in the semantic model settings but will not be able to start it again. At the same time, the first setting must also be enabled for the second setting to work.

Data model settings

The Data model section currently contains only one setting: **Users can edit data models in the Power BI service (preview)**, which allows editing of semantic models in the web environment. You can set this for specific groups of users, but they cannot adjust directly after activation. You must explicitly enable the **Users can edit data models in the Power BI service (preview)** option on individual workspaces within their settings (within My Workspaces, this option is enabled automatically for authorized users), as can be seen in Figure 1-7.

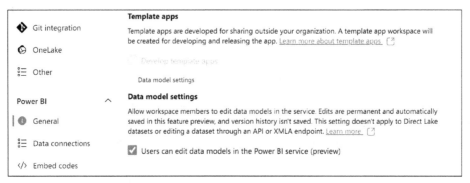

FIGURE 1-7 Data model settings in the Workspace settings

Modifications are currently supported in the following areas:

- Relationships
- DAX
- Measures
- Calculated tables
- Calculated columns
- Calculation croups
- RLS (row-level security)

So, the feature allows users to make quick interventions in the model without downloading .pbix files or having Power BI Desktop installed. On the other hand, all these modifications are saved immediately, so can influence what the end user is looking at. In addition, the capacity for background operations is used for these interventions, so with these adjustments, you can also influence the running of other background operations. The use of this functionality is then managed in the Fabric Capacity Metrics application as follows:

- Web modeling read operation
- Web modeling write operation

Scale-out settings

The Scale-out section also has a single setting: **Scale-out queries for large semantic models**. This setting can be enabled or disabled only, and it applies to all semantic models that support the Large Semantic Model Storage format. The function performs read-only replication of individual semantic models to ensure that responses to users will not be slowed down due to the simultaneous execution of multiple DAX queries originating exclusively from reports or dashboards. However, you can access this option only in Premium capacities (including Premium Per User). It can use capacity resources, so think in advance about which specific semantic models will need this functionality to avoid overload due to replications. In addition to read-only replicas, there is always one read-write replica to which all write operations are directed and from which read-only replications are performed.

OneLake settings

The OneLake section focuses on the accessibility of OneLake solutions. The first setting is **Users can access data stored in OneLake with apps external to Fabric**, and technically, connecting to any data in OneLake is forbidden if it is turned off. If this global setting is turned on, it is possible to access the data using, for example, the ADLS (Azure Data Lake Storage) API, OneLake Explorer, or Azure Databricks.

For OneLake Explorer, there is one more global setting: **Users can sync data in OneLake with the OneLake Explorer app**, which cannot be applied to only specific users in groups. The application allows users to synchronize data or files from workspaces or items available to their file explorer. Similarly, OneDrive has an app that technically enables users to manipulate the data directly from their environment. The data is not found with the user, and only after the user attempts to open it is the data downloaded for editing, deleting, previewing, and so on. It is also possible to add files through this application.

Git integration settings

The Git integration section contains three settings that control the integration options of Git and Fabric workspaces. Generally, this integration allows users to back up and version their work. Thanks to the capabilities of Git, they can also return to previous states of their work to collaborate with other developers when their work can be separated into different branches. Only Git in Azure Repos is supported for this integration right now. Users can use this integration to synchronize existing items from workspaces to Git. You can enable the **Users can synchronize workspace items with their Git repositories (preview)** setting for the whole organization or specific groups of users.

The **Users can export items to Git repositories in other geographical locations (preview)** setting allows individuals to use Git repositories that are not located in the exact geographic location of their workspaces. If this setting were turned off and the working proctor used the capacity of, for example, East Europe, but the Git repository was in West Europe, it would not be possible to connect these locations and perform synchronization between them.

The last setting here is **Users can export workspace items with applied Sensitivity Labels to Git repositories**. In the basic settings, workspace items marked with a Sensitivity Label cannot be synchronized with the GIT repository because these tags are not part of the synced metadata. This setting allows you to control who or which group of users can perform such synchronization.

NEED MORE REVIEW? **GIT CAPABILITIES WITH FABRIC ITEMS**

For more information about GIT capabilities, please visit *learn.microsoft.com/fabric/cicd/ git-integration/intro-to-git-integration*.

Choose a data gateway type

Preparing data, whether in Power BI or other parts of Fabric, means working with data sources, some of which may reside within the corporate environment. You can make on-premises data available from the cloud by using a *data gateway*. A gateway is an agent that is installed in your corporate network and acts as a bridge between the Power BI service and your corporate network. Additionally, a gateway handles credentials and authentication.

Most cloud data sources then can be refreshed in the Power BI service without a gateway, although one notable exception is the Web.Page function in Power Query.

In this section, "on-premises" loosely refers to a corporate network, which can include:

- On-premises data sources
- Cloud data sources that reside in IaaS (Infrastructure-as-a-Service) virtual machines
- Cloud data sources that reside within a virtual network (VNet)

Figure 1-8 shows a simplified data refresh diagram when using on-premises data sources.

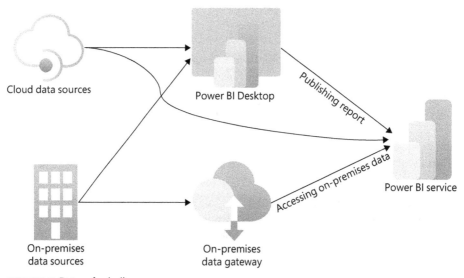

Cloud data sources

Power BI Desktop

Publishing report

Accessing on-premises data

Power BI service

On-premises data sources

On-premises data gateway

FIGURE 1-8 Data refresh diagram

When working in Power BI Desktop, you're supposed to have all the necessary access to the data sources you're working with—cloud or on-premises. Once you publish your report to the Power BI service, the cloud data sources may reach the Power BI service directly, whereas the on-premises data will need to go through a gateway for data to be refreshed in the Power BI service.

Tenant administration for gateways

Before you install a gateway, you need to ensure that you're allowed to install one, which depends on whether tenant administration for gateways is enabled in your tenant. You can change the setting in the Power BI service by choosing **Settings** > **Manage connections and gateways** > **On-premises data gateways**.

If the **Tenant administration for gateways** toggle is switched on, you'll see the **Manage gateway installers** option (Figure 1-9), which allows you to restrict users in your organization from installing gateways and to specify the users who can install gateways. Note that to be a gateway administrator, a user does not have to be allowed to install gateways (you'll learn more about gateway roles soon).

FIGURE 1-9 Manage gateway installers

Install a gateway

To install a gateway, select **Download** > **Data Gateway** in the Power BI service, which takes you to the gateway download page. The Power BI gateway is available in two modes:

- **Standard**   This gateway can be used by multiple users for all supported services, such as Power Automate. It's preferred in enterprise environments when several people are going to use the same data sources. Dataflows and paginated reports that connect to on-premises data also require Standard mode.

- **Personal**   Only you can use a gateway in Personal mode, and you can use it only for scheduling a refresh in Power BI. A gateway in Personal mode may be appropriate when you don't need to share data sources with others. R and Python scripts as data sources require a personal gateway. You can install only one personal gateway.

EXAM TIP

Be aware of the functionality difference between the two gateway installation modes and be prepared to decide which one is appropriate in any given situation.

Technically, there's a third choice: a virtual network (VNet) gateway, which is a Microsoft-managed service. It doesn't need to be installed, and like an on-premises gateway in Standard mode, it also allows you to share data sources with others. VNet gateways are outside the scope of this book, however.

In general, a data gateway should be installed on a machine that is always on and connected to the internet, because a gateway cannot access on-premises data sources from a machine that is powered off. You can install up to one gateway in each mode on the same computer, and you can manage multiple gateways from the same interface in the Power BI service. Installing Power BI gateways together with a self-hosted integration runtime (used for Azure Data Factory, for example) is not recommended.

If you want to practice working with a gateway, you need to install an on-premises data gateway. During the installation process, you must sign into your Power BI account, and you have to give your gateway a name. You also need to specify a recovery key that you can use to move or recover the gateway. After you install the gateway, you must add data sources and users to it.

Note that when installing a gateway in Standard mode, you can make it part of a *cluster*, which consists of one or more nodes grouped for high availability (avoiding having a single point of failure) and load balancing (automatic distribution of load across all nodes in a cluster). In general, it's recommended to have more than one gateway node in enterprise scenarios, as well as separate development or testing clusters. Even if there's only one node in a gateway cluster, the Power BI service will still call it a gateway cluster. For simplicity, this section uses the term "gateway" instead of "gateway cluster."

NEED MORE REVIEW? **ON-PREMISES GATEWAY INSTALLATION INSTRUCTIONS**

For more details on the data gateway installation process, including requirements and considerations, see "Install an on-premises data gateway" at *learn.microsoft.com/en-us/data-integration/gateway/service-gateway-install*.

Manage gateway settings

After you install a gateway, you'll be able to see it in the list of available gateways by selecting **Settings** > **Manage connections and gateways** > **On-premises data gateways**. From there, you can select your gateway, and then select **Settings** to change the following gateway settings:

- **Name**   Users will see this gateway name.
- **Department**   Users will see the department next to the gateway name.
- **Description**   A short explanation seen mostly by gateway admins.

- **Contact information**   This free text field can contain an email address or other useful information that users will see.

- **Distribute requests across all active gateways in this cluster**   This option is required to be on for load balancing.

- **Allow user's cloud data sources to refresh through this gateway cluster**   This setting allows merging and appending cloud and on-premises data sources together.

- **Allow user's custom data connectors to refresh through this gateway cluster**   This setting allows custom connectors to be used with the gateway. Custom connectors are outside the scope of this book.

Manage gateway users

To manage the users with whom a gateway is shared, select a gateway from the list of available gateways and then select **Manage users**.

When sharing a gateway with other users, you can select one of the following roles:

- **Connection Creator**   Allows the user to create data sources and connections on the gateway

- **Connection Creator with resharing**   Allows the user to create data sources and connections on the gateway as well as reshare gateway access

- **Admin**   Allows the user to create data sources and connections on the gateway, plus manage gateway access, configurations, credentials, and updates

At the very least, a gateway should have more than one administrator to avoid dependence on one person. You can see the gateway sharing options in Figure 1-10.

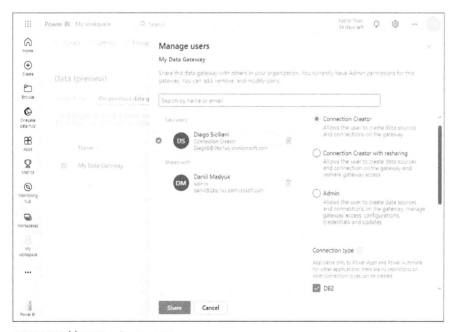

FIGURE 1-10 Manage gateway users

Add a data source to a gateway

After you have a gateway installed, you can add data sources to it in the Power BI service. To start, select **Settings** > **Manage connections and gateways**. At this point, you should see the page shown in Figure 1-11.

FIGURE 1-11 Data sources

You can start adding a new data source by selecting **New**. You'll then be prompted to select the gateway to add the data source to, assign a name to the data source, select the data source type, and so on (Figure 1-12).

FIGURE 1-12 New data source

Note that data source specifics, such as the server address, need to be the same in the list of gateway data sources and within the semantic model or dataflow. For example, if you can access a shared drive by typing either *sdrv01* or *sdrv01.internal.yourcompany.com* in Windows Explorer and in the gateway, you specify the address as *sdrv01.internal.yourcompany.com*, then you'll need to use *sdrv01.internal.yourcompany.com* in Power Query when authoring your queries.

Manage data source users

For a user to successfully use a gateway for accessing on-premises data, the person must be specified as a user for all on-premises data sources used in a semantic model or dataflow. In addition, all data sources must be added to one gateway, because you can use no more than one gateway for data refreshes.

To manage users of a data source, go to the list of data sources (**Settings** > **Manage connections and gateways**), select a data source, and then select **Manage users**. Three roles are available for users of data sources:

- **User** Allows the user to use the data source
- **User with resharing** Allows the user to use the data source and reshare with others
- **Owner** Allows the user to use the data source, as well as manage data source configurations and credentials

You can see the data source sharing options in Figure 1-13.

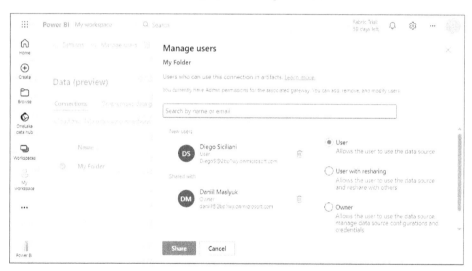

FIGURE 1-13 Manage data source users

Note that being a gateway administrator does not automatically make you a user of its data sources. To use a data source, you still need to be listed as its user, regardless of your gateway role.

Use a gateway

If you want to schedule a refresh of a report that uses on-premises data sources, you need to use a gateway. Figure 1-14 shows the **Gateway connections** section in the semantic model settings.

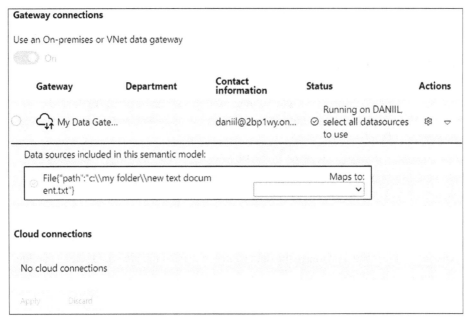

FIGURE 1-14 Gateway connection

To use a gateway, you'll need to ensure that you select the correct data sources from the **Maps to** dropdown and select **Apply**. If you're also using web data sources, you may have to enter credentials in the **Data source credentials** section in semantic model settings. Once all credentials are in place, you can use your gateway to refresh your semantic model.

Create a custom Power BI report theme

Power BI offers many ways to customize the look of your reports, one of which is formatting. Although the Power BI team designed a default theme that works in many circumstances, you might want to apply different formatting to your reports. Large companies often have their own brand books or at least a preferred color palette, and to be brand-compliant, your reports will need to follow the brand guidelines.

For example, you might want to select a particular font face for your reports; formatting each visual to apply the formatting is tedious, error-prone, and time-consuming. Even though you could use Format Painter, doing so will still be laborious and may not always produce the desired results. When you want your reports to be formatted in your way of choosing by default, you can use a custom report theme, which will save you a lot of time and apply formatting consistently for all new visuals and pages.

> **NOTE** **APPLYING A REPORT THEME**
>
> You can apply a report theme only in Power BI Desktop, not in the Power BI service. Dashboard themes, which are outside of scope of this book, are applied in the Power BI service.

In addition to the default theme, Power BI Desktop includes several other themes that you can see by selecting **View** > **Themes** (Figure 1-15). Furthermore, you can select **View** > **Themes** > **Theme gallery** to download more themes.

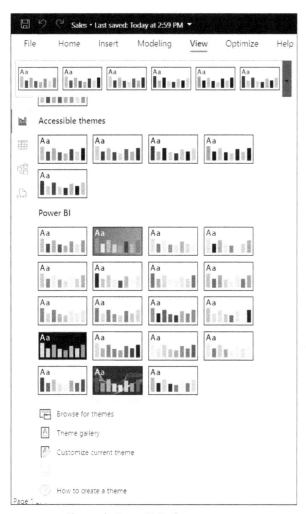

FIGURE 1-15 Themes in Power BI Desktop

When using themes, keep in mind that the theme will format only those formatting options that you didn't specify manually. If you want to revert the manually applied formatting to the theme formatting, select **Reset to default** in the formatting options.

You can also create your own theme in a few ways, such as:

- Use the Power BI Desktop theme editor
- Edit a theme JSON file
- Use third-party tools

Use the Power BI Desktop theme editor

You can customize the current theme directly in Power BI Desktop. To open the theme editor (Figure 1-16), select **View** > **Themes** > **Customize current theme**.

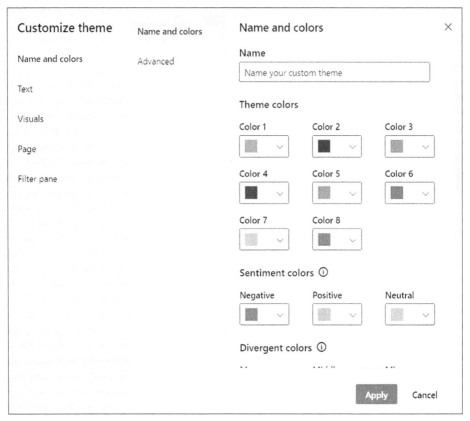

FIGURE 1-16 Customize theme

The Power BI Desktop theme customization feature allows you to change several categories of properties:

- **Name and colors**   Theme name, theme colors, sentiment color, divergent colors, and structural colors
- **Text**   General font options, as well as options specific to titles, cards and KPIs, and tab headers in the key influencers visual
- **Visuals**   Background, border, header, and tooltip formatting options
- **Page**   Wallpaper and page background colors and transparency
- **Filter pane**   Formatting options of the Filter pane and filter cards

Once you've made your customizations, select **Apply** to apply your changes to the current report theme.

Edit a theme JSON file

Note that the built-in theme editor does not contain all available properties you can format. To apply some other formatting by default, you need to edit the theme file, which is a JSON file. The first step is to export the current theme file from Power BI Desktop. To do so, select **View** > **Themes** > **Save current theme**.

> **NOTE** **SAVE CURRENT THEME UNAVAILABLE**
>
> If you cannot save the current theme, it's likely because you're using a default theme and with no customizations made to it. To export a default theme, apply at least one customization; even editing the report theme is sufficient.

When you open a Power BI theme file in a text editor, it will look similar to this:

```
{
    "name": "Exam Ref",
    "textClasses": {
        "label": {
            "fontSize": 12
        }
    },
    "dataColors": [
        "#0A89FF",
        "#0B1EAA",
        "#E7652D",
        "#78008A",
        "#DB329E",
        "#7A4ED4",
        "#ECC305",
        "#D4303C"
    ],
    "visualStyles": {
        "*": {
            "*": {
                "background": [
                    {
                        "transparency": 100
                    }
                ]
            }
        },
        "page": {
            "*": {
                "background": [
                    {
                        "color": {
                            "solid": {
                                "color": "#FFFFFF"
                            }
                        }
                    },
```

```
                    "transparency": 100
                }
            ]
        }
    }
}
}
```

You can make changes in the file and save it. To import it in Power BI Desktop, select **View** > **Themes** > **Browse for themes** and choose your theme JSON file. If the file was created correctly, you'll see the message shown in Figure 1-17; otherwise, you'll get an error message.

File successfully added	×
Your custom report theme is ready to use.	
	Got it

FIGURE 1-17 Import theme message

When editing a theme JSON file, you need to specify only the properties you want to change. Other properties will be inherited from the base theme included in Power BI Desktop when you created your report.

When you want to apply the same formatting to a class of properties, you can use an asterisk to denote all items within the class.

> **NOTE   REPORT THEME PROPERTIES**
>
> The full list of all properties available for formatting is outside of scope of this book. For more details, see "Properties within each card" at *learn.microsoft.com/en-us/power-bi/create-reports/desktop-report-themes#properties-within-each-card*.

If you need to edit a theme you imported, you can either export your theme and edit the JSON file or customize the theme in Power BI Desktop if the properties you want to edit are supported. Note that editing in Power BI Desktop changes only the properties you edit. Theme properties not editable in Power BI Desktop will not be changed, but you won't lose the theme properties you don't see.

Use third-party tools

In addition to the Power BI Desktop theme editor and manually editing JSON files, you can use third-party tools to create custom report themes. For example, you can use themes.pbix by POINT, which is available at *themegenerator.point-gmbh.com/en/Home*. As you can see in Figure 1-18, this theme generator offers a user interface that allows editing of more properties than the built-in Power BI Desktop theme editor. It also supports uploading of themes for editing.

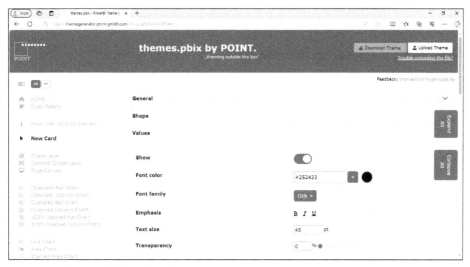

FIGURE 1-18 themes.pbix by POINT theme generator

Other examples of third-party theme generators include PowerBI.tips Theme Generator (*themes.powerbi.tips*) and Power BI Theme Generator by BIBB (*powerbithemegenerator.bibb.pro*).

Skill 1.2: Implement and manage a data analytics environment

Having created a set of items to support your solution, you will need to manage them. This includes managing the security element (who can access what, and what capabilities does that give them) as well as configuration of the items and capacities themselves. Keeping data under control is an essential building block of proper governance. Because data is also located within Fabric, however, you can use global solutions to secure the overall solution.

> **This skill covers how to:**
> - Implement workspace- and item-level access controls for Fabric items
> - Implement data sharing for workspaces, warehouses, and lakehouses
> - Manage Sensitivity Labels in semantic models and lakehouses
> - Configure Fabric-enabled workspace settings
> - Manage Fabric capacity

Implement workspace- and item-level access controls for Fabric items

The primary access control mechanism for Fabric is through workspace membership and roles. There are four workspace roles that users can be assigned to:

- **Admin**   Has full workspace administration access including workspace deletion
- **Member**   Can manage members with equivalent or lower permissions sets
- **Contributor**   Can create and manage content within the workspace
- **Viewer**   Has read-only access to the workspace

Creators of new workspaces are automatically assigned the Admin role.

Table 1-2 shows the capabilities that each workspace role allows.

TABLE 1-2 Workspace roles

Capability	Admin	Member	Contributor	Viewer
Update and delete the workspace	Yes			
Add or remove people, including other admins	Yes			
Add members or others with lower permissions	Yes	Yes		
Allow others to reshare items	Yes	Yes		
View and read content of data pipelines, notebooks, Spark job definitions, ML models and experiments, and event streams	Yes	Yes	Yes	Yes
View and read content of KQL databases, KQL querysets, and real-time dashboards	Yes	Yes	Yes	Yes
Connect to SQL analytics endpoint of a lakehouse or warehouse	Yes	Yes	Yes	Yes
Read lakehouse and data warehouse data and shortcuts with T-SQL through TDS endpoint	Yes	Yes	Yes	
Read lakehouse and data warehouse data and shortcuts through OneLake APIs and Spark	Yes	Yes	Yes	
Read lakehouse data through lakehouse explorer	Yes	Yes	Yes	
Write or delete data pipelines, notebooks, Spark job definitions, ML models and experiments, and event streams	Yes	Yes	Yes	
Write or delete KQL querysets, real-time dashboards, and schema and data of KQL databases, lakehouses, data warehouses, and shortcuts	Yes	Yes	Yes	

Capability	Admin	Member	Contributor	Viewer
Execute or cancel execution of notebooks, Spark job definitions, ML models and experiments	Yes	Yes	Yes	
Execute or cancel execution of data pipelines	Yes	Yes	Yes	Yes
View execution output of data pipelines, notebooks, and ML models and experiments	Yes	Yes	Yes	Yes
Schedule data refreshes via the on-premises gateway	Yes	Yes	Yes	
Modify gateway connection settings	Yes	Yes	Yes	

Membership of roles is managed through the **Manage access** option in the workspace (Figure 1-19).

FIGURE 1-19 The Manage access option

To add new members, search for their email addresses and select the roles they should be assigned to (Figure 1-20). As a best practice, control workspace membership and roles using Microsoft Entra groups as much as possible.

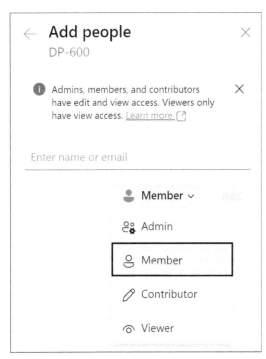

FIGURE 1-20 The dialog for adding people to workspace roles

If you have administrator access to the Fabric tenant it is also possible to manage workspace membership and roles via the Workspaces section of the admin portal (Figure 1-21).

Workspaces

View personal and group workspaces that exist in your organization. To change users' ability to create workspaces, see Tenant settings.

Name ⌄		Description ⌄	Type ⌄	State ⌄
✅ DP600	⋮		Workspace	Active
	☰ Details		Workspace	Active
	⊥ Access		Workspace	Active
	✎ Edit		Workspace	Active
	↳ Reassign workspace			

⟳ Refresh ⊥ Export ☰ Details ✎ Edit ⊥ Access ↳ Reassign workspace

FIGURE 1-21 The Workspaces view in the admin portal

You can also manage permissions at the item level. This allows users to access direct links to the content, even when they are not a member of the workspace. Item-level permissions will differ across item types. For example, items that are part of the Power BI experience can allow View access, Build access, and Share access. For storage-type items, such as warehouses and lakehouses, this more granular type of access control is referred to as data sharing.

Implement data sharing for workspaces, warehouses, and lakehouses

The warehouse and lakehouse items are primarily used by analytics engineers to indicate where in OneLake data should be stored. Both of these items have an additional data sharing permission type built into them, allowing sharing of data without having to grant workspace membership. These items can be accessed via the Data Hub or the Shared with Me sections in Fabric. The **Share** icon (Figure 1-22) appears when you hover over a warehouse or lakehouse item.

FIGURE 1-22 The Share icon

Click the **Share** icon to open the **Grant people access** dialog (Figure 1-23).

Three sharing options are available. **Read all SQL endpoint data** gives the user ReadData permission, allowing read-only access to data using the SQL Endpoint. **Read all Apache Spark** gives the user ReadAll permission. This option grants access directly to the underlying files in an item and is suitable for using Spark to read the data. The final option, **Build reports on**

the default dataset, does as it says. This is equivalent to Build permission being granted on a semantic model. For the default semantic model, however, the option to add users to this access option can only be done via the parent warehouse or lakehouse, not directly on the default semantic model.

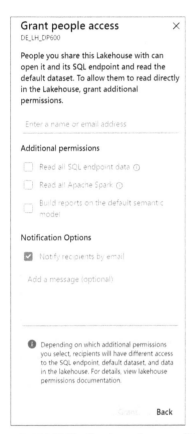

FIGURE 1-23 The Grant people access dialog for data sharing

IMPORTANT **READALL PERMISSIONS**

Remember that the second option is more permissive than the first, because **Read all SQL endpoint data** allows you to set additional layers of security such as object-level and row-level rules using the SQL endpoint, whereas these are not supported for Spark access.

If you need to update data sharing options, either to remove or update permissions, select the ellipsis next to the item and choose the **Manage permissions** (Figure 1-24).

FIGURE 1-24 The Manage permissions options for data sharing

Manage Sensitivity Labels in semantic models and lakehouses

Sensitivity Labels are an integral part of Fabric data security. As mentioned in the "Information Protection settings" section, to use these labels, you must set them in advance in Microsoft Purview and then enable them in the Tenant settings. If both conditions are met, it is possible to use individual items. Each label can allow specific users to perform different operations on items depending on their settings within Microsoft Purview. For example, one group of users can work with an item without restrictions, but another group can only read it. Thus, the settings made in Fabric are primarily intended to apply already existing policies and *not* to modify or create them.

Purview settings affecting label behavior

In general, so-called protected labels also exist within Sensitivity Labels. *Protected labels* are Sensitivity Labels with associated file protection policies and encryption settings that can be used to protect files and data. When using these protected labels within Fabric or the Power BI service, be aware that they do not in any way control access to the items or the items' use. The only thing the protected labels directly control there is the ability of users to change or remove them. In Power BI Desktop, protected labels can control access to files as determined by the options (View, Edit, Export) you set within the files. If you create a .pbix or .pbip file in cooperation with colleagues, after setting the protected label, one of you may no longer have permission to open this file.

As part of the Sensitivity Labels organizational settings, you can specify a *default label* that will be automatically assigned to each newly created Power BI item to help keep all content under control. You can change default settings within labels and set them separately for files, emails, and Power BI items. You can also change the default label applied to a Power BI item. Be aware that you can encounter multiple default labels at once, because they can be set by individual security groups or specific users. At such a moment, the one with a higher priority is automatically assigned, and the automatic assignment does not apply to external users.

The Sensitivity Label policy is another crucial mechanism for marking all items with a Sensitivity Label. If you turn on the **Require users to apply a label to their Power BI Content** option, for example, users assign a Sensitivity Label for each report, dashboard, or semantic model before saving.

Assigning Sensitivity Labels

Your ability to apply Sensitivity Labels depends on the environment and your permissions. Within Power BI Desktop, for example, you must be logged in to your account so that the label policies are recognized and the appropriate Tenant settings must be enabled. If they are, you can assign labels from the **Sensitivity** dropdown (Figure 1-25).

FIGURE 1-25 Assigning a Sensitivity Label in Power BI Desktop

In the Fabric Service environment, you can assign or change Sensitivity Labels from a number of locations. When an item is open, for example, click the label's name in the top bar to reveal an information menu that contains the settings for Sensitivity Labels and enables you to quickly edit them. Figure 1-26 shows the label information for a lakehouse. If the lakehouse is endorsed, then the name pattern is *<name>* + *<endorsement>* + *<Sensitivity Label>*.

FIGURE 1-26 A displayed Sensitivity Label for a lakehouse

You can also assign Sensitivity Labels an item's settings. If labels are not enabled in the Tenant settings, this option may not appear at all in the settings. The appearance of the settings may vary from artifact to artifact. For example, Figure 1-27 shows the settings in a semantic model, and Figure 1-28 shows the settings for a lakehouse.

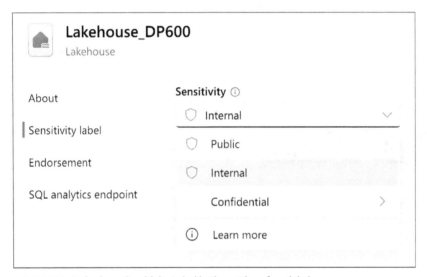

> ▷ Data source credentials
>
> △ Sensitivity label
>
> Classify the sensitivity of this semantic model Learn more
>
> | Internal   ⌄ |
>
> ⚠ Some sensitivity label settings, such as file encryption settings and content marking, are not enforced in Power BI. Learn more ↗
>
> Apply   Discard
>
> ▷ Parameters

FIGURE 1-27 Assigning Sensitivity Label in a semantic model's settings

Lakehouse_DP600
Lakehouse

About

Sensitivity label

Endorsement

SQL analytics endpoint

Sensitivity ⓘ

☐ Internal   ⌄

☐ Public

☐ Internal

   Confidential   ＞

ⓘ Learn more

FIGURE 1-28 Assigning a Sensitivity Label in the settings for a lakehouse

Inheritance of Sensitivity Labels

Earlier the "Information Protection settings" section discussed two important settings—**Automatically apply Sensitivity Labels to downstream content** and **Apply Sensitivity Labels from data source to their data In Power BI**—that have a significant influence on the inheritance of individual Sensitivity Labels.

The **Automatically apply Sensitivity Labels to downstream content** option is useful when you need to slightly separate items from Fabric and those from Power BI. Whether the label transfer occurs depends on which of these sources is upstream. Sensitivity Labels *will* be inherited when the transfer is from a:

- Power BI item to a Power BI item
- Fabric item to a Fabric item
- Fabric item to a Power BI item

The Sensitivity Labels will *not* be inherited when the transfer is from a Power BI item to a Fabric item.

In other words, the individual items you create within Power BI or Fabric and from other Fabric items in a line will inherit their labels. Likewise, automatically created semantic models inherit the Sensitivity Label of their parent lakehouse or data warehouse. In the same way, if you create a pipeline or notebook from a lakehouse, they will inherit their respective Sensitivity Labels immediately. If you create a lakehouse shortcut from a lakehouse with a Sensitivity Label to a lakehouse without a label, the label will also be transferred. The same behavior occurs from a notebook to a pipeline, from a KQL database to a KQL queryset, and from a KQL database to a pipeline.

Apply Sensitivity Labels from data source to their data In Power BI allows you to receive Sensitivity Labels directly from the data source. At the moment, however, this setting is only valid for semantic models.

Configure Fabric-enabled workspace settings

Fabric-enabled workspaces come with additional Fabric-specific options that you can configure. Figure 1-29 shows all the available options in the **Workspace settings** menu.

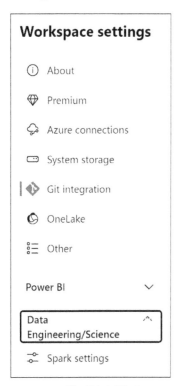

FIGURE 1-29 The Fabric Workspace settings menu

The **Git integration** option is visible for all workspaces; however, it is a premium feature and requires either a Premium Per User license or a Premium or Fabric capacity.

The **Data Engineering/Science** dropdown is a Fabric-specific configuration option. Here you can configure and manage settings for Spark workloads (notebooks) and Spark job definitions.

Choose the **Spark settings** option to reveal four tabs: **Pool**, **Environment**, **High Concurrency**, and **Automatic Log**.

In the **Pool** tab (Figure 1-30), you can set your default Spark pool for the workspace, as well as control the configuration for that pool.

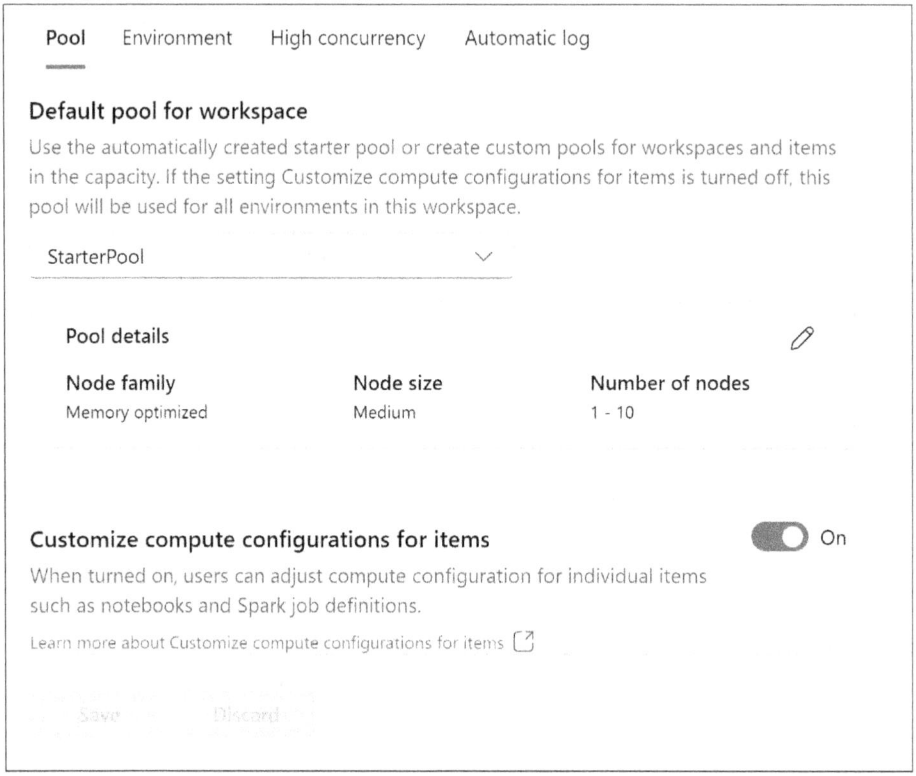

Pool   Environment   High concurrency   Automatic log

Default pool for workspace

Use the automatically created starter pool or create custom pools for workspaces and items in the capacity. If the setting Customize compute configurations for items is turned off, this pool will be used for all environments in this workspace.

StarterPool

Pool details

Node family	Node size	Number of nodes
Memory optimized	Medium	1 - 10

Customize compute configurations for items   On

When turned on, users can adjust compute configuration for individual items such as notebooks and Spark job definitions.

Learn more about Customize compute configurations for items

Save   Discard

FIGURE 1-30 The Pool tab of the Spark settings option in Workspace settings menu

StarterPools have always-on Spark clusters, meaning they are ready and available for your workloads without your having to wait for clusters to start. The StarterPool uses medium-size nodes. You cannot change the node size, but you can adjust the maximum nodes for autoscaling, as well as see the maximum limit for executors. Note that Admin access to the workspace is required to customize these options.

From the **Spark pool** dropdown, you also can create a new custom pool. Here you can control your node sizes as well as enable and disable the **Autoscale** option and set the minimum and maximum number of nodes. Bear in mind that the maximum number of nodes available is proportionate to the number of Spark VCores available in your Fabric capacity and the size of the nodes you configure. Table 1-3 details the VCore allocation for each SKU.

TABLE 1-3 VCore allocation for Fabric SKUs

Fabric Capacity SKU	Spark VCores
F2	4
F4	8
F8	16
F16	32
F32	64
F64	128
F128	256
F256	512
F512	1024
F1024	2048
F2048	4096

Table 1-4 lists the number of VCores assigned to the node sizes.

TABLE 1-4 VCore allocation for node sizes

Node Size	Spark VCores
Small	4
Medium	8
Large	16
X-Large	32
XX-Large	64

The smaller your nodes, the larger your VCore allocation, meaning there's opportunity for running more Spark jobs in parallel. Bigger nodes are more powerful and might run jobs more quickly, but they take up more of the VCore allocation. There is no one-size-fits-all approach to configuring Spark pools. Experiment with various configurations to find out what works best for you.

Environments are items you can create to provide flexible configurations for Spark jobs. You can set compute properties, Spark runtimes, and references to specific Python libraries. The **Environment** tab, shown in Figure 1-31, allows you to set the default environment for the workspace as well as the Spark runtime version if a default environment is not being set.

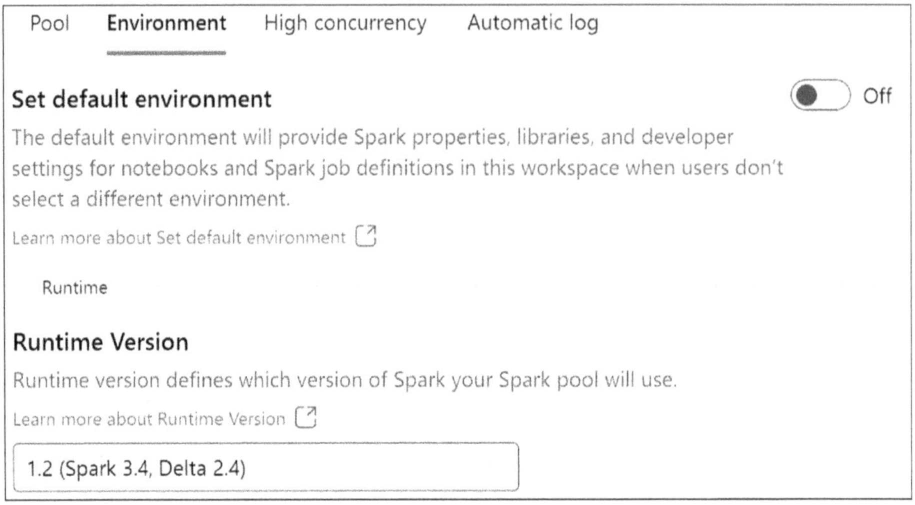

Pool	**Environment**	High concurrency	Automatic log

Set default environment   Off

The default environment will provide Spark properties, libraries, and developer settings for notebooks and Spark job definitions in this workspace when users don't select a different environment.

Learn more about Set default environment

  Runtime

Runtime Version

Runtime version defines which version of Spark your Spark pool will use.

Learn more about Runtime Version

  1.2 (Spark 3.4, Delta 2.4)

FIGURE 1-31 The Environment tab of the Spark settings option in Workspace settings menu

The **High Concurrency** tab (Figure 1-32) contains a single option of the same name. Toggle it on to allow multiple notebooks to use the same Spark resources.

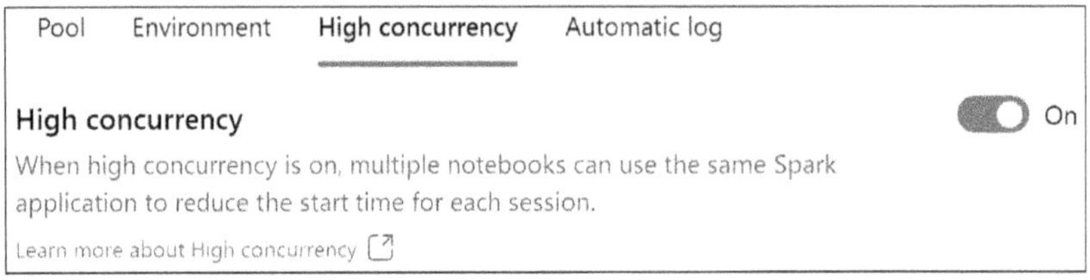

Pool	Environment	**High concurrency**	Automatic log

High concurrency   On

When high concurrency is on, multiple notebooks can use the same Spark application to reduce the start time for each session.

Learn more about High concurrency

FIGURE 1-32 The High concurrency tab of the Spark settings option in Workspace settings menu

The **Automatic log** tab (Figure 1-33) also contains a single toggle: **Automatically track machine learning Experiments and models**.

Pool	Environment	High concurrency	**Automatic log**

Automatically track machine learning experiments and models   On

Automatically log metrics, parameters, and models without coding explicit statements in your notebook.

Learn more about Automatically track machine learning experiments and models

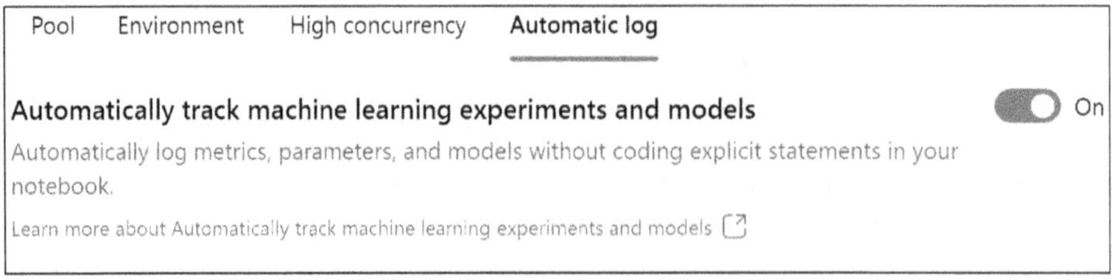

FIGURE 1-33 The Automatic log tab of the Spark settings option in Workspaces menu

Manage Fabric capacity

You can manage your Fabric capacity from the **Capacity admin** section of the Fabric Service or in the Azure portal. Each offers varying levels of functionality.

If you are a capacity admin, you can administer some settings via the **Details** tab of the **Capacity settings** page in the Admin portal (Figure 1-34).

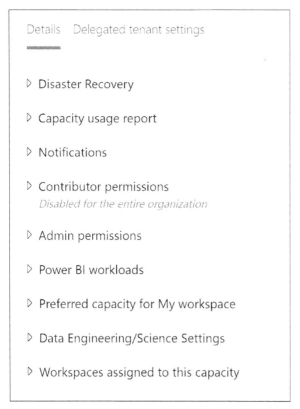

Details   Delegated tenant settings

▷ Disaster Recovery

▷ Capacity usage report

▷ Notifications

▷ Contributor permissions
  Disabled for the entire organization

▷ Admin permissions

▷ Power BI workloads

▷ Preferred capacity for My workspace

▷ Data Engineering/Science Settings

▷ Workspaces assigned to this capacity

FIGURE 1-34 The Details tab of the Fabric Capacity settings page

Disaster Recovery allows you to turn on the ability to replicate items to secondary regions, protecting you from disruption in case of service outages. By default, this option is off. Before turning it on, bear in mind that Disaster Recovery is a paid feature.

Capacity usage report links you to the Fabric Capacity Metrics app. If you do not already have this app set up, you will be prompted to install it.

To receive notification if your Fabric capacity is nearing its limits, use the **Notifications** option (Figure 1-35) to configure alerts to an email distribution list of your choice.

In the **Contributor permissions** section, you can provide a list of either specific users or security groups who will be allowed to add or remove workspaces in the capacity. By default this is set to off.

FIGURE 1-35 The Notifications section of the Details tab from the Fabric capacity settings page

The **Admin permissions** section is where you add or remove capacity administrators.

The **Power BI workloads** section (Figure 1-36) provides a whole host of settings related to your Power BI semantic models.

FIGURE 1-36 The Power BI Workloads section of the Details tab from the Fabric Capacity settings page

In the **Preferred capacity for My workspace** section you can set the capacity as the default for My Workspace. By default, this is option off.

The **Data Engineering/Science Settings** option opens a separate dialog where you can toggle whether the capacity allows customized Spark pools on workspaces belonging to the capacity.

Workspaces assigned to this capacity is the section where you manage which workspaces can use the capacity. You can add and remove workspaces.

The Fabric **Capacity** settings page also includes a **Delegated tenant settings** tab (Figure 1-37). All available options here are Tenant settings that can be devolved and overruled at a capacity level.

FIGURE 1-37 The Delegated tenant settings tab from the Fabric Capacity settings page

Beyond the Capacity Admin section of the Fabric Service, you can also manage elements of your Fabric Capacity in the Azure portal. Here you are able to pause and resume your capacity or even delete it.

Skill 1.3: Manage the analytics development lifecycle

In the enterprise environment, with multiple developers and analysts collaborating, it's especially important to follow a development lifecycle and to keep automation and reusability in mind. Version control, for example, can help avoid rework and prevent loss of Fabric assets. The development lifecycle may look different for different parts of Fabric, and in this skill you'll learn strategies you can put in place for Power BI and other Fabric items, as well as find out about reusable Power BI assets that can save development time and improve consistency.

Data lineage gives you an overview of where your data flows from, where it is within the environment, and what items are used. If you influence one of the items, however, that change can impact all those following. You will also learn how to perform an impact analysis on downstream items. This way, you can prevent potential unpleasant effects.

This skill covers how to:

- Implement version control for a workspace
- Create and manage a Power BI Desktop project (.pbip)
- Plan and implement deployment solutions
- Perform impact analysis of downstream dependencies from lakehouses, data warehouses, dataflows, and semantic models
- Deploy and manage semantic models by using the XMLA endpoint
- Create and update reusable assets, including Power BI template (.pbit) files, Power BI data source (.pbids) files, and shared semantic models

Implement version control for a workspace

You can manage your code and back up your work by connecting a workspace to Git, which will allow a two-way synchronization between Git and the workspace. Additionally, you can revert to prior states and collaborate with others more efficiently.

> **NOTE PREREQUISITES**
>
> Git integration requires a workspace to have a Premium or Fabric capacity license, and the **Users can create Fabric items** setting must be enabled in the Fabric admin portal. For more information on the admin portal, see "Skill 1.1: Plan a data analytics environment."
>
> At the time of writing, you can use only Azure DevOps as a Git host. This section assumes that you already have an Azure DevOps account registered to your Fabric user.

To configure Git integration in a workspace:

1. Select **Workspace settings** > **Git integration** to open the Git Integration section of the Workspace Settings menu (Figure 1-38).
2. Choose your parameters from the **Organization**, **Project**, **Git repository**, and **Branch** dropdowns. Optionally, you can enter a folder name for the **Git folder** setting as well.
3. Click **Connect and sync**.

Once you finish connecting, your content from the branch, if any, will be synced, and the new **Git status** column will display *Synced* status. Additionally, you'll see the branch name and last sync time and commit.

Note that even if your Git content was saved with data, you'll need to refresh your semantic models for them to contain data. If you used on-premises data in your semantic models, you must use a data gateway, as described in "Skill 1.1: Plan a data analytics environment."

FIGURE 1-38 Git integration

Remember, any changes can be synchronized both ways. For example, you can make changes to a report, which will turn the report's Git status to *Uncommitted*. To commit your changes to Git, select **Source control**, select the item you want to commit changes of, and click **Commit** (Figure 1-39).

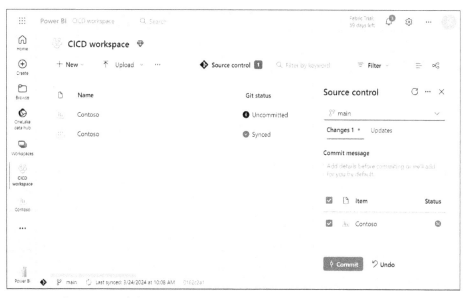

FIGURE 1-39 Source control changes

If, on the other hand, there are updates in Git, the Git status of the relevant items will be *Update Required*, and the items will appear in the **Updates** section of **Source control**. You can then select **Update all** to sync with Git.

If you already had content in your workspace and Git when you configured integration, you'll see a message like in Figure 1-40.

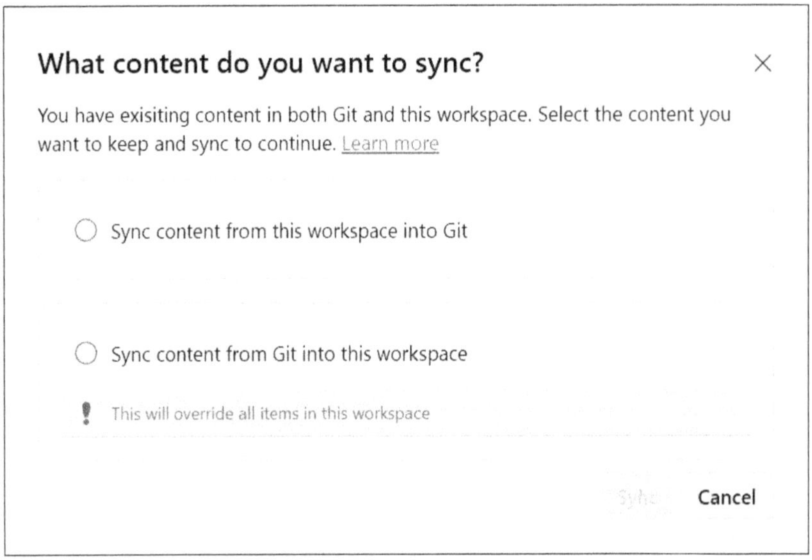

What content do you want to sync?   ✕

You have exisiting content in both Git and this workspace. Select the content you want to keep and sync to continue. Learn more

◯ Sync content from this workspace into Git

◯ Sync content from Git into this workspace

❗ This will override all items in this workspace

Sync   **Cancel**

FIGURE 1-40 If you already had content present when you configured Git integration, you might have a Content sync conflict to resolve.

To resolve the potential conflict, you can sync content from your workspace into Git or from Git into your workspace, which will override all items in the workspace.

> **NOTE SYNCING CHANGES**
>
> To see any content changes locally, you'll need to use your local Git client to sync.

Create and manage a Power BI Desktop project (.pbip)

You can use Power BI Desktop projects for easier source control and continuous integration and continuous delivery (CI/CD) implementation. Additionally, you can edit projects with a text editor and generate them programmatically.

To create a Power BI Desktop project in Power BI Desktop, select **File** > **Save as** and choose **.pbip** as the file type. For example, if you save a report called Contoso as a Power BI project, you'll see a structure similar to the following:

- Contoso.Dataset
    - .pbi
        - cache.abf
        - editorSettings.json
        - localSettings.json

- definition
  - cultures
    - (Model cultures)
  - roles
    - (Model roles)
  - tables
    - (Model tables)
  - database.tmdl
  - model.tmdl
  - relationships.tmdl
- definition.pbidataset
- diagramLayout.json
- item.config.json
- item.metadata.json
- Contoso.Report
  - .pbi
    - localSettings.json
    - definition.pbir
  - item.config.json
  - item.metadata.json
  - report.json
- .gitignore
- Contoso.pbip

Note that the list above isn't exhaustive, and you may have fewer or more items, depending on your project contents. Also, it's possible to have more than one report folder related to the same semantic model folder, if you create a new report on the existing semantic model in the Power BI service.

Power BI projects lend themselves well to source control, because they separate the report and semantic model, unlike .pbix files. If you want to make changes programmatically or using a text editor, simply edit the relevant file. For example, to make changes to a visual, you can edit report.json inside the Contoso.Report folder. Note that Power BI Desktop isn't aware of changes made outside of Power BI Desktop; if you had a report open, you'd need to close and open it again.

NEED MORE REVIEW?   PROJECT FILES LIMITATIONS

For more details on Power BI Desktop projects, including considerations and limitations, see "Power BI Desktop projects" at *learn.microsoft.com/en-us/power-bi/developer/projects/projects-overview*.

Plan and implement deployment solutions

As with many areas of Fabric, you have multiple options available to you when planning and implementing the deployment of your solution.

Your first decision is to decide how many environments you need to deploy across. A typical development lifecycle will have three environments:

- **Development** Where new content is designed and created
- **Test** Where new content is tested, either via load and performance testing that uses more production-realistic data or testing functional and nonfunctional requirements required by the solution
- **Production** Where you share the finished product with users across your business

There are many variations on the stages outlined above. Some organizations may have a Pre-Production environment where they perform testing on real data before they are happy to move items to production. Some organizations may undertake their development and testing activities in one single environment, thus reducing the number of environments.

There is not necessarily one right answer here, but you should make your decisions based on the requirements specific to you.

For each environment, you will need to create a separate workspace.

Your next decision is which method to use for the deployments. Fabric includes a built-in **Deployment Pipelines** feature that can help.

You can create your pipelines from either the **Deployment Pipelines** page (Figure 1-41), which is accessed from the sidebar, or by using the **Create Deployment Pipeline** option available in workspaces that are not currently assigned to a deployment pipeline (Figure 1-42).

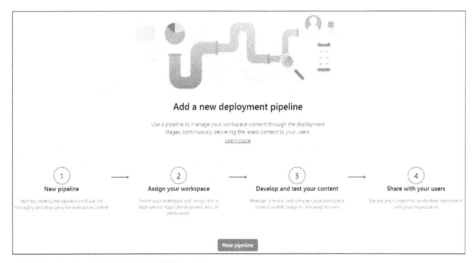

FIGURE 1-41 The Deployment Pipelines page

FIGURE 1-42 The Create deployment pipeline option available in workspaces

When creating a new deployment pipeline, you will be prompted to provide a name and an optional description. You will then be given the option to customize your deployment pipeline stages, as shown in Figure 1-43.

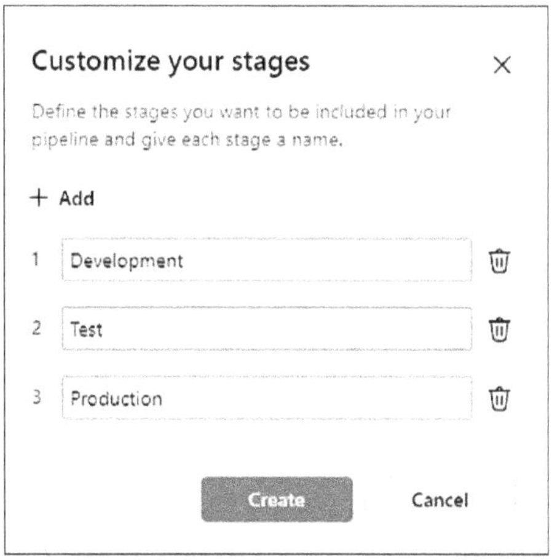

Customize your stages ×

Define the stages you want to be included in your pipeline and give each stage a name.

+ Add

1 Development 🗑

2 Test 🗑

3 Production 🗑

[**Create**] Cancel

FIGURE 1-43 The Customize your stages dialog

In the **Customize your stages** dialog you can remove or create additional stages according to your needs. A pipeline requires a minimum of two stages, but you can have up to 10.

With the deployment pipeline created you will need to assign the relevant workspace to each stage. When this is done, you will see the items currently created in each lifecycle stage. The **Compare** icon indicates any differences between the lifecycle stages. A green checkmark signifies that the workspaces are in sync and there are no changes to deploy (Figure 1-44). An orange X indicates that outstanding changes need deployment (Figure 1-45).

FIGURE 1-44 The Compare icon showing workspaces are in sync

FIGURE 1-45 The Compare icon showing changes need to be deployed

When the Compare icon is orange, a **Compare** option becomes available, which will give further context as to which items have outstanding changes. In the source lifecycle stage

(Figure 1-46 left), you will see **New** and **Different** tags to indicate brand-new items or existing item with changes, respectively. The target stage (Figure 1-46 right) displays Different tags for existing items that do not match the source stage and **Not in previous stage** tags with items that were deleted in the source stage.

FIGURE 1-46 Comparing a source lifecycle stage (left) with a target (right) lifecycle stage reveals item-by-item differences between the two.

Items marked as Different also display a **Review Changes** icon; click it to view the code of the item at each stage side by side, so you can understand what changes were made (Figure 1-47).

FIGURE 1-47 The Change Review dialog shows the differences in the source and target code.

To deploy the changes, you can choose to deploy the entire workspace, or you can select and deploy only specific items. Deploying specific items makes sense when some items are still works in progress due to either development or testing tasks. In this case, deploying whole workspaces would risk deploying unfinished items in error. On deployment you will be prompted to add a note, enabling you to provide commentary regarding the items and the changes you have made. This is useful when looking back over the history of deployments.

After the first deployment of an item to a stage, you can configure deployment rules. *Deployment rules* enable you to configure variables that allow you to change data sources and parameter values as you move your items through the development lifecycle. Perhaps you carry out development and testing on a different set of data to your production environment; you could set up deployment rules to hot swap these sources easily.

The alternative to using the deployment pipelines native to Fabric is to use a service that sits outside of Fabric. Considering the Fabric Git integration with Azure DevOps, using the deployment pipelines that you can build in Azure DevOps would be an obvious choice. Here you have a more code-intensive approach to building a deployment pipeline: You define steps using YAML to deploy items that are being managed in a Git repository. Using a service such as Azure DevOps allows you to integrate additional change management processes, such as an approval process, code validation, and automated testing. This is a more complex and advanced approach to deployment, but if your organization is already using such pipelines for other deployments or if you require a more robust governance wrapper around your deployments, it could be a good option to explore.

Perform impact analysis of downstream dependencies from lakehouses, data warehouses, dataflows, and semantic models

Individual items within the Fabric environment and the Power BI service are often linked logically. In **Lineage view** (Figure 1-48), the links are displayed to show how one item uses the data of another or works with them, and so on. These links help users understand connections and the potential impact of changing from one item to all the following items. Lineage view is available for users with a Power BI Pro or Premium Per User license and Contributor permission in the workspace. Bear in mind, however, Lineage display mode takes longer to render than the regular List view. If you don't need information about lineage between items, you're better off using List view.

FIGURE 1-48 Lineage view of a workspace

Lineage view provides an overview of which items will be affected by the possible removal or modification of an upstream item, which may be in another workspace. Downstream items will be shown only if they are in the same workspace, which means users lose the opportunity to find out what will be affected. For that, Lineage view provides an option called **Show impact across workspaces** (Figure 1-49). Select its icon to perform an impact analysis on downstream items and display individual items in one place (Figure 1-50).

FIGURE 1-49 The Show impact across workspaces icon

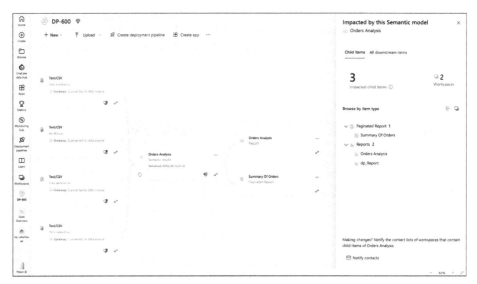

FIGURE 1-50 List of all child items across all workspaces

Part of the impact analysis is a quick overview of affected items, and this also might show workspaces to which the user does not have access. You can choose whether to see direct children or even the entire hierarchical tree by switching between the **Child Items** and **All Downstream Items** tabs. The overview also shows the number of workspaces, the categorization of items, and the possibility of listing individual workspaces. Select the **Notify Contacts** button to send a custom notification message to contacts listed in an item's settings (Figure 1-51).

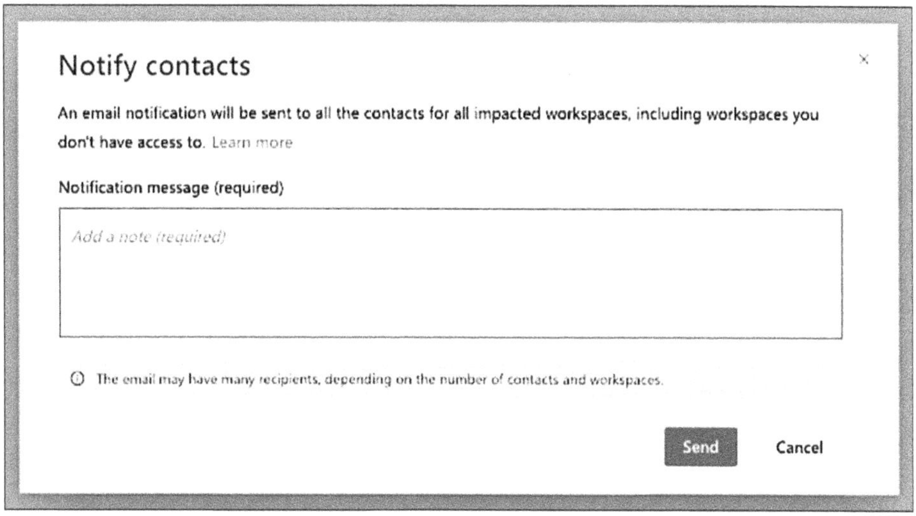

Notify contacts
An email notification will be sent to all the contacts for all impacted workspaces, including workspaces you don't have access to. Learn more
Notification message (required)
Add a note (required)
The email may have many recipients, depending on the number of contacts and workspaces.
Send
Cancel

FIGURE 1-51 Notify contacts about affected workspaces.

You can perform an impact analysis on semantic models, lakehouses, warehouses, notebooks, pipelines, and other Fabric items, as well as on data sources, as shown in Figure 1-52. Note that if the source is DataFlow Gen1, then the icon for impact analysis will not be available.

Text/CSV
Gateway: Connected to data source.
Orders Analysis
Semantic model
Refreshed: 10/02/24, 13:21:50
Text/CSV
Gateway: Connected to data source.

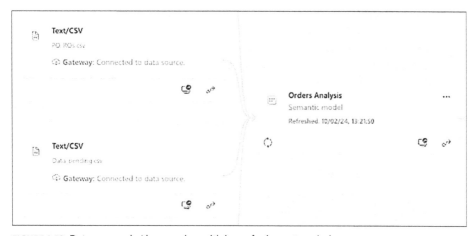

FIGURE 1-52 Data sources in Lineage view with icons for impact analysis

Impact analysis is automatically performed even when you try to republish an item as a new one. In this case, you will see a "Replace this dataset?" message in Power BI Desktop informing that the change will affect the list of items (Figure 1-53).

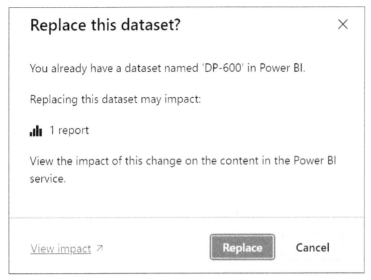

FIGURE 1-53 Impact analysis inside Power BI Desktop while republishing content

Deploy and manage semantic models by using the XMLA endpoint

When you use a Fabric, Power BI Premium, or Embedded capacity, you can use the XML for Analysis (XMLA) endpoint to connect to your semantic models. By using XMLA endpoints, you can get data from a Power BI semantic model and use a client tool other than Power BI to interact with the data. For example, you can visualize the data in Excel, or you can use a third-party tool to edit your semantic model.

To use the XMLA endpoints for deployment and management of semantic models, you must enable the **Allow XMLA endpoints and Analyze in Excel with on-premises semantic models** option in the Power BI admin portal. The **XMLA endpoint** setting in the capacity settings must also be set to **Read Write**.

When making a connection by using the XMLA endpoint, you connect to a Power BI workspace as if it were a server with semantic models acting as databases. To get the workspace connection address, go to the Workspace settings menu and select **Premium** > **Workspace connection** > **Copy** (Figure 1-54).

The address will have the following format:

powerbi://api.powerbi.com/v1.0/myorg/Your Workspace Name

You can use the address as a server address when making a connection in your client tool. Most client tools will allow you to select a semantic model after you connect to your workspace. Some client tools require setting an initial catalog; in this case, use the name of a semantic model you want to connect to.

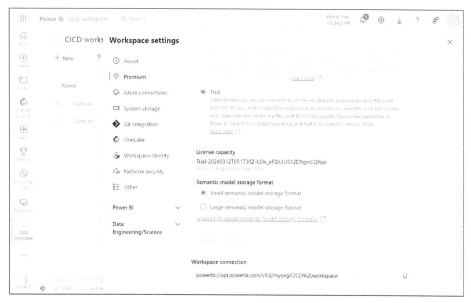

FIGURE 1-54 The Premium section of Workspace settings menus

NOTE USING AZURE B2B AND XMLA ENDPOINT

If you're a B2B user in someone's tenant and want to connect to their dataset by using the XMLA endpoint, you'll need to replace *myorg* with their domain name, so the workspace connection string will look like *powerbi://api.powerbi.com/v1.0/contoso.com/ Your Workspace Name*.

When you connect to a workspace from Tabular Editor, you can select a semantic model and edit it. You can also deploy a new semantic model to a workspace using Tabular Editor. Here are the steps to do so:

1. Create a new model or open an existing one from a file, database, or a folder, making edits as necessary.

2. Select **Model** > **Deploy**.

3. Enter the workspace connection string in **Server**, and select **Next**.

4. Select an existing semantic model or enter the new semantic model name in **Database Name**, and select **Next**.

5. Select the elements you want to deploy, and select **Next**, Select **Deploy**.

6. Refresh your semantic model.

Tabular Editor will deploy metadata only, which is why you need to refresh your semantic model as the last step if your changes include more than measure updates.

Note that you can use other tools, such as Visual Studio or ALM Toolkit, to deploy and manage semantic models. A description of all these tools is outside the scope of this book.

Create and update reusable assets, including Power BI template (.pbit) files, Power BI data source (.pbids) files, and shared semantic models

When you work in an organization with multiple report developers, often you need to develop reports in a consistent fashion. This section reviews several tools available in Power BI:

- Templates
- Power BI data source files
- Shared semantic models

Templates

You can create templates in Power BI Desktop so that others can use your template as a starting point for their own reports. Besides the time that can be saved by using a template, greater consistency will exist between reports in the organization.

Power BI templates (.pbit files) contain:

- Queries, including parameters
- Data models, including DAX formulas, relationships, and so on
- Report pages, visuals, bookmarks, and so on

Power BI templates do not include the data or credentials.

To create a Power BI template from an existing report, select **File** > **Export** > **Power BI template**. You'll be prompted to enter an optional template description and save the file.

To use a Power BI template, you can open its file as you normally would, or you can open Power BI Desktop first, then select **File** > **Import** > **Power BI template**. Either way, you'll be prompted to specify the parameter values, if any, and then Power BI will load the data and create a report for you, which you can then edit further, save, and publish to the Power BI service.

PBIDS files

If you've already connected to data in Power BI Desktop, you can export .pbids files, which have data source connection details embedded in them. They can be useful when you want to make it easier for report creators to connect to specific data sources.

To export a PBIDS file in Power BI Desktop, start by going to Data source settings by selecting **Transform data** > **Data source settings**. You'll see a list of data sources like the one in Figure 1-55.

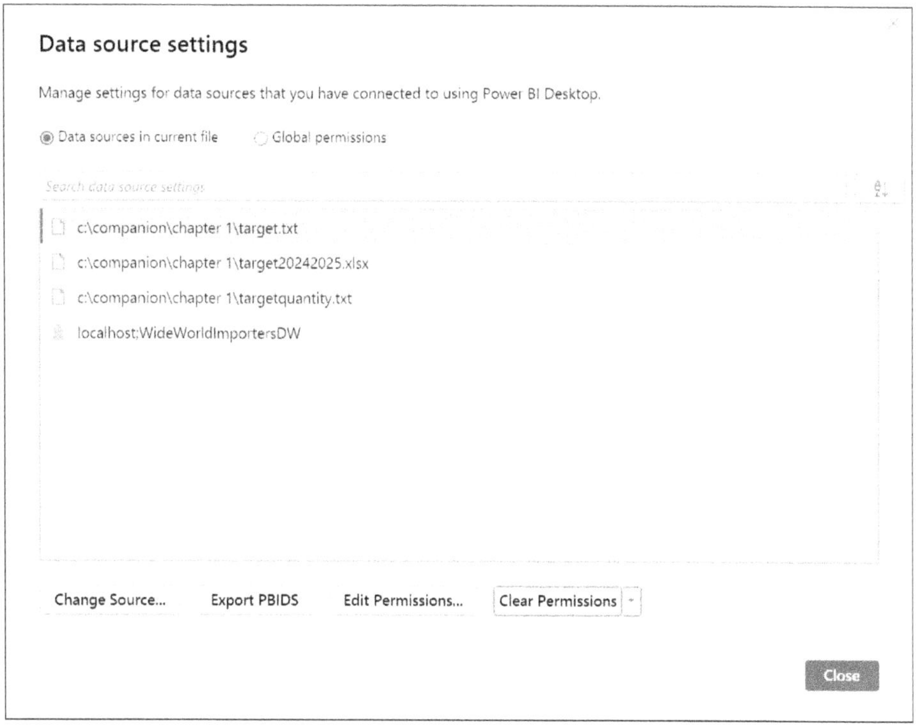

FIGURE 1-55 Data source settings

To export a PBIDS file for a data source, select the data source from the list, and then select **Export PBIDS**, which will prompt you to save the new .pbids file.

For example, if you export a folder data source, you'll get a .pbids file with code similar to the following:

```
{
  "version": "0.1",
  "connections": [
    {
      "details": {
        "protocol": "tds",
        "address": {
          "server": "localhost",
          "database": "WideWorldImportersDW"
        },
        "authentication": null,
        "query": null
      },
      "options": {},
      "mode": null
    }
  ]
}
```

When you open a .pbids file, the experience is the same as when you connect to the data source in a new Power BI Desktop file.

NOTE **CREDENTIALS**

PBIDS files do not contain credentials, so users still need to be able to access the data sources.

Shared semantic models

A shared Power BI semantic model is a semantic model in Fabric used by a report from a different workspace. A semantic model creator can allow others to build reports from their semantic model by using the Build permission. Using shared semantic models has several benefits:

- You ensure consistent data across different reports.
- When connecting to a shared semantic model, you are not copying any data needlessly.
- You can create a copy of an existing report and modify it, which takes less effort than starting from scratch.

NOTE **USING SHARED SEMANTIC MODELS**

Sometimes different teams want to see the same data by using different visuals. In that case, it makes sense to create a single semantic model and different reports that all connect to the same semantic model.

You can connect to a shared semantic model from either Power BI Desktop or the Power BI service:

- In Power BI Desktop, select **OneLake data hub** > **Power BI semantic models** on the **Home** tab.
- In the Power BI service, when you are in a workspace, select **New** > **Report** > **Pick a published semantic model**.

Either way, you will then see a list of shared semantic models you can connect to, as shown in Figure 1-56.

After you are connected to a shared semantic model in Power BI Desktop, some user interface buttons may be unavailable or missing because this connectivity mode comes with limitations. For example, when you connect to a shared semantic model, Power Query Editor is not available and the Data view is missing. In the lower-right corner, you'll see the name and workspace you're connected to (Figure 1-57).

To change the semantic model you are connected to, you can select the **Transform Data** label and then **Data source settings**, which will bring you back to the list of semantic models available to you.

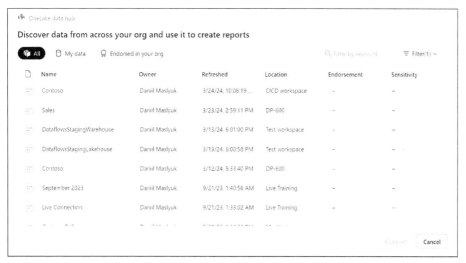

FIGURE 1-56 List of available semantic models

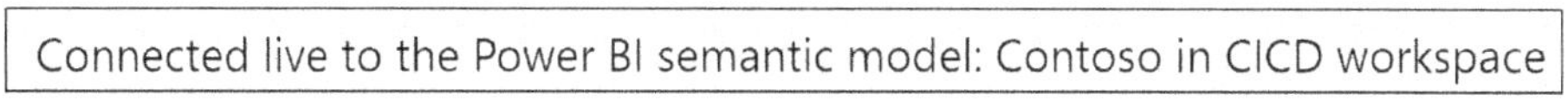

Connected live to the Power BI semantic model: Contoso in CICD workspace

FIGURE 1-57 Power BI Desktop connected to a Power BI semantic model

Note that you can still create measures, and they will be saved in your .pbix file but not in the shared semantic model itself. That means other users who connect to the same shared semantic model will not see the measures you created. These measures are known as *local* or *report-level* measures.

Chapter summary

- Plan which Fabric items are suitable for your solution and what types of capacity are available for you to purchase.

- Tenant settings can only be operated by a user with the appropriate authorization, and you should check these possible settings regularly, as new ones are constantly being added.

- Most settings can be turned on or off for specific security groups, and some settings are logically related, so one setting may also require another. Therefore, it is essential to consider who can access specific options and when. For example, consider who can use Fabric items and who can't, because its content should be, for example, only Power BI or it should only consume the resulting created content.

- When working with on-premises data, you need to install and use an on-premises data gateway. For data behind corporate virtual networks (VNets), you can use a VNet gateway, which is an online service from Microsoft.

- You can change the look of a report by selecting one of the preset themes or defining your own theme. To create your own theme, you can use Power BI Desktop, edit a JSON file, or use a third-party tool.

- Assign workspace roles to people to allow them to access and use Fabric items in a workspace.

- Give people differing levels of access to data from outside of a workspace.

- Sensitivity Labels come from Microsoft Purview and are only used in Fabric. Their direct abilities are thus dependent on their original definition.

- Labels may behave differently in Fabric and Power BI Desktop because they are separate environments, and standard file policies are applied in Power BI Desktop.

- Labels can be assigned to any Fabric item and thus ensure that everything will be subject to the same rules. Thanks to specific settings, it is also possible to restrict any security labels from being exported to Git.

- Configure Fabric specific settings on your workspace.

- Manage the Fabric capacity being used for your solution's workload.

- With Git integration in Fabric, you can sync workspaces to branches and folders in Git, allowing you to perform source control and CI/CD activities.

- Power BI Desktop projects enable source control and text and programmatic editing of Power BI semantic models and reports.

- Plan and set up deployment pipelines for your solution.

- To use Lineage view, you must have at least Contributor permission within the workspace. Within it, you can use Impact Analysis.

- Impact Analysis provides an overview of the direct child items of the examined item but, at the same time, allows for the display of the entire inheritance tree of items, even through individual workspaces.

- Impact analyses can be performed on Fabric or Power BI items and on the data sources themselves to find out what will be affected by their change.

- The XMLA endpoint offers a way to deploy and manage semantic models by using third-party tools such as Tabular Editor.

- Power BI Desktop allows you to create reusable content, such as templates and data source files. Semantic models that are used for more than one report or across workspaces become shared semantic models, leading to improved data consistency and less data duplication.

Thought experiment

In this thought experiment, demonstrate your skills and knowledge of the topics covered in this chapter. You can find the answers in the section that follows.

You are an enterprise data analyst at Contoso responsible for creating and distributing Power BI reports, as well as administrating the analytics environments. Contoso uses Microsoft Fabric and Azure DevOps. Management requested that you build and share some of your reports with a wider audience.

Based on background information and business requirements, answer the following questions:

1. A user who does not have an assigned workspace role on your workspace would still like to access data in your warehouse to analyze with SQL. You have row-level security applied in the warehouse and need to make sure this is respected. How should you provide access, without also giving visibility of other items in the workspace?

   A. Give the user Viewer access on the workspace.

   B. Give the user Read All Apache Spark access.

   C. Give the user Read All SQL Endpoint access.

   D. Give the user Build Reports on the default semantic model access.

2. You need to create a deployment pipeline for your solution in the Fabric Service. Which of the following steps would you *not* need to follow?

   A. Assign workspaces to development lifecycle stages.

   B. Associate the deployment pipeline to a Git repository.

   C. Configure deployment rules to switch data sources as you move items through your stages.

   D. Create a pipeline and a separate workspace per required lifecycle stage.

3. Within your organization, Golden Semantic Models use data from the Fabric warehouse. You want to ensure that users can easily find these semantic models within OneLake data hubs and that they are at the forefront. So, what do you need to do?

   A. Set models as promoted and discoverable.

   B. Set models as certified and discoverable.

   C. Feature semantic models on a homepage.

   D. Name them with a prefix of 0_.

4. You need to ensure that all new reports created in your organization follow the same formatting guidelines consistent with the corporate branding. How should you address the problem? The solution should minimize the overall time spent on formatting.

   A. Direct users to the brand portal so they know what font and colors should be applied.

   B. Tell users to use the Format Painter to copy formatting between visuals for consistency.

   C. Create a report template with a corporate theme.

5. Your organization has a brand team that dictates the style of reports, and you want all new reports to use the same date table. Which tool should you use to improve the adherence to the brand team's guidelines?

   A. Power BI templates

   B. Power BI report themes

   C. Power BI data source files

   D. Shared semantic models

6. You collaborate on a report and a semantic model with a developer from a different team. You're using Power BI project files, and both the report and semantic model are published to a workspace. How should you ensure you're both aware that there are changes the other developer has made? Your solution must minimize effort.

   A. Sync the workspace with Git.

   B. Use SharePoint and check out files.

   C. Send files via email.

Thought experiment answers

1. The answer is **C**, give the user Read All SQL Endpoint access. Viewer access on the workspace would allow the user to interact with other items in the workspace so doesn't fit the requirement. Read All Spark data allows underlying access to the delta files, and whilst this would allow querying using SQL, it would also allow the use of Spark, which does not respect row-level security, so would be too permissive. Build access on the semantic model would give access to the correct data, and with the correct permissions applied, but would only allow interaction through a semantic model, not by using SQL. The correct answer is to give access using Read All SQL Endpoint access. This only gives access to the data, respects the security applied, and allows the user to connect via a SQL client to query the data.

2. The answer is **B**. Git repositories can be associated at a workspace level but not to a deployment pipeline. Although associating your workspace with a Git repository would be a recommended practice, it is not a requirement of a pipeline.

3. The answer is **B**. Certification is at a higher level than Promoted. At the same time, when activated that semantic model will be discoverable. You will make it possible to find it in the OneLake data hub even without users already having access to the given workspace. If they already have permissions, even in Power BI Desktop, when trying to connect to semantic models from the OneLake data hub, they will see Certified content in the first place.

4. The answer is **C**. Creating a report from a template that already includes a theme will mean that all new reports have the same formatting applied, and it won't require any extra effort from report builders. Option A may result in inconsistent formatting due to different report builders applying guidelines differently. Option B still requires the knowledge of corporate branding requirements, and it will demand more manual effort compared to a corporate Power BI template with a theme included.

5. The answer is **A**. Power BI templates can hold Power BI themes and have some pre-defined data model elements, such as the Date table. Power BI report themes can only be used for styling, and a data source file cannot contain any styling elements, so options B and C are wrong. A shared dataset can contain a Date table, although it won't contain a theme, so option D is also wrong.

6. The answer is **A**. If there are changes that aren't synced with your local copies, your Git tool will let you know and allow you to see what the changes are. Options B and C will result in more effort because they won't necessarily tell you which changes were made.

CHAPTER 2

Prepare and serve data

For data to be used to get answers, it needs to be modeled, prepared, cleaned, orchestrated, and provided so that the right users can get to it when they need it. As part of the preparation process, you often need to decide what transformation tool to use, whether to duplicate the data, how the partitions should be created, which transformations to use, and how to control the transformations to ensure the correct continuity of individual operations between individual states. At the same time, you want to undertake these steps via the most efficient means possible, ensuring optimal usage of your Microsoft Fabric resources.

Skills covered in this chapter:

- Skill 2.1: Create objects in a lakehouse or warehouse
- Skill 2.2: Copy data
- Skill 2.3: Transform data
- Skill 2.4: Optimize performance

Skill 2.1: Create objects in a lakehouse or warehouse

With data coming from various sources and in multiple formats, you need somewhere to store it so that it can then be processed into the appropriate form, format, and style of storage most suitable for its subsequent use. You need to get the data into a unified OneLake environment, which then makes it possible to use no-code, low-code, and even full-code transformations to process the data. Once the data is in OneLake, it is not duplicated in multiple places, because OneLake uses shortcuts to point to specific locations of data rather than creating additional instances of that data when it's needed by other items.

> **This skill covers how to:**
> - Ingest data by using a data pipeline, dataflow, or notebook
> - Create and manage shortcuts
> - Implement file partitioning for analytics workloads in a lakehouse
> - Create views, functions, and stored procedures
> - Enrich data by adding new columns or tables

Ingest data by using a data pipeline, dataflow, or notebook

Fabric provides three basic ways to retrieve data from existing storage and systems: *data pipelines*, *dataflows*, and *notebooks*. Each item uses a different user approach and targets different types of users.

Data pipelines

A *data pipeline* is an item from the Data Factory experience that acts as an orchestration component. It can run other items and services and be scheduled to run at specific times. To start creating a pipeline, select **New** > **Data pipeline**, give the pipeline a name, then select **Create**. In Figure 2-1, you can see the blank canvas of the data pipeline editor.

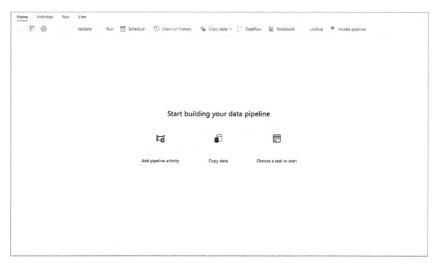

FIGURE 2-1 Blank data pipeline canvas in the data pipeline editor

Within the Fabric services, the **Copy Activity** feature uses the **Data Movement service** and allows you to get data from child nodes, bring it to the Fabric environment, and save it. You can specify the data be saved in the original data format or first converted to another format or directly to Delta Parquet tables within Lakehouse Explorer. You can set up **Copy Activity** by selecting either:

- **Add pipeline activity** (works on the canvas)
- **Copy data** (launches a wizard)

Neither method requires code from you to retrieve the data and convert it to the desired format. In addition to lakehouses, **Copy Activity** can also work and ingest data from other Fabric items, such as warehouses.

> **NOTE   CSV FILE SAMPLE**
>
> If you want to try the following examples on your own, you can find the CSV file at *github.com/tirnovar/dp-600/blob/main/data/sales*.

EXAMPLE OF HOW TO INGEST DATA TO LAKEHOUSE BY PIPELINE

To upload data, open or create a pipeline in the workspace. In this pipeline, you can ingest your data by following these steps:

1. Select **Copy data** from the blank canvas (Figure 2-2).

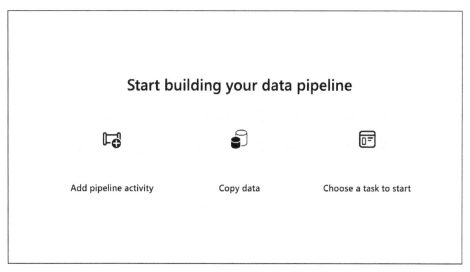

FIGURE 2-2 Quick actions appear only if the pipeline is empty.

2. Search and choose data sources, such as **Azure Data Lake Storage Gen2** shown in Figure 2-3.

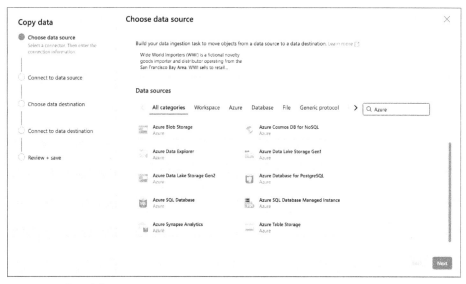

FIGURE 2-3 Filtered data sources

3. Select **Create a new connection** (Figure 2-4), fill in your URL, and sign in.

FIGURE 2-4 Create a new connection. Blank fields in the wizard preview require values in the proper format to help you.

4. Choose data to import. For example, Figure 2-5 shows a file named Sales selected.

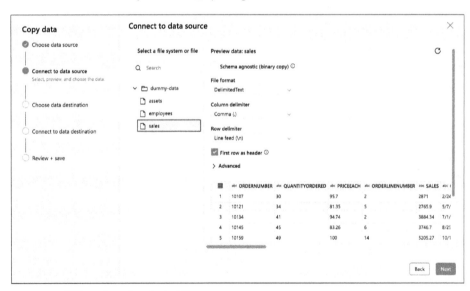

FIGURE 2-5 CSV preview of a selected file

5. Select **Lakehouse** as a data destination. You can use the search feature to quickly find a specific data destination (Figure 2-6).

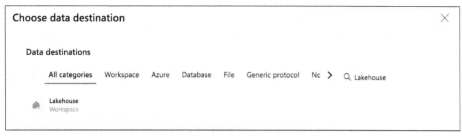

FIGURE 2-6 Searching for lakehouse in data destinations

6. Select the existing lakehouse or create a new one (Figure 2-7).

FIGURE 2-7 Creating a new lakehouse

7. Map data to columns in a table or create a new table and define column names and their data types (Figure 2-8).

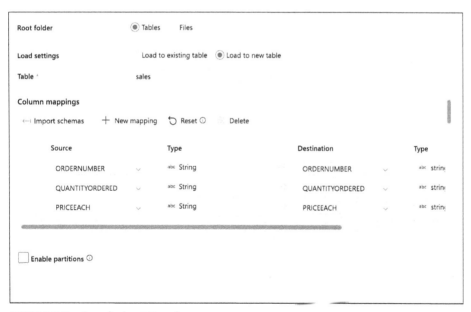

FIGURE 2-8 Preview of column mapping

8. Select **Save + Run**.

The pipeline will be immediately blocked among the items to be launched. After a while, the status of the ongoing data migration and the operation's result will be displayed.

Dataflows

An item that uses Power Query Online, DataFlow Gen2 allows you to use all existing data connectors, including a connection to on-premises data using an on-premises data gateway. Figure 2-9 shows how DataFlow Gen2 looks when you open it for the first time.

FIGURE 2-9 Empty canvas of DataFlow Gen2

While working with data, DataFlow Gen2 uses two additional items for staging: An automatically generated lakehouse serves as **Staging Storage**, and a warehouse serves as **Staging Compute** and can be used to write to the data destination. Figure 2-10 illustrates the process.

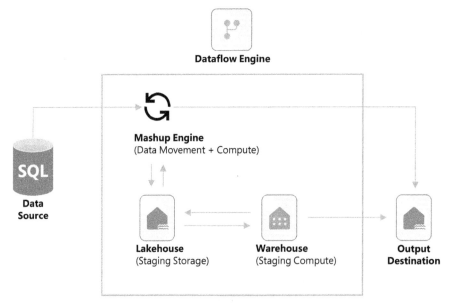

FIGURE 2-10 Dataflow engine schema

When data enters the dataflow engine, the mashup engine based on staging can distribute the data to Staging Storage and Staging Compute or directly transform it and then save it to a destination. You can set data destinations within dataflows separately for each query. Your current destination choices are lakehouse, warehouse, **Azure SQL** database, and Azure Data Explorer (Kusto). If queries have disabled staging, these items are unused, and everything is calculated in memory (Figure 2-11), which on a smaller data sample can better impact the consumed CUs capacity and, simultaneously, the speed. If you have a larger sample of data or a sample requiring more transformations and even combining data from different sources, then the impact can be precisely the opposite.

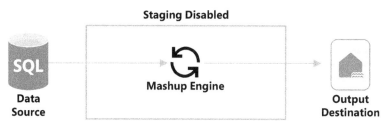

FIGURE 2-11 Disabled staging

Because dataflows use Power Query Online, you can create transformations using a graphical interface or directly with the M language in **Advanced editor**, **Script view**, or **Step script**.

NEED MORE REVIEW? **M FORMULA LANGUAGE**

For a definition of M formula language, please visit *learn.microsoft.com/powerquery-m*.

EXAMPLE OF HOW TO INGEST DATA TO LAKEHOUSE BY DATAFLOWS

To open a new DataFlow Gen2:

1. Select the "Get data from another source" link in DataFlow Gen2.

2. Search for **Azure Data Lake Storage Gen2** (Figure 2-12) and select it from the **New sources** section.

3. Create a new connection in a new window (Figure 2-13), select **Next**, and then select **Create.**

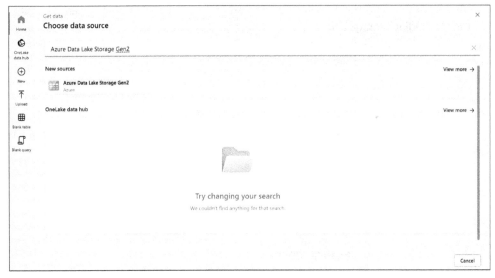

FIGURE 2-12 Choose a data source wizard

FIGURE 2-13 Connection settings

4. Filter the files. If you have the file names, you can filter by the **Name** column in Figure 2-14; otherwise, you can use the column **Folder Path** to select the data container/folder destination.

5. If you are selecting just one file, you can directly select the value **[Binary]** in the Content column, and Power Query will extract data for you. Otherwise, use the **Combine** icon next to the column name (two arrows pointing down), set the file origin if necessary, and select **OK**. Figure 2-15 shows a preview of the data.

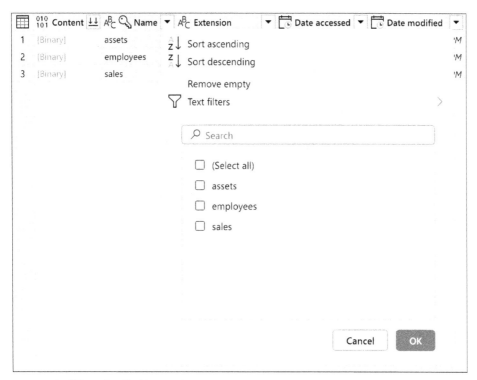

FIGURE 2-14 Filter using the Name column.

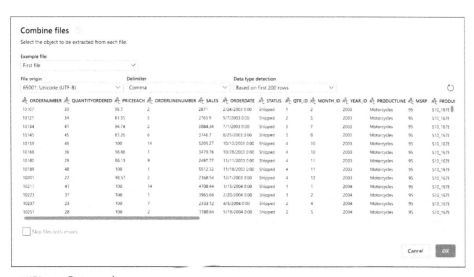

FIGURE 2-15 Data preview

6. Prepare the data, select the **plus** icon (right corner) to add a data destination, and then choose **Lakehouse** (Figure 2-16).

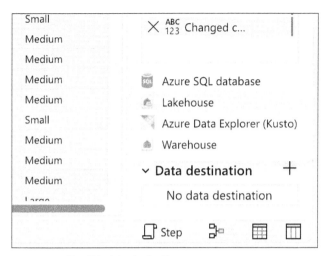

FIGURE 2-16 Possible data destinations

7. Create your connection for all lakehouses, or use the one you already have.

8. Search for your lakehouse (Figure 2-17), and choose a table to insert data or create a new one.

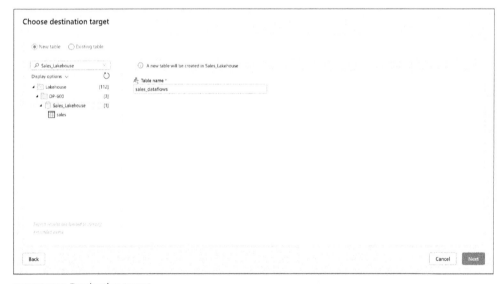

FIGURE 2-17 Destination target

9. Disable **Use automatic settings**. Select **Replace** and **Dynamic schema**. Set data types of all inserted columns or select columns that will be used with selected data types as a schema for the new table. You can see the full settings in Figure 2-18.

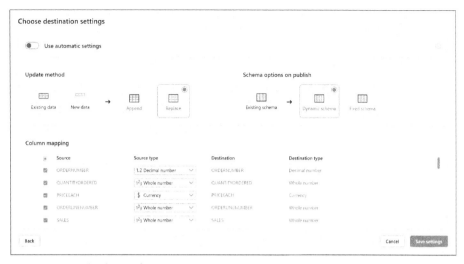

FIGURE 2-18 Destination settings

10. Disable staging of the query by right-clicking a query in the **Queries** pane and toggling off **Enable staging.**

11. Publish the dataflow, and refresh it.

The table is created and filled with data as soon as the dataflow is updated. You can update your dataflow manually, or you can set regular updates. Because users often need to branch out individual transformation processes, timing all items separately can be problematic. That's why using the orchestration capabilities of a data pipeline is good, as they can also run dataflows.

Notebooks

Notebooks are items that are used primarily for creating Apache Spark jobs and machine learning experiments. A notebook itself does not allow you to perform data transformations using the UI. Instead, you must use of one of the supported scripting languages:

- PySpark (Python)
- Spark SQL
- Spark (Scala)
- SparkR (R)

You can use these languages in individual code cells that can be executed independently regardless of their order or run sequentially. If a notebook is started using a pipeline, for example, then all cells are executed in their order. Individual code cells can reuse previous cells' variables and outputs, so combining individual scripting languages is possible to obtain a result. In addition to these languages, you can also use Markdown notepads. However, it is possible to create notes in code cells according to the rules of the chosen language.

Notebooks are extended with the **Data Wrangler** tool, which allows you to perform transformation and explorer operations with data using a graphical interface similar to Power Query. It currently allows editing data loaded as **pandas DataFrame** and **Spark DataFrame**.

Notebooks allow the use of many libraries, which are ready-made collections of code for the user. You can use three types of libraries:

- **Built-in**   These are pre-installed libraries for each Fabric Spark runtime, according to its settings. For specific details, consult "Apache Spar Runtimes in Fabric" at *learn.microsoft. com/en-us/fabric/data-engineering/runtime.*

- **Public**   These libraries are stored in public repositories like PyPI or Conda. Public libraries must be installed within individual notebook runs or in advance in the runtime via a custom environment or workspace default environment.

- **Custom**   These are libraries created within the organization or provided by any developer. You can use .whl libraries for Python, .jar for Java, or .tar.gz for R.

You can use the code below to inline call pieces of libraries for notebook purposes. The first line imports the full library, and the second imports only specifically named functions from a library:

```
import {name-of-package-from-library} [as {user-defined-name-of-package}]
from {name-of-package-from-library} import {name-of-function}
```

Also, thanks to libraries, notebooks can get data from a large number of source locations and can also get it to a lot of destinations. Thus, notebooks use Fabric capacity for their operation, and the admin should monitor this use of capacity to prevent a possible shortage.

NEED MORE REVIEW?   **DATA WRANGLER**

To find more information about Data Wrangler, please read "How to accelerate Data Prep with Data Wrangler in Microsoft Fabric" at *learn.microsoft.com/fabric/data-science/data-wrangler.*

EXAMPLE OF HOW TO INGEST DATA TO A LAKEHOUSE BY A NOTEBOOK

Open a blank notebook, and follow these steps:

1. Insert the following code into the first cell:

```
azure_data_lake_gen2_name = "<name-of-your-ADLG2>"
blob_container_name = "<container-name>"
file_name = "<file-name>"
path = f'abfss://{blob_container_name}@{azure_data_lake_gen2_name}.dfs.core.
windows.net/{file_name}'
```

2. Fill variables by your content.

3. Create a new **Code cell**.

4. Insert the following code:

```
df = spark.read.format('csv').options(header='True',inferSchema='True').load(path)
```

5. Add a lakehouse by selecting **Lakehouse** in Explorer.

6. Select **Add** in the left of the window (Figure 2-19).

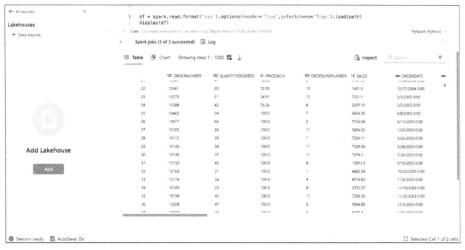

FIGURE 2-19 Preview of data in a notebook

7. In the popup, choose if you want to create a new lakehouse or use an existing one (Figure 2-20).

Add Lakehouse

○ New lakehouse

◉ Existing lakehouse

Add   Cancel

FIGURE 2-20 Add lakehouse options

8. Your decision in step 7 will stop the current Spark session. You need to confirm this by selecting the **Stop now** button.

9. Create a new **Code cell**, and insert the following code:

```
df.write.mode("overwrite").format("delta").saveAsTable('salesByNotebook')
```

10. Select **Run all**.

Once selected, the lakehouse will create a new table named salesbyNotebook with the schema defined by the data frame. In addition, you can use the function saveAsTable to save; the input would look like save('Table/salesByNotebook'). There is often no need to overwrite all data stored in tables, so you can use mode('append') just to add new rows. If you want to save data not as a table but as a file, you can use save('Files/<name-of-folder-for-files>'). The result would then look like:

```
df.write.format("csv").save("Files/SalesData")
df.write.format("parquet").save("Files/SalesData")
```

Create and manage shortcuts

Shortcuts are objects in OneLake that point to other storage locations. They appear as folders in OneLake; any experience or service with access to OneLake can use them. OneLake shortcuts behave similarly to Microsoft Windows shortcuts. They're independent objects from the target to which they are just pointing. If you delete a shortcut, the target remains unaffected. The shortcut can break if you move, rename, or delete a target path.

Shortcuts can be created in **lakehouse** or **KQL (Kusto Query Language)** databases, and you can use them as data directly in OneLake. Any Fabric service can use them without necessarily copying data directly from a data source. Shortcuts can be created as:

- Table shortcut
- File shortcut

Thanks to the ability to create shortcuts with data stored directly in OneLake, you can reuse data between lakehouses stored in different workspaces. These shortcuts can be generated from a **lakehouse**, **warehouse**, or **KQL** database. They can also access data for notebook transformations or other Fabric items.

EXAMPLE OF HOW TO CREATE A SHORTCUT INSIDE A LAKEHOUSE

You can create a shortcut if you own a lakehouse by following these steps:

1. Open Lakehouse Explorer.
2. Right-click a directory within the **Explorer** pane, or select the **ellipsis** icon that appears when you hover over the Tables or Files main folder.
3. Select **New shortcut** (Figure 2-21).

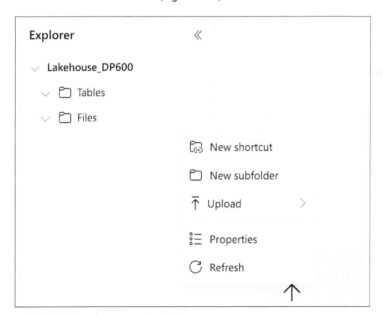

FIGURE 2-21 Creating a new shortcut

4. Select a source of data, such as **Azure Data Lake Storage Gen2** (Figure 2-22).

FIGURE 2-22 Shortcut wizard

5. Fill in the connection settings.
6. Name the shortcut, and set the subpath to your data.
7. Select the new shortcut folder to preview the data (Figure 2-23).

FIGURE 2-23 Data preview

As you can see in Figure 2-24, shortcuts are indicated by a folder icon similar to the one used for Tables and Files but with an added link symbol. This icon is attached to the original icon and can recognize data connected as shortcuts. To delete a shortcut, select the **ellipsis** icon displayed after hovering over the shortcut name and select the **Delete** option.

FIGURE 2-24 Icon previews

Implement file partitioning for analytics workloads in a lakehouse

A crucial technique in data management, *data partitioning* involves dividing a large dataset into smaller, more manageable subsets known as *partitions*. Each partition holds a portion of the data, which can be stored and processed independently.

Partitions are represented as folders that contain Parquet files that all meet the same partition condition. A partition condition uses data in a selected column (or columns) because multiple partitions are supported. Based on them, you can create a partition folder with an exact name pattern: *<partition-name>=<value>*. For example, Figure 2-25 shows a preview of COUNTRY partitions. Note that a partition folder must contain at least one file; empty partition folders are automatically removed.

← sales (file view)			
Name	**Date modified**	**Type**	**Size**
📁 COUNTRY=Australia	3/10/2024 8:29:51 …	Folder	1 items
📁 COUNTRY=Austria	3/10/2024 8:29:52 …	Folder	1 items
📁 COUNTRY=Belgium	3/10/2024 8:29:53 …	Folder	1 items
📁 COUNTRY=Canada	3/10/2024 8:29:52 …	Folder	1 items
📁 COUNTRY=Denmark	3/10/2024 8:29:53 …	Folder	1 items
📁 COUNTRY=Finland	3/10/2024 8:29:52 …	Folder	1 items
📁 COUNTRY=France	3/10/2024 8:29:51 …	Folder	1 items
📁 COUNTRY=Germany	3/10/2024 8:29:53 …	Folder	1 items
📁 COUNTRY=Ireland	3/10/2024 8:29:54 …	Folder	1 items

FIGURE 2-25 Deployed COUNTRY partitions

Not every column can be used as a partition column, because partition columns must have one of the following data types:

- String
- Integer
- Boolean
- DateTime

If a column contains empty values, one more partition with a condition equal to __HIVE_DEFAULT_PARTITION__ will be created.

Delta tables are also filed by composition so that the same principle can be applied to them. However, the **Copy Activity** options within pipelines, DataFlow Gen2, and notebooks currently allow you to create partitions using **Copy Activity** (only for tables) and notebook (for tables and files).

EXAMPLE OF IMPLEMENTING PARTITIONS BY COPY ACTIVITY IN A PIPELINE

Open the new data pipeline in the same workspace as a lakehouse, which will be used as a data destination, and then follow these steps:

1. Add a **Copy Activity** by selecting **Add pipeline activity** > **Copy data**. Under **Source**, select **Sample dataset**, select **Browse**, and then choose a dataset, such as NYC Taxi – Green (Parquet), as shown in Figure 2-26.

FIGURE 2-26 Inserting a sample dataset as a data store type

2. Under **Destination**, select a destination **lakehouse**.
3. Open **Advanced options**.
4. Enable **partitions**.
5. Add partitions columns (Figure 2-27).

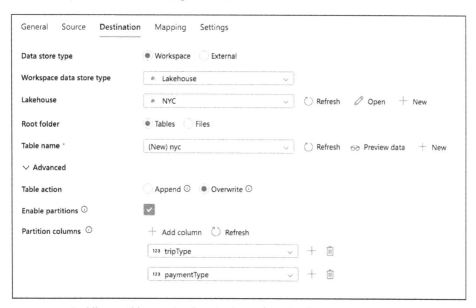

FIGURE 2-27 Enabling partitions and assigned columns from the data source

6. Select **Run**.

This run's result will look the same in the Lakehouse Explorer as the run without partitions. The difference occurs when you select the created table's **ellipsis** and select **View files**. The result will then look similar to Figure 2-28.

FIGURE 2-28 Implemented partitions on a table with a blank value

EXAMPLE OF IMPLEMENTING PARTITIONS USING FABRIC NOTEBOOKS

Create and open a new notebook in a workspace where is also a lakehouse that might be used as a data destination, and then follow these steps:

1. Connect to the lakehouse with the data ingested by the previous pipeline.

2. Delete all default cells, and create one new **Code cell**.

3. Insert the following code:

```
df = spark.sql("SELECT * FROM nyc")
df.write.partitionBy("vendorID","tripType","paymentType").mode("overwrite").
parquet("Files/nyc")
```

4. Select **Run**.

The function `partitionBy` from step 3 creates partitions based on the column names inserted, which in this case are vendorID, tripType, and paymentType. These appear both in Lakehouse Explorer (Figure 2-29) and a notebook's Lakehouse Preview.

FIGURE 2-29 Preview of partitions in Lakehouse Explorer

Create views, functions, and stored procedures

Fabric lakehouses that use SQL analytic endpoints and warehouses both support the creation of views, functions, and stored procedures. Three components are integral parts of a **SQL** database:

- **View**   A virtual table whose content is pre-defined by a query
- **Function**   A user-defined function that accepts parameters, performs an action, such as a complex calculation, and returns the result as a scalar value or a table
- **Stored procedure**   A block of T-SQL code stored in a database that the client can execute

All of them can be created using the SQL query editor either directly in the SQL analytic endpoint interface via the SQL query of the mentioned items or by using SQL Management Studio or Azure Data Studio. You can create views and stored procedures using templates also. To access them, hover over their respective folder, and then select the **ellipsis** icon that appears (Figure 2-30). Note that the **Refresh** option in the resulting menu refreshes only the preview of the data, not the data itself.

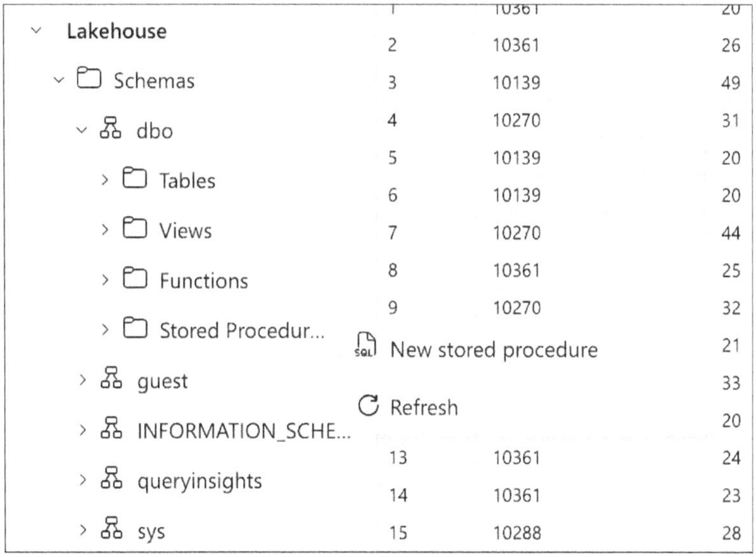

∨ Lakehouse	1	10361	20
	2	10361	26
∨ ☐ Schemas	3	10139	49
∨ ⬚ dbo	4	10270	31
	5	10139	20
> ☐ Tables	6	10139	20
> ☐ Views	7	10270	44
> ☐ Functions	8	10361	25
	9	10270	32
> ☐ Stored Procedur...	▢ New stored procedure		21
> ⬚ guest			33
	↻ Refresh		20
> ⬚ INFORMATION_SCHE...			
	13	10361	24
> ⬚ queryinsights	14	10361	23
> ⬚ sys	15	10288	28

FIGURE 2-30 Quick options for creating a Stored Procedure

> **NOTE   CSV FILE SAMPLE**
>
> The data in the following examples are created from the CSV file found at *github.com/tirnovar/dp-600/blob/main/data/sales*.

Views

You can create a view in two ways: using a **SQL command** in the SQL query editor or a **visual query**, which is a no-code option that uses Diagram view in Power Query and is shown in Figure 2-31.

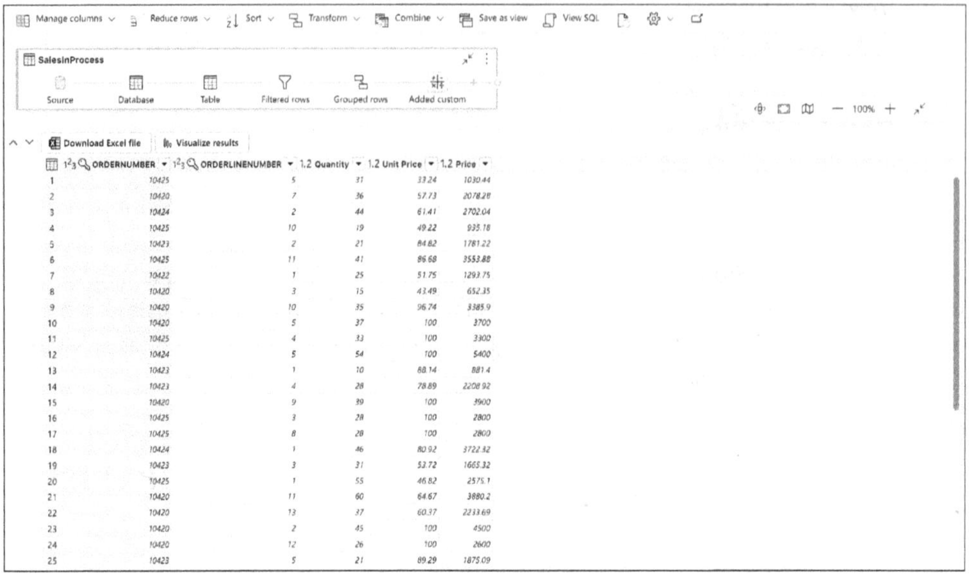

FIGURE 2-31 Diagram experience with data preview of a visual query

You can open the entire Power Query Online window, but you risk using an untranslatable operation. Power Query provides you with a data preview during each transformation step, allowing you to navigate your data easily and see what is happening. If you only use operations that Power Query can convert to SQL, you can save your results by selecting the **Save as view** button. (If you use a nontranslatable operation, an information banner will immediately tell you.) The **Save as view** popup is shown in Figure 2-32.

Another approach is to use the SQL query editor, where you can write and execute all your queries. These queries can also be stored as a personal queries alias, **My queries**, or as **Shared queries**, which all users with the right to access that item (SQL endpoint or warehouse) can see and potentially use if they have permission to execute SQL queries. This option contains a **Save as view** button next to the **Run** button. You can save any selected part of the code to create a new view. You can, therefore, test even more complex queries or perform different queries simultaneously. When you find a specific part of the code that suits you and returns the correct results, you can create a view from it, as shown in Figure 2-33.

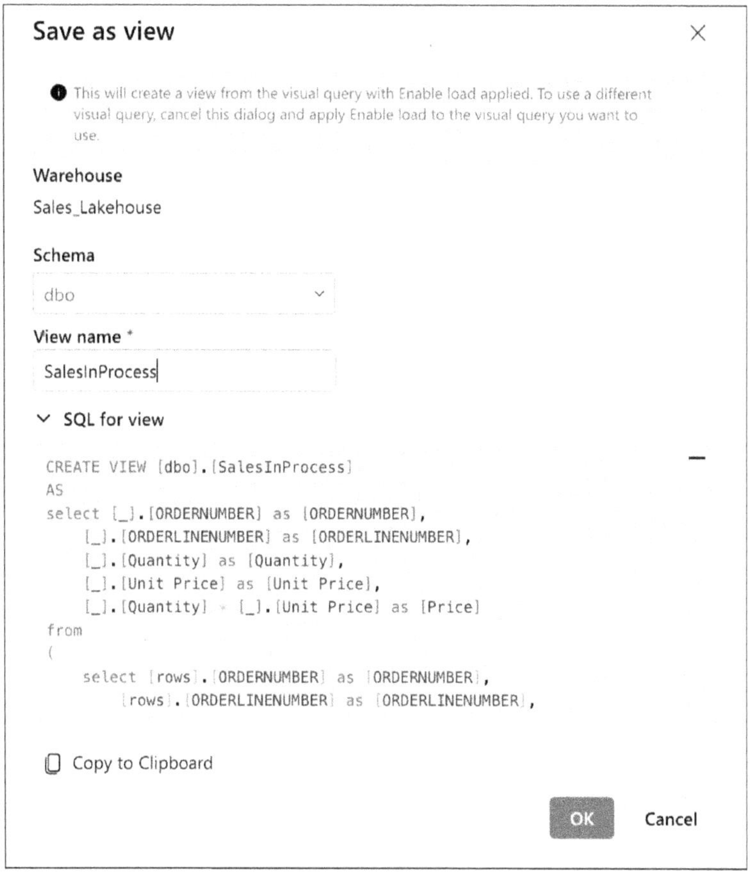

Save as view
This will create a view from the visual query with Enable load applied. To use a different visual query, cancel this dialog and apply Enable load to the visual query you want to use.
Warehouse
Sales_Lakehouse
Schema
dbo
View name *
SalesInProcess
SQL for view
CREATE VIEW [dbo].[SalesInProcess]
AS
select [_].[ORDERNUMBER] as [ORDERNUMBER],
[_].[ORDERLINENUMBER] as [ORDERLINENUMBER],
[_].[Quantity] as [Quantity],
[_].[Unit Price] as [Unit Price],
[_].[Quantity] * [_].[Unit Price] as [Price]
from
(
select [rows].[ORDERNUMBER] as [ORDERNUMBER],
[rows].[ORDERLINENUMBER] as [ORDERLINENUMBER],
Copy to Clipboard
OK
Cancel

FIGURE 2-32 SQL Preview in the Save as view

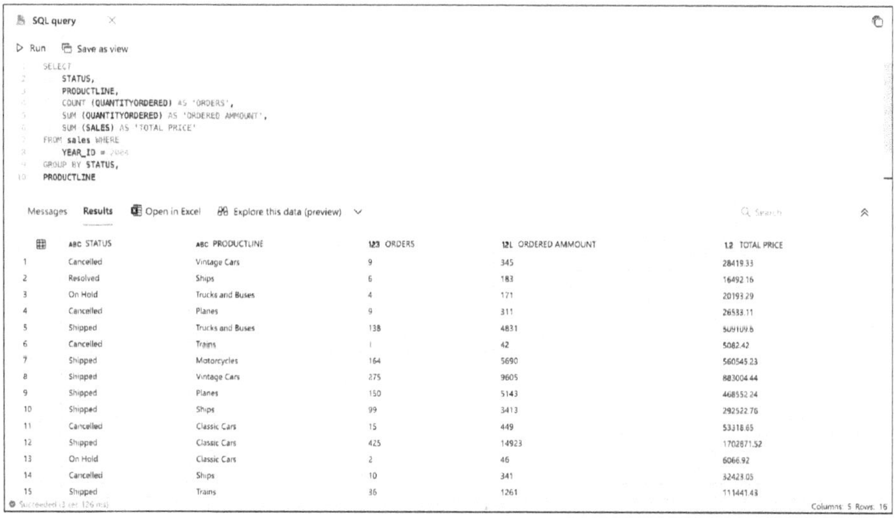

SQL query
Run
Save as view
SELECT
STATUS,
PRODUCTLINE,
COUNT (QUANTITYORDERED) AS 'ORDERS',
SUM (QUANTITYORDERED) AS 'ORDERED AMMOUNT',
SUM (SALES) AS 'TOTAL PRICE'
FROM sales WHERE
YEAR_ID = 2004
GROUP BY STATUS,
PRODUCTLINE
Messages
Results
Open in Excel
Explore this data (preview)
STATUS
PRODUCTLINE
ORDERS
ORDERED AMMOUNT
TOTAL PRICE
1 Cancelled Vintage Cars 9 345 28419.33
2 Resolved Ships 6 183 16492.16
3 On Hold Trucks and Buses 4 171 20193.29
4 Cancelled Planes 9 311 26533.11
5 Shipped Trucks and Buses 138 4831
6 Cancelled Trains 1 42 5082.42
7 Shipped Motorcycles 164 5690 560545.23
8 Shipped Vintage Cars 275 9605 883004.44
9 Shipped Planes 150 5143 468552.24
10 Shipped Ships 99 3413 292522.76
11 Cancelled Classic Cars 15 449 53318.65
12 Shipped Classic Cars 425 14923 1702871.52
13 On Hold Classic Cars 2 46 6066.92
14 Cancelled Ships 10 341 32423.05
15 Shipped Trains 36 1261 111441.43
Columns: 5 Rows: 16

FIGURE 2-33 Selected T-SQL that will be used as a view

As with a visual query, you still need to set the view's name (Figure 2-34). You can also take another look at the code that will be used.

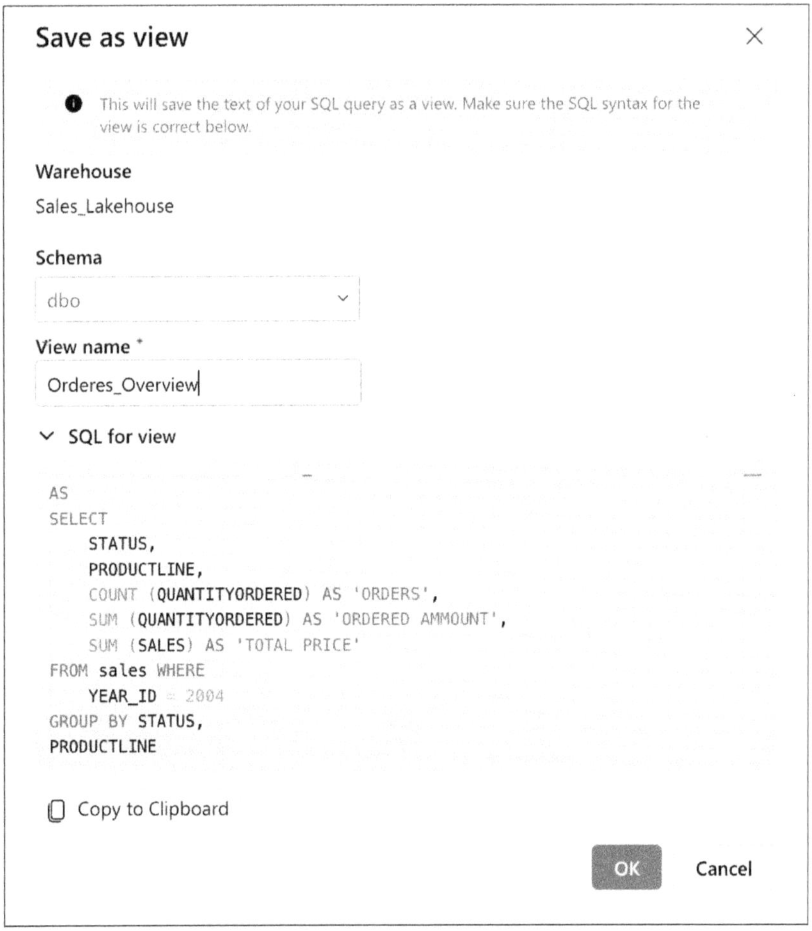

Save as view   ✕

    ⓘ   This will save the text of your SQL query as a view. Make sure the SQL syntax for the
        view is correct below.

Warehouse
Sales_Lakehouse

Schema
dbo   ⌄

View name *
Orderes_Overview

⌄ SQL for view

```
AS
SELECT
    STATUS,
    PRODUCTLINE,
    COUNT (QUANTITYORDERED) AS 'ORDERS',
    SUM (QUANTITYORDERED) AS 'ORDERED AMMOUNT',
    SUM (SALES) AS 'TOTAL PRICE'
FROM sales WHERE
    YEAR_ID = 2004
GROUP BY STATUS,
PRODUCTLINE
```

  ⎙ Copy to Clipboard

                                              [OK]   Cancel

FIGURE 2-34 T-SQL preview in Save as view window

Of course, you have the option to create views directly using CREATE VIEW using the following syntax:

```
CREATE [ OR ALTER ] VIEW [ schema_name . ] view_name [  ( column_name [ ,...n ] ) ]
AS <select_statement> [;]
<select_statement> ::=
  [ WITH <common_table_expression> [ ,...n ] ]
  <select_criteria>
```

> **NEED MORE REVIEW?** **T-SQL VIEWS**
>
> For more information about views, please visit *learn.microsoft.com/sql/t-sql/statements/create-view-transact-sql*.

Functions

Functions cannot be defined using a visual query, so you must use the T-SQL syntax directly within the SQL query option using the function syntax:

```
CREATE FUNCTION [ schema_name. ] function_name ( [ { @parameter_name [ AS ] parameter_
data_type [ = default ] } [ ,...n ]])
RETURNS TABLE
    [ WITH SCHEMABINDING ] [ AS ]
RETURN [ ( ] select_stmt [ ) ] [ ; ]
```

Alternatively, you could use another tool, such as Azure Data Studio or SQL Management Studio.

> **NEED MORE REVIEW?** **FUNCTIONS**
>
> For more information about functions, please visit *learn.microsoft.com/sql/t-sql/statements/ create-function-sql-data-warehouse.*

Stored Procedures

Stored procedures cannot be created using a visual query either. T-SQL syntax must be used here as well:

```
CREATE [ OR ALTER ] { PROC | PROCEDURE } [ schema_name.] procedure_name
    [ { @parameter data_type } [ OUT | OUTPUT ] ] [ ,...n ]
AS
{ [ BEGIN ] sql_statement [;][ ,...n ] [ END ] } [;]
```

You can also create stored procedures using a shortcut that prepares the piece of code. To use this shortcut, follow these steps:

1. Open Warehouse Explorer.
2. Right-click the **Stored Procedures** folder or the **ellipsis** that appear after hovering over it.
3. Select **New stored procedure**.

To use this shortcut as a SQL query in Warehouse Explorer:

1. Open Warehouse Explorer.
2. Expand more options at the **New SQL query**.
3. Select **Stored procedure**.

Both approaches create the code shown in Figure 2-35 as a new SQL query. You can then edit your code and prepare it to do exactly what you need.

```
SQL query 1        ✕

▷ Run      🗐 Save as view
1    CREATE PROC [dbo].[storedproc1]
2    @param1 int,
3    @param2 int
4    AS
5    BEGIN
6    SELECT @param1, @param2
7    END
8    |
```

FIGURE 2-35 Create a stored procedure template

NEED MORE REVIEW?   **STORED PROCEDURES**

For more information about stored procedures, please visit *learn.microsoft.com/sql/t-sql/statements/create-procedure-transact-sql*.

NOTE   **AZURE DATA STUDIO AND SQL MANAGEMENT STUDIO**

A SQL endpoint and warehouse can be connected using Azure Data Studio or SQL Management Studio. These tools provide you with various ready-made templates for creating views, functions, and stored procedures from their environment.

Enrich data by adding new columns or tables

As you prepare the data based on the input scenarios, it may sometimes correspond to how it will need to look in the end. Often, though, additional columns or tables will need to be added and existing ones modified or removed. Microsoft Fabric, within its ingest items and T-SQL, allows you to enrich the data and thus compile the resulting views containing precisely what is needed.

Remember that Warehouse Explorer and SQL endpoint currently do *not* support ALTER TABLE ADD COLUMN within the lakehouse and warehouse data items. Therefore, extending tables with additional columns by T-SQL is impossible; instead, you must delete the table and create it again. Within Lakehouse Explorer, however, you can edit the Delta tables schema using notebooks or SparkJobs.

The withColumn() and select() functions can extend existing DataFrames. The select() function allows you to define the columns you want to keep from the existing DataFrame. At the same time, it allows the columns defined below to be renamed, be retyped, or to perform some function with them, such as explode(). This feature allows you to select the same column twice, expanding the DataFrame with a new column. The function `withColumn()` returns a new DataFrame by adding a column or replacing the existing one with the same name.

Consider a few examples of using these functions:

```
df.select("id","name") # Will select only two columns from whole DataFrame
df.select("*",(df.UnitPrice-df.ProductionPrice).alias('ProductMargin')) # Calculates new
column based on two existing and will contain all previous columns
df.withColumn('ProductMargin', df.UnitPrice - df.ProductionPrice) # Calculates new
column based on two existingwithColumn('UnitPrice', df.UnitPrice + 10) # Replaces
current column UnitPrice with new values
```

> **NEED MORE REVIEW?** **FUNCTION EXPLODE()**
>
> For the Spark definition of function `explode()`, please visit *spark.apache.org/docs/3.1.3/api/ python/reference/api/pyspark.sql.functions.explode.html.*

To modify the existing schema of existing tables using the schema of extended DataFrames, you can use two options parameters of the `options()` function:

- `mergeSchema` Expands the existing schema with the schema of the Spark frame being written
- `overwriteSchema` Overwrites the schema of the existing Delta table with the schema of the written Spark frame

For example, you could use:

```
df.write.mode("overwrite").option("mergeSchema", "true").saveAsTable("sales")
df.write.model("overwrite").option("overwriteSchema", "true").saveAsTable("sales")
```

> **IMPORTANT** **REMOVING EXISTING COLUMNS BY** `overwriteSchema`
>
> Suppose an existing column is eliminated by `overwriteSchema` but not existing Parquet (like meanwhile Append mode). In that case, the data will not be discarded and will still be part of existing Parquet files. Only from the schema's point of view does the given column no longer exist, and it is not usually possible to query it.

As shown in the previous section, you can create a table using **Copy Activity**, **DataFlow Gen2**, or **notebooks** directly based on the data. You can also ingest data using a data pipeline, dataflow, or notebook. At the same time, you can create a new table using **T-SQL within the Warehouse Explorer**.

1. Select **New SQL query** to expand it**.**
2. Select **Table** (Figure 2-36).

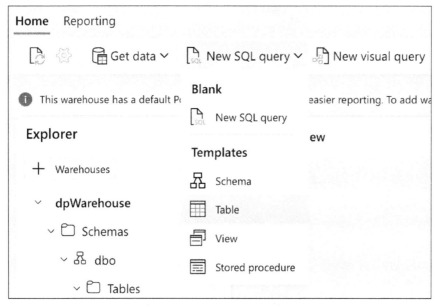

FIGURE 2-36 All current T-SQL template options in Warehouse Explorer

3. Edit the inserted code as shown in Figure 2-37.

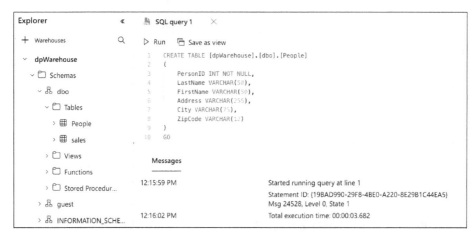

FIGURE 2-37 Creating a table with T-SQL

4. Select **Run** to create the table.

Unfortunately, this same progression does not work within SQL endpoint in Lakehouse Explorer. If you want to create a table without data, you can use PySpark and a similar syntax in SparkSQL. Changing from SQL data types to Spark data types is important; for example, use the STRING data type instead of VARCHAR (Figure 2-38).

FIGURE 2-38 Creating a table with PySpark

Skill 2.2: Copy data

This section will show how to add your copy tasks to a pipeline and then how you can schedule either the pipeline or those individual tasks to run on a schedule.

Copying data or transferring it between individual locations always involves decisions—the first being whether copying is necessary or whether an alternative to duplicating data is available. If copying is the only option, then you must select an appropriate method. If the copying is to be carried out regularly, then the possibilities of orchestrating the entire solution must also be addressed so that the timing is correct and there are no collisions or possible copying of incomplete data.

> **This skill covers how to:**
> - Choose an appropriate method for copying data from a Fabric data source to a lakehouse or warehouse
> - Copy data by using a data pipeline, dataflow, or notebook
> - Implement fast copy when using dataflows
> - Add stored procedures, notebooks, and dataflows to a data pipeline
> - Schedule data pipelines
> - Schedule dataflows and notebooks

Choose an appropriate method for copying data from a Fabric data source to a lakehouse or warehouse

Copying data always involves a critical decision about the method to use. It is always necessary to know what happens to the data during transmission, whether it should be enriched or modified during the process, and who the target audience will be who will create or manage the solution.

It would be best if you also decided whether data duplication is necessary. This topic is quite critical for Microsoft Fabric, especially from the Lakehouse Explorer point of view, because it can directly refer the user to the use of shortcuts. Thanks to them, you do not need to duplicate the data. Transformations that will be performed afterward will automatically work the most current variant of data because a shortcut provides a link to the location of the data and thus the resulting data does not have to be copied and maintained twice. However, the Warehouse Explorer does not support this.

In case it is necessary to duplicate data or perform any transformation directly during the move, it is important to validate if there is a connector for the data source. Microsoft Fabric provides three options: DataFlow Gen2, pipelines, and notebooks can access data within OneLake and thus can copy it. Of course, when you select a lakehouse as a data source, for example, the Copy Activity within a pipeline offers only lakehouses in the current workspace. Still, you can use the SQL endpoint of the given lakehouse and connect to it using the **Azure SQL Database connector**. The connection to the SQL endpoint can also be used within warehouse stored procedures, which can load data from the lakehouse to the warehouse.

You should also consider who will manage the resulting solution. More code means more freedom in solving the problem, but at the same time, there are higher demands on the technical skills of the people managing the given solution. Therefore, look at the team composition for which you're selecting and creating a solution. If users understand Power Query and create transformations, notebooks with PySpark will probably be entirely new to them. It would require high input resources to use or manage it entirely.

Lastly, consider whether changing the data storage style would be best, taking into account the data format and possibly partitions and folder structures. For example, DataFlow Gen2 currently supports saving the result of transformations only as a table. If these JSON files need to be transferred between lakehouses without changes, the DataFlow Gen2 option will not be very suitable. In this case, the Copy Activity within the data pipeline, which allows files to be moved, would serve much better. At such a moment, files can only be copied within one workspace because a SQL endpoint would not help with the files, and storing data in specific partitions would not be possible. However, a notebook is not limited to data in one workspace and can be highly efficient, although it does require working with PySpark or another of its supported languages.

Of course, extreme emphasis should be place on the thriftiness of the chosen solution so that it is not using an excessive amount of capacity units. If you find it does, search for a more economical option. Each of the options has its pros and cons, so your decision will depend on several factors at the same time. As you weigh these, remember: Users often choose and prefer the option that they understand and that will provide them with a quick solution to their problems, even if more efficient options may exist.

NEED MORE REVIEW? **MICROSOFT FABRIC DECISION GUIDE FOR COPY ACTIVITY, DATAFLOWS, AND SPARK NOTEBOOK**

For more information about deciding between Copy Activity, dataflow, or Spark Notebook, please visit *learn.microsoft.com/fabric/get-started/decision-guide-pipeline-dataflow-spark*.

Copy data by using a data pipeline, dataflow, or notebook

Copying data within Microsoft Fabric, specifically within Lakehouse Explorer and Warehouse Explorer, has two possible origins: creating the given item that will be used for copying or opening the item to which the data will be copied. Both paths lead to the same goal, but the second can save the user a few extra clicks, through the fact that the user first opens the end item and creates copy items from it. This route automatically sets the destination to itself. For example, in DataFlow Gen2, all queries will automatically be set to store data in the Lakehouse Explorer from which it was created.

For the following examples, data obtained as samples within Lakehouse are used. This is how you can get them:

1. Create a new lakehouse or open a completely blank one.

2. Select **Start with sample data** (Figure 2-39), and wait for a moment.

Start with sample data

Automatically import tables
filled with sample data.

FIGURE 2-39 The Start with sample data option

EXAMPLE OF HOW TO COPY DATA BETWEEN LAKEHOUSES BY PIPELINE

You can use **Copy Activity** to copy data between lakehouses by following these steps:

1. Create and open a new lakehouse.

2. Select **New data pipeline** from **Get data** options (Figure 2-40), and choose a name for the pipeline.

3. Select **Lakehouse** and **Existing lakehouse**, and then choose the one that contains your data from the existing lakehouses (Figure 2-41). If you cannot see Lakehouse it is in a different workspace.

4. Select the **publicholidays** table (Figure 2-42).

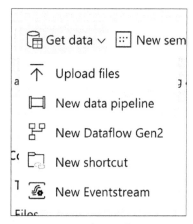

FIGURE 2-40 Get data options

FIGURE 2-41 Choose data source

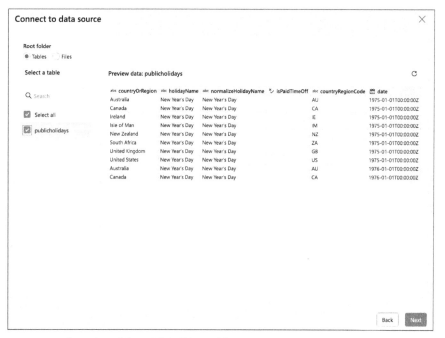

FIGURE 2-42 A preview of the publicholidays table

5. Select the target via **Lakehouse** > **Load to a new table**, and check if every column has been mapped correctly with the proper data type. In this step, you can also set partitions. However, you cannot currently use **Copy Activity** on Delta tables, which are already partitioned.

6. Select **Run**. In Figure 2-43, you can see the result of loading data into the lakehouse.

FIGURE 2-43 Successful run of a pipeline

EXAMPLE OF HOW TO COPY DATA BETWEEN LAKEHOUSES BY DATAFLOW GEN2

You can use **DataFlow Gen2** to copy data between lakehouses by following these steps:

1. Open Lakehouse.

2. Select **New DataFlow Gen2** from the **Get data** options.

3. Rename **Dataflow**.

4. As shown in Figure 2-44, navigate through **Get data** > **New** > **Microsoft Fabric** and select **Lakehouse**.

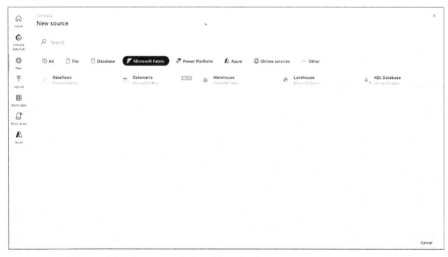

FIGURE 2-44 Microsoft Fabric sources in DataFlow Gen2

5. Select the connection **Lakehouse (None)**; if you haven't created a connection yet, you must sign in to do so.

6. Select the table that will be copied in the source lakehouse, and select the **Create** button.

7. Power Query Online will preview data, as shown in Figure 2-45. Notice in the bottom-right corner that the created query has already been connected to the initial lakehouse.

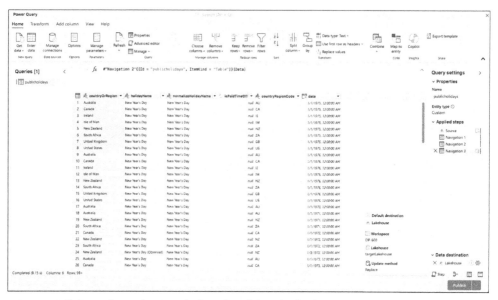

FIGURE 2-45 Data preview and automatically assigned data destination

8. If you want to change the data destination or its setup, open the Data Destination wizard. Select **Publish.**

Dataflow starts right after being saved, and you can find the copy result in the refresh history. To access refresh history, select the **ellipsis** icon and select the **Refresh History** option. More details about the completed operation will also be displayed when you select the **DateTime** in the **Start time** column. Figure 2-46 shows this detailed preview.

EXAMPLE OF HOW TO COPY DATA BETWEEN LAKEHOUSES BY NOTEBOOK

A third option is to copy data between lakehouses by notebooks. To do so, follow these steps:

1. Open Lakehouse.

2. From **Open notebook** (Figure 2-47), select **New notebook**.

3. If your lakehouses are in the same workspace, then you can load data into the **DataFrame** by Spark SQL by referencing the lakehouse with the original data and the table that contains data that you want to copy. Figure 2-48 shows a preview of the display() function results. The display() function creates a more user-friendly table that allows sorting columns but contains only the first 1,000 rows. You can change this limit in options. Note that a rendered table can also be downloaded.

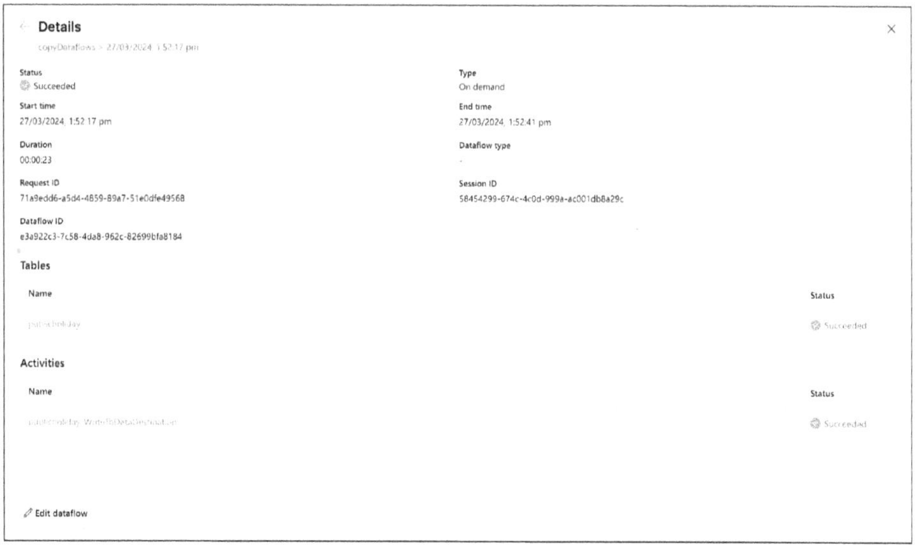

FIGURE 2-46 DataFlow Gen2 refresh history

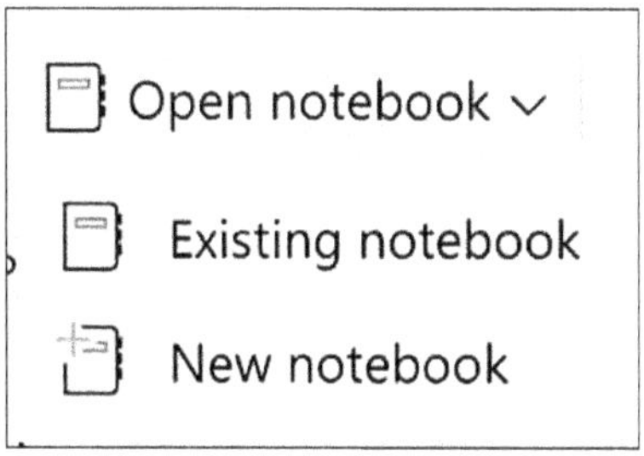

FIGURE 2-47 Open notebook options

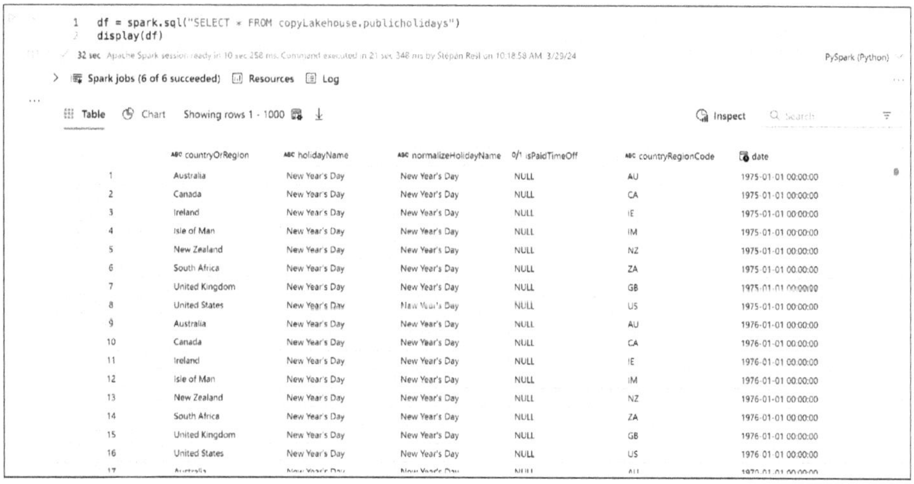

FIGURE 2-48 Displayed data from loaded DataFrame

4. Write the DataFrame data into the default lakehouse to ensure that data will be loaded even when someone updates the table schema in the origin lakehouse. You can use `overwriteSchema` (Figure 2-49), as was discussed in the section "Enrich data by adding new columns or tables."

FIGURE 2-49 Writing data from a DataFrame into a lakehouse as a table

5. If your lakehouses are in a different workspace, using the **Azure Blob File System (ABFS)** is better. ABFS can help you get data from any lakehouse. Navigate to the **lakehouse with the original data**. Select the **ellipsis** icon to open more table options. The full path is visible in Figure 2-50.

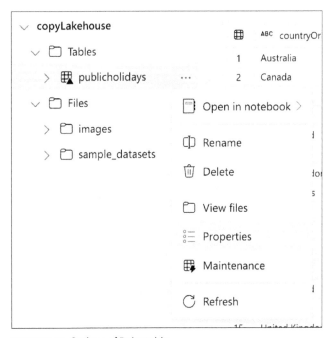

FIGURE 2-50 Options of Delta table

6. Copy the URL in the ABFS Path (Figure 2-51). The second "s" means that Transport Layer Security (TLS) will always be used.

7. Return to the created notebook and use `spark.read.load()` to load data into DataFrame through ABFS Path. Figure 2-52 provides the full code for this load.

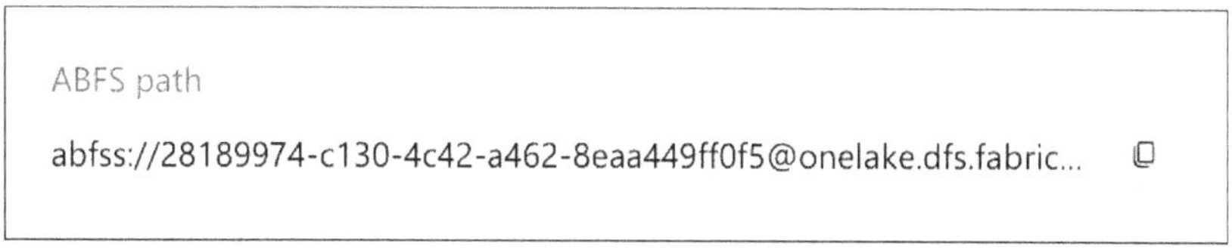

FIGURE 2-51 ABFS Path

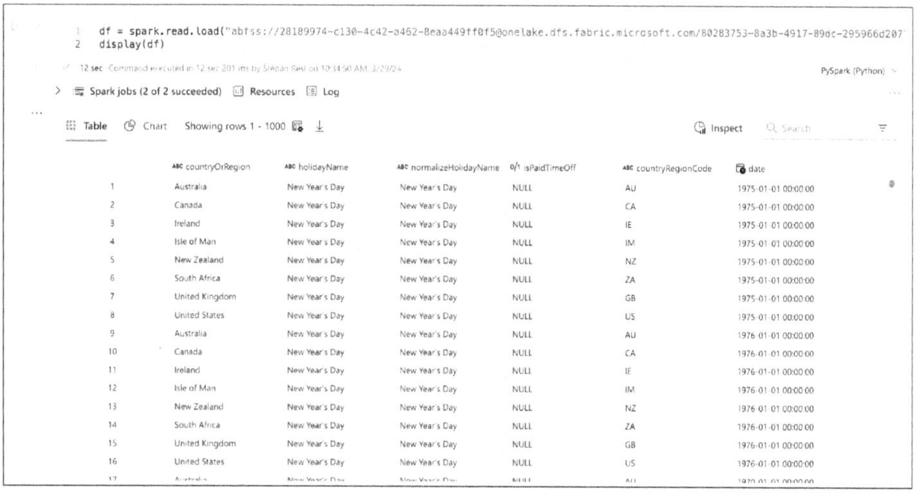

	countryOrRegion	holidayName	normalizeHolidayName	isPaidTimeOff	countryRegionCode	date
1	Australia	New Year's Day	New Year's Day	NULL	AU	1975-01-01 00:00:00
2	Canada	New Year's Day	New Year's Day	NULL	CA	1975-01-01 00:00:00
3	Ireland	New Year's Day	New Year's Day	NULL	IE	1975-01-01 00:00:00
4	Isle of Man	New Year's Day	New Year's Day	NULL	IM	1975-01-01 00:00:00
5	New Zealand	New Year's Day	New Year's Day	NULL	NZ	1975-01-01 00:00:00
6	South Africa	New Year's Day	New Year's Day	NULL	ZA	1975-01-01 00:00:00
7	United Kingdom	New Year's Day	New Year's Day	NULL	GB	1975-01-01 00:00:00
8	United States	New Year's Day	New Year's Day	NULL	US	1975-01-01 00:00:00
9	Australia	New Year's Day	New Year's Day	NULL	AU	1976-01-01 00:00:00
10	Canada	New Year's Day	New Year's Day	NULL	CA	1976-01-01 00:00:00
11	Ireland	New Year's Day	New Year's Day	NULL	IE	1976-01-01 00:00:00
12	Isle of Man	New Year's Day	New Year's Day	NULL	IM	1976-01-01 00:00:00
13	New Zealand	New Year's Day	New Year's Day	NULL	NZ	1976-01-01 00:00:00
14	South Africa	New Year's Day	New Year's Day	NULL	ZA	1976-01-01 00:00:00
15	United Kingdom	New Year's Day	New Year's Day	NULL	GB	1976-01-01 00:00:00
16	United States	New Year's Day	New Year's Day	NULL	US	1976-01-01 00:00:00

FIGURE 2-52 Preview of data from the lakehouse in another workspace

8. Write data into the **default lakehouse**, as was shown in step 4.

Implement fast copy when using dataflows

When you choose DataFlow Gen2 to copy data, you have the additional choice of using the **fast copy** option. Fast copy allows you to continue using Power Query in dataflows but also takes advantage of the scalable backend of the pipeline Copy Activity to allow you to ingest larger volumes of data more efficiently.

There are some limitations to using fast copy. For example, it supports only five data source connectors at this writing:

- Azure Data Lake Storage Gen2
- Azure Blob Storage
- Azure SQL Database
- Lakehouse
- PostgreSQL

For Azure Data Lake Storage Gen2 and Azure Blob storage, only CSV and Parquet files are supported. Data in your source also needs to meet certain size requirements. CSV and Parquet files must have a minimum size of 100 MB, and database sources require a minimum of 5 million rows.

Also, only a limited number of transformations are possible:

- Combine files
- Select or remove columns
- Change data types
- Rename a column

If you require more complex transformations, then you can negate this limitation by enabling staging, loading data to a staging lakehouse, and adding additional transformations steps to queries that reference the staged data.

The first step for using fast copy is to enable it in your dataflow. To do this, select **Options** from the **Home** tab of the **Power Query** ribbon (Figure 2-53), and from the subsequent dialog select **Allow use of fast copy connectors** from the **Scale** tab (Figure 2-54).

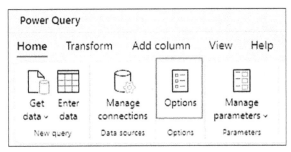

FIGURE 2-53 The Options button in the Home tab of the Power Query ribbon

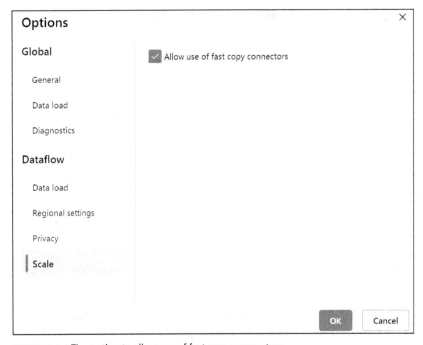

FIGURE 2-54 The option to allow use of fast copy connectors

Once you publish your dataflow and run it, you will be able to see whether the fast copy engine was triggered or not by looking at the dataflow's **refresh history**. Figure 2-55 shows an example where the fast copy engine was not used, even though fast copy had been enabled. The Engine field is left blank, whilst an error is highlighted at the bottom of the summary because the dataflow did not meet the expected criteria. This meant the dataflow still ran, and succeeded, but fell back on the dataflow's engine. (To generate this example, I added a custom column, which is an unsupported transformation.)

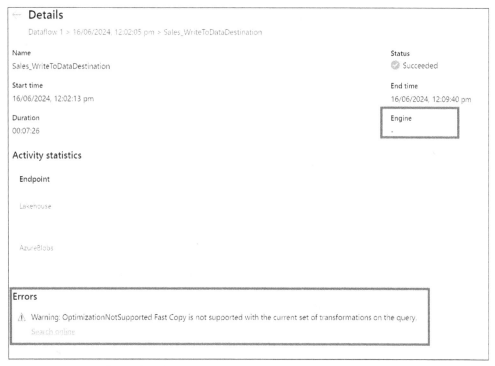

FIGURE 2-55 The dataflow refresh history shows the Engine field is empty and has a warning listed in the errors

While you are developing your dataflow, Power Query offers clues as to whether fast copy will work or not. The indicator in the **Applied steps** pane, historically used to indicate whether a step is supported by query folding or not, now also includes an assessment of whether your steps will support fast copy.

The example in Figure 2-56 shows the final step has a red indicator because the step has broken fast copy, whilst all other steps now show amber to indicate that fast copy won't be used due to breaking steps elsewhere in the query.

Removing the breaking step changes the indicators to show that fast copy is supported, as demonstrated in Figure 2-57.

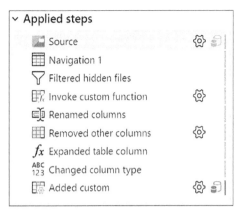

FIGURE 2-56 The Applied steps pane has an indicator to show if fast copy will be used

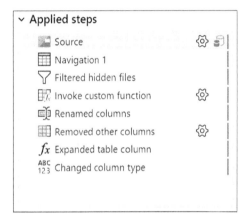

FIGURE 2-57 The Applied steps indicator showing fast copy will be used

Rather than wait for an entire dataflow to execute to check if fast copy was used, you can set queries in your dataflow to use the **Require fast copy** option, which you can find in a query's context menu (Figure 2-58). With this setting, the conditions for using fast copy are assessed before the dataflow refreshes. If the conditions are not met, the dataflow will "fail fast," as opposed to falling back to the dataflows engine.

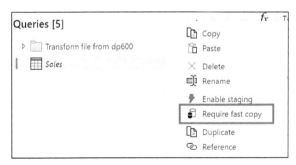

FIGURE 2-58 The Require fast copy option

Having updated the example dataflow to ensure fast copy will be used, you can now see the outcome of this in the dataflow refresh history. In Figure 2-59, you can see that the Engine field in the **Refresh history** pane now shows CopyActivity and no longer displays any errors or warnings.

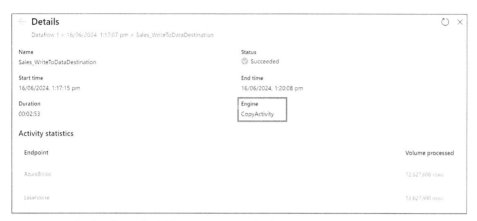

FIGURE 2-59 The dataflow refresh history shows that the fast copy engine has been used

You can also see that the duration of dataflow is less than 3 minutes, compared to over 7 minutes when fast copy wasn't triggered. Fast copy rapidly imported the same volume of data, from the same source—clearly demonstrating that fast copy can speed up your workload.

Add stored procedures, notebooks, and dataflows to a data pipeline

You can use data pipelines, from the Data Factory experience, to orchestrate transformation tasks within your Fabric solution.

When creating a new pipeline, the landing page will greet you with the option to **Add a pipeline activity** to start building your data pipeline, as shown in Figure 2-60.

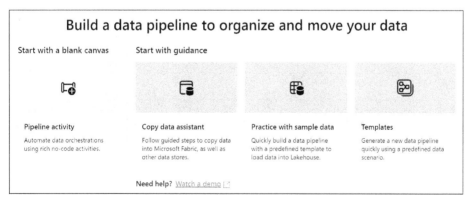

FIGURE 2-60 You can add a pipeline activity from the data pipeline landing page

Selecting the **Add pipeline activity** option launches a context menu with a list of activities you are able to add. Under the **Move and transform group**, you will see an option to add a Dataflow activity (Figure 2-61).

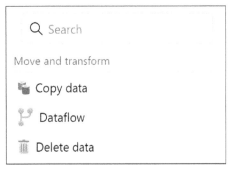

FIGURE 2-61 Dataflow appears under the Move and transform group

The option to add notebooks and stored procedures falls under the **Transform group**, shown in Figure 2-62.

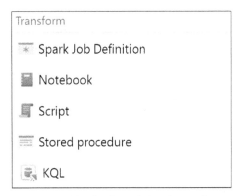

FIGURE 2-62 Notebooks and stored procedures appear under the Transform group

If you need to add an activity to an existing pipeline that already has tasks in it, you won't see this option. Instead, you can select the activities via the **Activities** menu option (Figure 2-63).

FIGURE 2-63 The Activities menu option

Adding a stored procedure to a data pipeline

Selecting your chosen activity adds it to the data pipeline canvas. For example, suppose you first want to add a stored procedure (Figure 2-64).

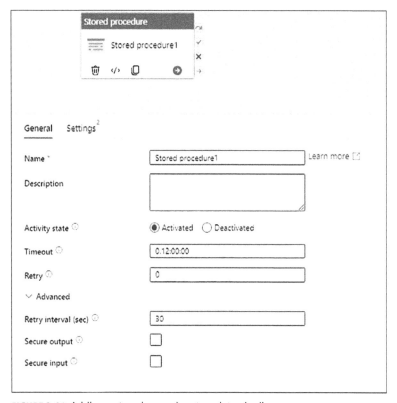

FIGURE 2-64 Adding a stored procedure to a data pipeline

With the activity selected, a configuration window is available at the bottom of the screen. The **General** tab allows you to set the following options:

- **Name** Provide something descriptive here that either matches the name of the stored procedure or describes what the stored procedure does, rather than leaving the default value.

- **Description** Provide a more detailed description of what the stored procedure does.

- **Activity state** Set whether the activity is activated or not. Deactivated activities are skipped when a pipeline runs.

- **Timeout** Set a time limit for the activity to run. The default is 12 hours.

- **Retry** Set the number of repeat attempts that should be made if the activity fails.

- **Retry interval (sec)** Set how long the activity should wait between retries.

- **Secure output**   Turn this option on to exclude the outputs from the activity from capture in logging. Turn it off to include the output.
- **Secure input**   Turn on this option to exclude inputs to the activity from logging.

The second tab, Settings (Figure 2-65), is where you set details for the stored procedure.

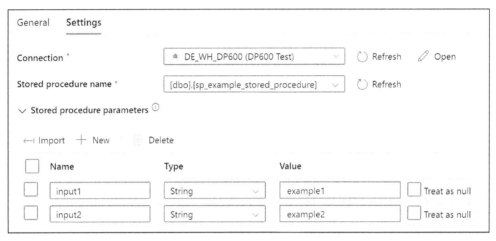

FIGURE 2-65 The Settings tab for a stored procedure activity

The **Settings** tab allows you to set the following options:

- **Data store type**   Selecting *Workspace* will allow you to pick a stored procedure from a warehouse in your current workspace. The *External* option allows you to connect to an alternative Azure SQL Database source.
- **Warehouse/Connection**   The heading for this option will change dependent on the preceding selection. If Workspace was selected as the data store type, you will have a dropdown to select your warehouse. If External was selected, you will be prompted to select a connection to an external source or to define a new connection.
- **Stored procedure name**   Based on your Warehouse/Connection choice you have a dropdown to select the relevant stored procedure.
- **Stored procedure parameters**   Selecting the *Import* button will bring in any parameters associated with the stored procedure. You can assign values to the parameters. These can be dynamic content if you wish.

Adding a dataflow to a data pipeline

Adding a dataflow activity to a pipeline follows a similar pattern. The **General** tab for a dataflow activity is identical to that of a stored procedure (Figure 2-66).

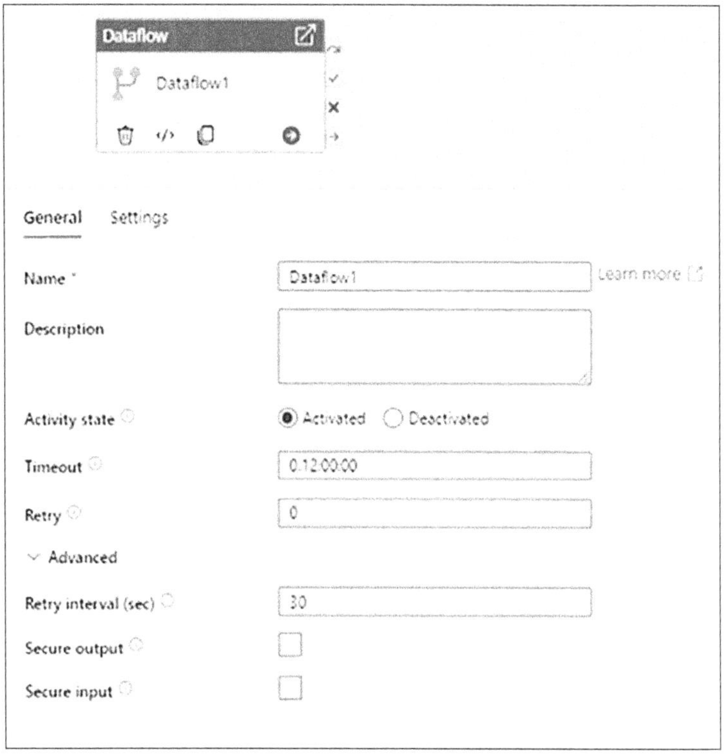

FIGURE 2-66 Adding a dataflow to a data pipeline

The **Settings** tab differs though, as you can see in Figure 2-67.

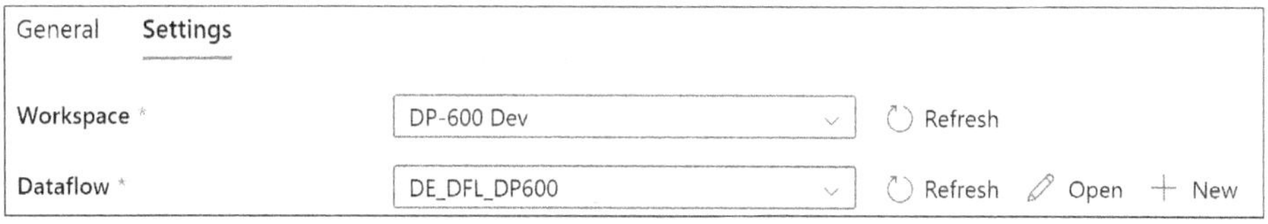

FIGURE 2-67 The Settings tab for a dataflow activity

The **Workspace** option allows you to pick which workspace you wish to select a dataflow from. Unlike some other activities, you are not bound to the same workspace that the data pipeline belongs to.

After you select a workspace, the **Dataflow** option allows you to select from the available dataflows. Both of these options accept dynamic content as input

Adding a notebook to a data pipeline

Finally, you can add a notebook as an activity to the data pipeline. Once again, the **General** tab for this activity matches that of the other data transformation tasks (Figure 2-68).

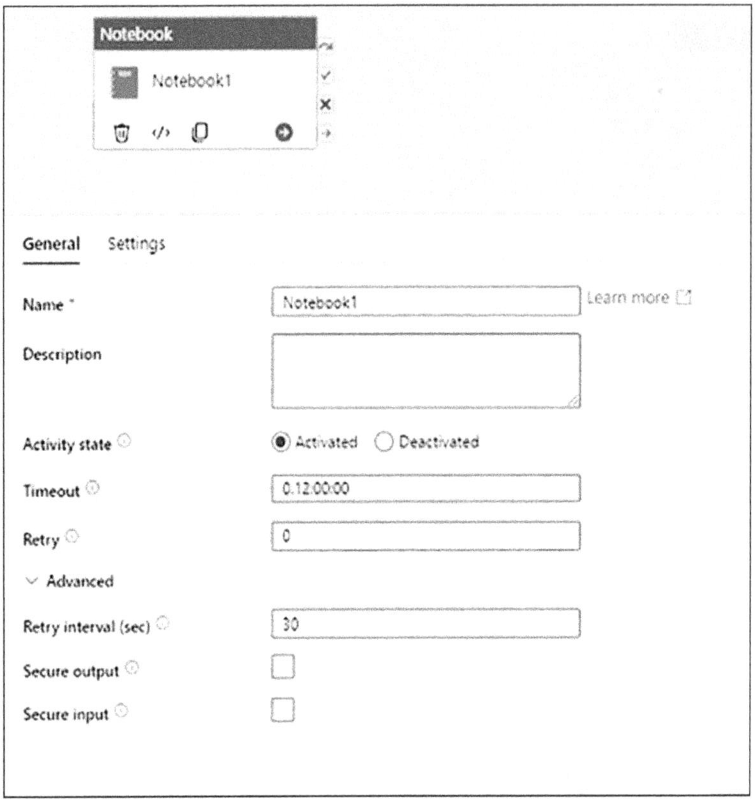

FIGURE 2-68 Adding a notebook to a data pipeline

Figure 2-69 shows the **Settings** tab for a notebook activity.

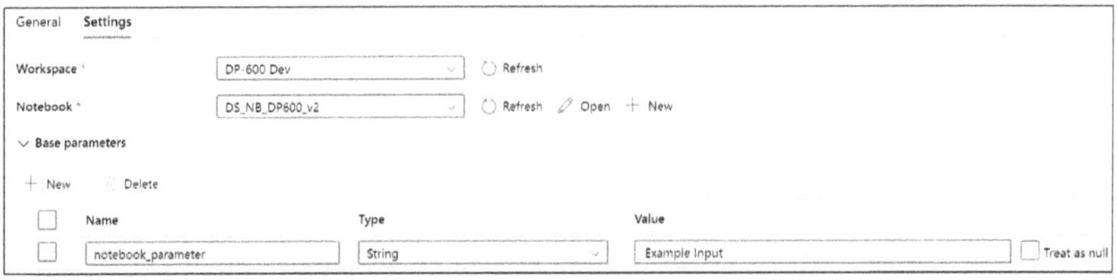

FIGURE 2-69 The Settings tab for a notebook activity

As you can with dataflows, you can choose notebooks from other workspaces by using the dropdown, which then cascades to the Notebook dropdown and allows you to choose the relevant notebook. Like stored procedures, notebooks also accept parameters as inputs. These are configured under the **Base parameters** section. The **Value field** for the Workspace, Notebook, and Base parameters all accept dynamic content.

Schedule data pipelines

There are two available options in the Fabric user interface for scheduling a data pipeline. From the workspace, you can select **Schedule** from the **ellipsis** menu available next to the pipeline (Figure 2-70).

FIGURE 2-70 Selecting the Schedule option from the data pipeline workspace

Alternatively, from an open data pipeline, a **Schedule** button is available in the **Home** tab of the menu bar (Figure 2-71).

FIGURE 2-71 Selecting the Schedule option from the data pipeline

Select either option to launch the dialog shown in Figure 2-72.

Here you can set the following options:

- **Scheduled run**   Toggle whether a schedule is on or off.
- **Repeat**   Set the frequency of the schedule. The options here are *by the minute*, *Hourly*, *Daily*, or *Weekly*. Depending on your selection here, you will be prompted with further configuration options with which you set corresponding details giving more specifics about the frequency.
- **Start date and time**   Specify when the data pipeline schedule begins.
- **End date and time**   Specify when the data pipeline schedule stops.
- **Time zone**   Set to ensure the schedule is on local time.

With all options configured, select the **Apply** button to set the schedule.

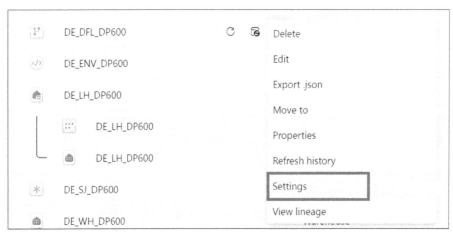

FIGURE 2-72 The Schedule dialog for a data pipeline

Schedule dataflows and notebooks

To schedule dataflows and notebooks, you could add them to a data pipeline and set a schedule on that pipeline, following the steps presented in the previous two sections. However, you can schedule each of these items independently as well.

To schedule a dataflow, select the **Settings** option from the **ellipsis** menu (Figure 2-73).

DE_DFL_DP600		C		Delete
DE_ENV_DP600				Edit
DE_LH_DP600				Export .json
	DE_LH_DP600			Move to
	DE_LH_DP600			Properties
DE_SJ_DP600				Refresh history
				Settings
DE_WH_DP600				View lineage

FIGURE 2-73 Selecting the dataflow Settings option from the workspace

From here, expand the **Refresh** section to reveal the scheduling options (Figure 2-74).

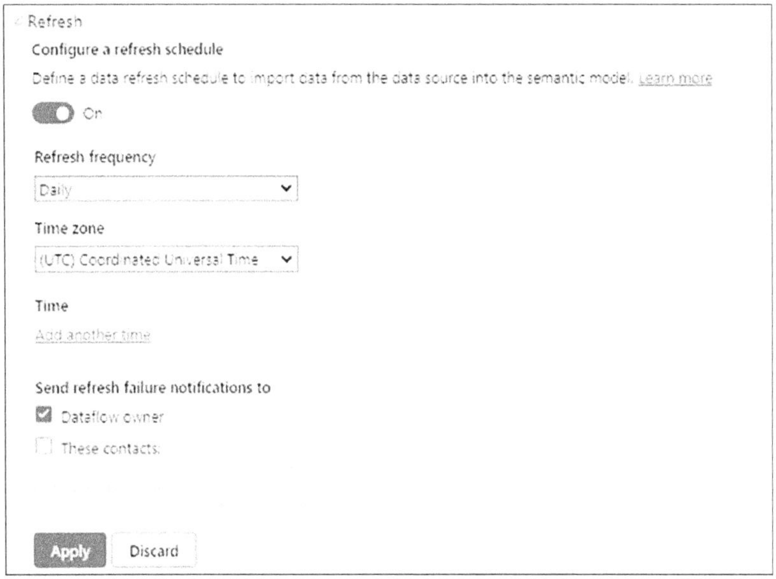

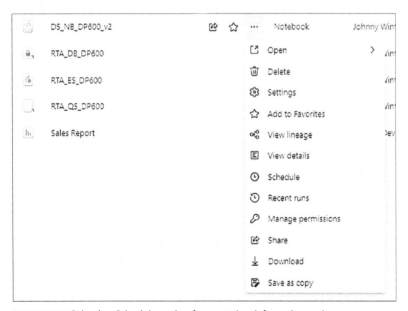

FIGURE 2-74 The Refresh scheduling options for a dataflow

From here you can toggle the schedule on or off, select either *Daily* or *Weekly* for **Refresh frequency**, select the time zone, and add the time of the refreshes. Selecting a Weekly refresh also allows you to select the days of the week. You can also add a list of contacts to be notified in case the dataflow refresh fails.

There are two routes to setting a schedule for running a notebook. Again, you can access the **Schedule** option via the **ellipsis** menu from the workspace (Figure 2-75).

FIGURE 2-75 Selecting Schedule option for a notebook from the workspace

The alternative is to select the **Schedule** option from the **Run** tab of the menu bar in the notebook (Figure 2-76.)

FIGURE 2-76 The Run tab of the notebook menu bar

The **Schedule** dialog for a notebook is identical to the dialog for scheduling a data pipeline (Figure 2-77). All configuration options are as described in the "Schedule data pipelines" section of this chapter.

DS_NB_DP600_v2
Notebook

About

Endorsement

Schedule

No previous history
The scheduled refresh is turned off

🕐 Schedule

Scheduled run

○ On   ● Off

Repeat

Select a freque ⌄

Start date and time   **End date and time**

dd/mm/yyyy   dd/mm/yyyy

Time zone

(UTC) Dublin, Edinburgh, Lisbon, London ⌄

Apply

FIGURE 2-77 The Schedule dialog for a notebook

Skill 2.3: Transform data

When data comes from individual systems, it often needs to be cleaned, edited, combined with historical or other data, and prepared for information extraction. This skill includes guidance on how to structure your data to make it suitable from an analytics solution, discussing concepts around data modeling techniques, as well as practical advice on how to achieve some of the transformations you will need to use.

This skill covers how to:

- Implement a data cleansing process
- Implement a star schema for a lakehouse or warehouse, including Type 1 and Type 2 slowly changing dimensions
- Implement bridge tables for a lakehouse or warehouse
- Denormalize data
- Aggregate or de-aggregate data
- Merge or join data
- Identify and resolve duplicate data, missing data, or null values
- Convert data types by using SQL or PySpark
- Filter data

Implement a data cleansing process

Data cleansing is integral to data preparation, ensuring data is ready for subsequent use and processing. As part of this, data quality is addressed when the data must meet the necessary criteria or measures of:

- **Validity**   Whether data contains only values and data types that conform to defined rules and restrictions. This means that if you expect to receive numerical values but sometimes get a number and sometimes text, then the data type restriction is not met, and this needs to be taken care of as part of data cleansing. Likewise, if you expect the numeric values to range from 0 to 100 and the returned value is −40 or 1,000, then the data is outside the expected range, and again, this needs to be resolved.

- **Accuracy**   Whether the data matches the expected incoming values set as thresholds based on historical data or a forecast. It can also be said that accuracy is a description of random errors or deviations that are or can be found in the data. You can measure this criterion using the standard deviation: The smaller the standard deviation, the more accurate the data you have. Various graphical representations, such as the Box and Whisker plot, are often used for this criterion, focusing on data distribution. This lets you quickly see the distance of quartiles from extremes and possible outliers. In the same way, this criterion can also be viewed in the way that it should tell you whether the data that arrives can exist at all. An example is that a city called XYZ or Microsoft exists in a particular state.

- **Completeness**   Whether all the necessary data is present. This criterion is difficult to fix with corrective transformations, because you cannot determine exactly what state the data would be in at any given moment if it arrived or what it would contain. It is, therefore, very often expressed as the number of missing values. This can take different forms, but two are typical. The first is the number of null or blank values within a given column—the number of missing values in the sequence. The second option can be thought of as having a sequence of numbers 1 to 100 and missing the numbers 3, 17, 31, 56, and 89. These numbers can also represent entire missing rows, meaning that the data is potentially incomplete and needs to be verified to determine whether it should exist.

- **Consistency** Whether the data under the same circumstances or conditions data are the same. An example of this could be that each customer has a delivery address, but at the same time, two addresses are registered, one of which refers to "156th Ave. NE, Redmond" and the other to "156th Ave., Redmond." At a given moment, deciding which address is correct or currently valid is necessary. Different kinds of inconsistency have different approaches to resolution. For example, you might decide that only the most recent addresses will always be used or the introduction of addresses as slowly changing dimensions (see the next section), so that it is possible to work correctly in the future even with a change of addresses when the customer moves.

- **Uniformity** Whether the same units are used. An example of this could be that all prices are converted to a central currency for subsequent calculations or whether some central value or column needs to be added so that it is not necessary to always multiply the value with the data using the exchange rate of the given moment. Another example could relate to converting all units of measurement to a uniform one, so everything is in liters, kilograms, and so on. Uniformity is also about conforming to the same number of decimal places or setting the lowest order to be used.

The data quality resulting from these criteria or metrics helps the subsequent transformations and information mining because the data can be relied upon. To ensure everyone can rely on the data, however, you must follow steps to prepare the data so that your criteria are met or are as accurate as possible.

> *NOTE* **DATA QUALITY STEPS**
>
> The steps to enhance data quality include removing irrelevant data, de-duplication, correcting structural errors, eliminating missing data, eliminating outliers, standardizing, normalizing, and more.

Before you can begin your data quality steps, you must go through another crucial phase: a data audit. An audit's goal is to identify what errors appear in the data and ensure that if a new type of error occurs, it will be recorded and incorporated into subsequent steps. Microsoft Fabric provides capabilities that can significantly assist with this audit. Specifically, you can use data profiling to provide a summary overview of the data. You can learn more about data profiling in the "Profile data" section of Chapter 4, "Explore and analyze data."

Therefore, it is essential to know how the data looks initially, what problems or errors must be dealt with, and how to set the data cleansing process accordingly. As you've learned, cleansing requires more than changing data types, filtering, or removing unnecessary columns. Therefore, within Microsoft Fabric, the resulting cleansing process will usually be created within **notebooks** or **DataFlow Gen2**, as these provide you with complete options for transformations and data profiling.

Implement a star schema for a lakehouse or warehouse, including Type 1 and Type 2 slowly changing dimensions

A *star schema* is a data modeling pattern associated with analytics. It is sometimes referred to as a dimensional model or Kimball method, as it was pioneered by Ralph Kimball.

For your analytics implementation in Fabric, a star schema is the recommended approach whether you are using a lakehouse or a warehouse as your preferred storage choice.

Historically, the choice of star schema was largely made for query performance reasons. Whilst technology has moved on and this is now less of a concern, the structure of a star schema still offers the benefit that it organizes your data in a way that makes it easily accessible for users, by grouping together data into an intuitive set of entities for explorative analysis.

Two main types of tables are created in a star schema—fact and dimension:

- **Fact tables are used for measurement.** They store in them the numbers recorded as part of a business process event. These numbers will typically be summarized and/or trended allowing analysts to answer questions relating to the how much, how many, how long, or how often of a particular event.

- **Dimension tables provide context.** They include the descriptive attributes about a particular event allowing analysts to answer questions about the who, what, when, where, and how related to an event.

Figure 2-78 shows a high-level view of a star schema, illustrating how the tables interact with each other. A fact table sits at the center of the design, surrounded by dimension tables at each of the star's points.

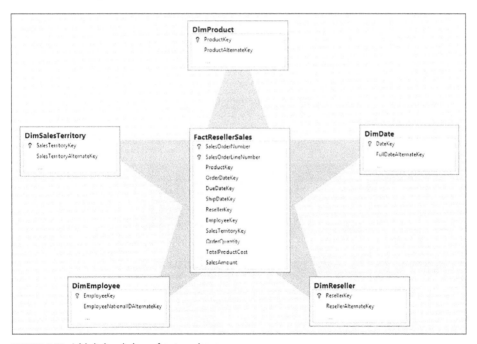

FIGURE 2-78 A high-level view of a star schema

Fact tables typically are long and thin, because they contain many rows (multi-billions would not be uncommon in this day and age) but do not have many columns. The columns ordinarily consist of the measurements you need to record (quantity, cost, amount, and similar) and then the foreign keys of the dimension tables the fact table is related to.

Conversely, a dimension table is often described as being short and wide. Here you would expect to see fewer records, but many columns that have the descriptive attributes for the entity the table represents. The wide nature of dimension tables can often be attributed to the denormalized nature of these entities (see the "Denormalize data" section for more details).

Dimension tables themselves can fall into their own special categories. Descriptive data relating to a particular record in a dimension table may well change over time. These dimensions are referred to as *slowly changing dimensions* (*SCDs*). When creating your solution you need to make decisions on how you will handle these changes over time.

Kimball defined eight types of SCD. The scope of the DP-600 exam is concerned with Types 1 and 2 only, but for completeness we will also describe type 0:

- **Type 0 SCD** Dimension that is created once, is never updated, and will never change. A good example is a time dimension. There will only ever be 24 hours in a day and 60 minutes in an hour. If your implementation requires a time table, you can likely populate this as a one-off exercise and never have to do any further maintenance or updates.

- **Type 1 SCD** Dimension that always maintains the current version of a record. If you have a dimension table with employee records in it and an employee's job title changes, then a Type 1 SCD will simply update that record and overwrite the job title field with the new value.

- **Type 2 SCD** Dimension that tracks history over time. If a change is made to a record, rather than overwrite the existing record, a new one is created with the new details on it. Typically these records will have a start date and end date to denote the valid period for the record, and it is also a common practice to include a Boolean field to indicate whether the record is current or not.

Figure 2-79 shows an example of how a Type 1 SCD table would look before and after an update for an employee's record.

Before

EmployeeKey	EmployeeID	EmployeeName	EmployeeJobTitle
1	123456	Kim Abercrombie	Manager
2	234567	Manish Chopra	Data Engineer
3	345678	Sven Freitag	Data Analyst

After

EmployeeKey	EmployeeID	EmployeeName	EmployeeJobTitle
1	123456	Kim Abercrombie	Manager
2	234567	Manish Chopra	Data Engineer
3	345678	Sven Freitag	Analytics Engineer

FIGURE 2-79 Comparing a Type 1 SCD dimension table before and after an update

In the example, the job title for employee Sven Freitag has changed from Data Analyst to Analytics Engineer. Because this is a Type 1 SCD, the EmployeeJobTitle field has been overwritten.

Figure 2-80 shows how the same change would look if the employee table had been designed as an SCD Type 2 table.

Before

EmployeeKey	EmployeeID	EmployeeName	EmployeeJobTitle	ValidFrom	ValidTo	IsCurrent
1	123456	Kim Abercrombie	Manager	2020-01-01	NULL	1
2	234567	Manish Chopra	Data Engineer	2020-01-01	NULL	1
3	345678	Sven Freitag	Data Analyst	2020-01-01	NULL	1

After

EmployeeKey	EmployeeID	EmployeeName	EmployeeJobTitle	ValidFrom	ValidTo	IsCurrent
1	123456	Kim Abercrombie	Manager	2020-01-01	NULL	1
2	234567	Manish Chopra	Data Engineer	2020-01-01	NULL	1
3	345678	Sven Freitag	Data Analyst	2020-01-01	2024-03-12	0
4	345678	Sven Freitag	Analytics Engineer	2024-03-12	NULL	1

FIGURE 2-80 Comparing a Type 2 SCD dimension table before and after an update

In the SCD Type 2 approach, you can see that a new record has been created to reflect the new job title for Sven Freitag. The ValidTo date for the previous version of Sven's employee record has been set to the date of the change, and the IsCurrent field has been set to 0, the Boolean value for false.

The choice you make for how to design your dimension tables will have an impact on the analysis that is able to be performed on your data. Expanding the example, imagine that you have a fact table that records the number of sick days taken by each employee. An analyst wishes to understand if certain job roles have an impact on the number of sick days being taken. Although Sven Freitag has been an Analytics Engineer for only a short period of time, a Type 1 SCD will report *all* of his sickness absences against the job title of Analytics Engineer.

If the employee dimension table is designed as a Type 2 SCD, then any sickness absence that occurs between 2020-01-01 and 2024-03-12 would be recorded against the job title Data Analyst for Sven. Any absences on or after 2024-03-12 would be recorded against the job title Analytics Engineer.

Generally, a Type 1 approach is easier to implement; however, it could be argued that a Type 2 approach gives you a more accurate answer for the analysis being performed in the example. Ultimately, the correct choice will be driven by the nature of your data and the specific requirements of your solution.

Implement bridge tables for a lakehouse or warehouse

A *bridge table* is a special kind of table used in a dimensional model to help resolve many-to-many relationships. Typically, the cardinality of a relationship between a fact table and a dimension table is one to many. This means that one record from a dimension table relates to many records in a fact table, and each record in a fact table relates to only one record in the dimension table. Sometimes, however, your data will not follow this pattern. Consider the tables in Figure 2-81, which show the transactions for bank accounts.

FactBankTransactions

BankAccountKey	TransactionDate	TransactionAmount
123	2024-03-17	100.00
123	2024-03-18	50.00
123	2024-03-19	20.00
456	2024-03-19	45.50

DimBankAccount

BankAccountKey	AccountNumber	AccountHolder
123	654321	Samantha Smith
123	654321	Ben Smith
456	987654	Heidi Steen

FIGURE 2-81 Tables holding data related to bank account transactions

The account number 654321 appears to be a joint account and has two account holders. This means you have many (more than one) Bank Account records related to many Bank Transaction records. If you were to query these tables to ascertain the total transaction value for the Smiths' account using SQL, this would return a value of 340.00, because the many-to-many relationship has caused the query to duplicate the data, rather than returning the correct value of 170.00. The following code block demonstrates this SQL query:

```
SELECT
    SUM(fbt.TransactionAmount) AS TransactionAmount
FROM
    FactBankTransactions fbt
    INNER JOIN DimBankAccount dba
      ON fbt.BankAccountKey = dba.BankAccountKey
WHERE
    dba.AccountNumber = 654321
```

Although you could resolve this issue by several methods using SQL to group the data in a way to return the correct answer, none of these will be useful once data is being queried via a semantic model. Instead, you should separate Bank Account and Account Holder into two separate tables and use a bridge table to help resolve the cardinality of the relationship. When implementing this in a warehouse or lakehouse, the tables would resemble those in Figure 2-82.

When implementing the relationships between these tables in a semantic model, you must make sure you allow a bidirectional filter between DimBankAccount and the bridge table to allow filters to propagate through from the DimAccountHolder table, as shown in Figure 2-83.

FactBankTransactions

BankAccountKey	TransactionDate	TransactionAmount
123	2024-03-17	100.00
123	2024-03-18	50.00
123	2024-03-19	20.00
456	2024-03-19	45.50

DimBankAccount

BankAccountKey	AccountNumber
123	654321
456	987654

DimAccountHolder

AccountHolderKey	AccountHolder
1	Samantha Smith
2	Ben Smith
3	Heidi Steen

BridgeBankAccountHolder

BankAccountKey	AccountHolderKey
123	1
123	2
456	3

FIGURE 2-82 Tables implemented using a bridge table pattern

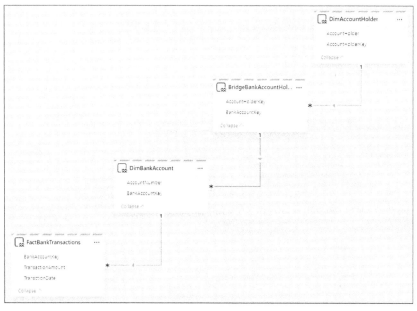

FIGURE 2-83 The semantic model view of a bridge table pattern

A bridge table pattern is ultimately a technique used for semantic model optimization. However, implementing the bridge table in your lakehouse or warehouse makes sense, allowing this pattern to be used in default semantic models or custom semantic models downstream from there.

To achieve a bridge table, you should make sure that concepts such as BankAccount and AccountHolder are treated as separate entities and then create a query that is the product of the two tables, covering all combinations of the primary keys of the two entities. The result of this query can be written down and persisted as a table in either your lakehouse or warehouse.

Denormalize data

The denormalization of data is another important concept of dimensional modeling and star schemas. The idea of *normalizing data* was conceived to avoid data redundancy and the duplication of data. This also helped with consistency of data as a piece of information would be stored in only one place, so if it were to change, it required updating in only one place. Normalized data is a common pattern in online transactional systems.

However, these types of systems are not optimized for analytics. Normalization means breaking up a particular concept or entity into many small tables linked with primary and foreign keys. This means querying data requires many joins. Querying and aggregating data across many joins is inefficient.

Denormalization of data into a star schema aims to address the performance bottleneck caused by having to do a lot of joining. It makes querying and aggregating data simpler and more performant. To demonstrate an example of denormalization, in Figure 2-84 product information is broken down into a normalized hierarchy of tables.

Product

ProductId	ProductName	ProductSubcategoryId
123	MP3 Player	1
456	Wireless Keyboard	11
789	SLR Camera	24

ProductSubcategory

ProductSubcategoryId	ProductSubcategoryName	ProductCategoryId
1	MP4&MP3	1
11	Computer Accessories	2
24	Digital SLR Cameras	4

ProductCategory

ProductCategoryId	ProductCategoryName
1	Audio
2	Computers
4	Cameras and Camcorders

FIGURE 2-84 A set of related normalized tables

Any query that wants to group product data by its Product Category will have to go via at least two table joins.

Denormalization removes this requirement by grouping this data into one wide table. You could achieve this using the following SQL query:

```
SELECT
    p.ProductId,
    p.ProductName,
    ps.ProductSubcategoryName,
    pc.ProductCategoryName
FROM    Product p
    INNER JOIN ProductSubcategory ps
        ON p.ProductSubcategoryId = ps.productSubcategoryId
    INNER JOIN ProductCategory pc
        ON ps.ProductCategoryId = pc.ProductCategoryId
```

The output of this query is shown in Figure 2-85.

Product

ProductId	ProductName	ProductSubcategoryName	ProductCategoryName
123	MP3 Player	MP4&MP3	Audio
456	Wireless Keyboard	Computer Accessories	Computers
789	SLR Camera	Digital SLR Cameras	Cameras and Camcorders

FIGURE 2-85 A denormalized Product table

This can then be saved and persisted as a table in your lakehouse or warehouse, allowing the facilitation of more efficient queries with fewer table joins. If more products that share subcategories and categories are added to the table, you will see some values repeated, but the overhead of this data redundancy is outweighed by the benefits of being able to gather all product data required for analysis from a single table.

Aggregate or de-aggregate data

Aggregation and de-aggregation are both common transformations applied to data when modeling for analytics use cases.

Aggregation is a technique to reduce the row count of a table by grouping and summarizing data to a higher granularity. Consider a call center that takes hundreds of calls per hour. For performance monitoring purposes, the lower-level detail of these calls, such as who the customer is or the exact minute the call took place, might not be pertinent pieces of data. See Figure 2-86 for an example table of call data.

You can reduce the number of records if you group by Date, Hour, Operator, and Call Type, whilst representing the number of records by counting the number of rows in the original data (Figure 2-87).

CallId	Date	Time	Customer	Operator	Call Type
123	2024-03-19	10:05	Customer 1	David Pelton	Query
456	2024-03-19	10:15	Customer 2	Tanja Plate	Sale
789	2024-03-19	10:15	Customer 3	Cassie Hicks	Query
101	2024-03-19	10:20	Customer 4	Vikas Jain	Sale
112	2024-03-19	10:30	Customer 5	David Pelton	Complaint
131	2024-03-19	10:45	Customer 6	Tanja Plate	Cancellation
415	2024-03-19	10:50	Customer 7	Cassie Hicks	Query
161	2024-03-19	10:50	Customer 8	Vikas Jain	Sale
718	2024-03-19	10:55	Customer 9	David Pelton	Query
192	2024-03-19	10:59	Customer 10	Tanja Plate	Sale

FIGURE 2-86 A table of example call center data

Date	Hour	Operator	Call Type	Calls
2024-03-19	10	David Pelton	Query	2
2024-03-19	10	David Pelton	Complaint	1
2024-03-19	10	Tanja Plate	Sale	2
2024-03-19	10	Tanja Plate	Cancellation	1
2024-03-19	10	Cassie Hicks	Query	2
2024-03-19	10	Vikas Jain	Sale	2

FIGURE 2-87 An aggregated table of example data from Figure 2-86

This aggregation reduced the row count by over one third and precalculated the number of calls per operator and call type.

You can aggregate this data further if you pivot the call type column into individual fields with their own call totals (Figure 2-88).

Date	Hour	Operator	Queries	Complaints	Sales	Cancellations	Total Calls
2024-03-19	10	David Pelton	2	1	0	0	3
2024-03-19	10	Tanja Plate	0	0	2	1	3
2024-03-19	10	Cassie Hicks	2	0	0	0	2
2024-03-19	10	Vikas Jain	0	0	2	0	2

FIGURE 2-88 Call Type data is pivoted

The volume of data was reduced by another third, going from the original raw data of 10 rows down to four rows, whilst still retaining the ability to analyze and trend the data by date, hour, operator, and call types. The data transformation experiences in stored procedures (using T-SQL), notebooks (using PySpark or SparkSQL), and Dataflows all provide the functionality to perform this type of aggregation.

Conversely, you may face situations where the source data you are provided with has already been aggregated, but to a granularity or shape that does not allow the analysis that you need to do.

Again, consider a call center. The example data in Figure 2-89 shows the number of calls each operator has received by each hour of their shift.

Date	Operator	09:00	10:00	11:00	12:00	13:00	14:00	15:00	16:00
2024-03-19	David Pelton	2	3	1	4	1	4	3	2
2024-03-19	Tanja Plate	3	3	3	2	1	5	3	1
2024-03-19	Cassie Hicks	4	2	3	1	2	3	1	2
2024-03-19	Vikas Jain	4	2	2	3	1	4	2	1

FIGURE 2-89 Example call center data shows calls per hour

With the data in this shape, it becomes difficult to trend the call data over periods of time or to sum the data to see the total number of calls taken during the day.

Here it makes sense to unpivot the data, treating the hour of the day as a descriptive attribute of the data (and possibly turning it into a foreign key field that can be joined to a time dimension). This allows the number of calls to be recorded in a single column that can be easily summed for analysis. Figure 2-90 shows the outcome.

Date	Operator	Hour	Calls
2024-03-19	David Pelton	09:00	2
2024-03-19	Tanja Plate	09:00	3
2024-03-19	Cassie Hicks	09:00	4
2024-03-19	Vikas Jain	09:00	4
2024-03-19	David Pelton	10:00	3
2024-03-19	Tanja Plate	10:00	3
2024-03-19	Cassie Hicks	10:00	2
2024-03-19	Vikas Jain	10:00	2
2024-03-19	David Pelton	11:00	1
2024-03-19	Tanja Plate	11:00	3
2024-03-19	Cassie Hicks	11:00	3
2024-03-19	Vikas Jain	11:00	2
2024-03-19	David Pelton	12:00	4
2024-03-19	Tanja Plate	12:00	2
2024-03-19	Cassie Hicks	12:00	1
2024-03-19	Vikas Jain	12:00	3
2024-03-19	David Pelton	13:00	1
2024-03-19	Tanja Plate	13:00	1
2024-03-19	Cassie Hicks	13:00	2
2024-03-19	Vikas Jain	13:00	1
2024-03-19	David Pelton	14:00	4
2024-03-19	Tanja Plate	14:00	5
2024-03-19	Cassie Hicks	14:00	3
2024-03-19	Vikas Jain	14:00	4
2024-03-19	David Pelton	15:00	3
2024-03-19	Tanja Plate	15:00	3
2024-03-19	Cassie Hicks	15:00	1
2024-03-19	Vikas Jain	15:00	2
2024-03-19	David Pelton	16:00	2
2024-03-19	Tanja Plate	16:00	1
2024-03-19	Cassie Hicks	16:00	2
2024-03-19	Vikas Jain	16:00	1

FIGURE 2-90 Data from Figure 2-89 is de-aggregated

Merge or join data

As part of your analytics solution you will inevitably reach a point where you will want to merge data, join data, or both. The "Denormalize data" section hinted already about the necessity to join data, when you created a single table to join a hierarchy of tables into one entity. There are certainly other reasons you might want to join data together, be it for denormalization or for bringing together data from disparate sources so you can perform calculations on them.

There are different ways to join data, as shown in Figure 2-91:

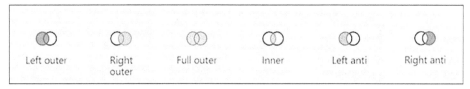

FIGURE 2-91 Types of data joins

Each of these join types achieve a different result:

- A **left outer** join keeps all records from the first table selected and any records that match in a second table. If the record doesn't exist in the second table, the query returns a null value.

- A **right outer** join keeps all records from the second table selected and any records that match in the first table. If the record doesn't exist in the first table, the query returns a null value. This type of join is rarely seen in practice as it is common practice to always select the table you would like to keep all records for first and perform a left outer join.

- A **full outer** join retains all records from both tables, and a null value is generated on either side of the join for any nonmatching records.

- An **inner join** is perhaps the most common type of join used, and it returns only records that match in both tables. An inner join can be used as a means to discard records you don't want to keep in a query, as the join condition can act as a way to filter data if you are joining to a table that only contains the desired set of records.

- **Left anti** and **right anti joins** are also filtering joins. A left anti join keeps only records that do not exist in the second table, whilst a right anti join keeps only records that do not exist in the first table.

Joining data is possible in all of the data transformation items in Fabric. When you join two tables in a dataflow, it is referred to as a *merge*. The screenshot in Figure 2-91 is taken from the **Merge** dialog (though the concepts behind the merge types are relevant across all experiences).

To merge tables in a dataflow, first select a merging option from the ribbon menu of the **dataflow editor**. You will be given two choices: **Merge queries**, which will add additional columns to the currently selected table, and **Merge queries as new**, which will create a brand-new table with the joined tables combined. Figure 2-92 shows the dialog for merging tables in a dataflow.

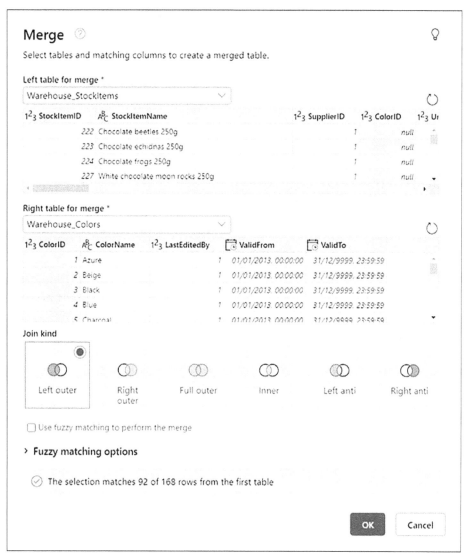

FIGURE 2-92 The Merge dialog in the dataflow editor

The left table for the merge is selected in the first section of the dialog, and the right table in the second section. To define the join condition, the common key is selected (in the example ColorID), with the **Join kind** selected from the options below this.

To achieve the same result using T-SQL, you would use the following code:

```
SELECT
    *
FROM
    Warehouse_StockItems wi
    LEFT OUTER JOIN Warehouse_Colors wc
        ON wi.ColorID = wc.ColorID
```

You would change the join type in row 5 of this code snippet to achieve the join result of your choice.

If you were to do this in a notebook using PySpark, you could use the following code:

```
df_items = spark.sql("SELECT * FROM Warehouse_StockItems")

df_colors = spark.sql("SELECT * FROM Warehouse_Colors")

df_join = df_items.join(df_colors, df_items["ColorID"] == df_colors["ColorId"], "left")

display(df_join)
```

This snippet declares each of the base tables as DataFrames before creating a third DataFrame that joins the two together. The join type is specified in the third argument of the join function.

Identify and resolve duplicate data, missing data, or null values

You may find that the source data you ingest into your solution has duplicate records, missing data, or null values contained in it. As a result of the transformations you apply to your data, you might even create these results yourself. There are several means by which you can identify this, and regardless of your chosen method of data transformation, check at each step in your data processing stages for duplicates, missing data, or null values.

To identify duplicates, you first need to understand what denotes the uniqueness of a given record. Categorical data is likely to be repeated across multiple rows of a given dataset, so some element of duplication is expected. But a *unique record* will have one or more key fields that define it as a standalone record. You will use this field (or fields) to understand whether you have any duplicates.

For dataflows, you can enable column profile tools that will show quality details and value distributions. Figure 2-93 shows a table in the dataflow editor with the profile tools switched on.

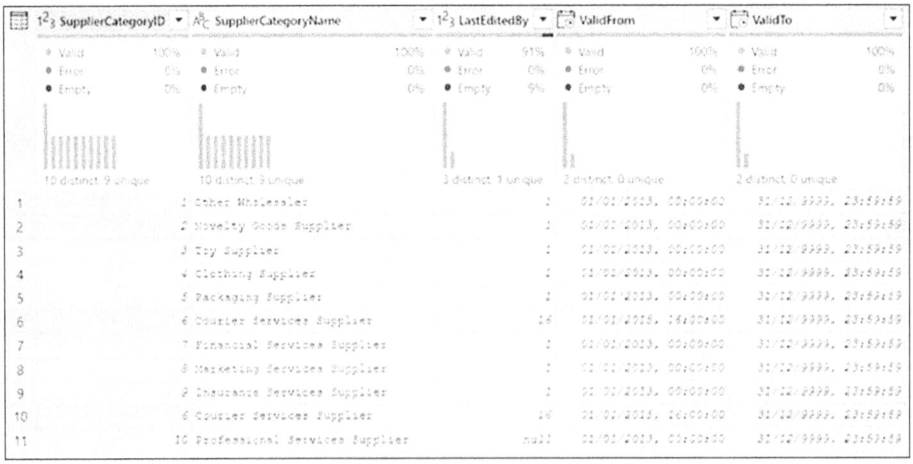

FIGURE 2-93 Column profiling in the dataflow editor

For Figure 2-93's example SupplierCategory table, the ID and Name fields should be unique, but two facts indicate the presence of duplicates: the distinct and unique count of rows are not equal and the value distribution graphic does not show a flat line.

Checking for duplicates in SQL and PySpark is less straightforward and really a case of analyzing the data yourself. Figure 2-94 shows one method for identifying duplicates using SQL.

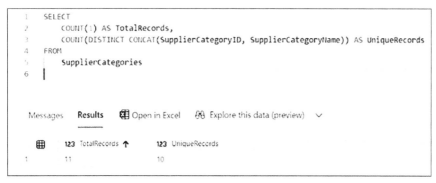

```
1   SELECT
2       COUNT(1) AS TotalRecords,
3       COUNT(DISTINCT CONCAT(SupplierCategoryID, SupplierCategoryName)) AS UniqueRecords
4   FROM
5       SupplierCategories
6   |
```

Messages **Results** ▦ Open in Excel ◷ Explore this data (preview) ∨

	123 TotalRecords ↑	123 UniqueRecords
1	11	10

FIGURE 2-94 Identifying the existence of duplicates using SQL

Figure 2-95 shows an alternative method that helps identify the offending values.

```
1   SELECT
2       SupplierCategoryID,
3       SupplierCategoryName,
4       COUNT(1) AS TotalRecords
5   FROM
6       SupplierCategories
7   GROUP BY
8       SupplierCategoryID,
9       SupplierCategoryName
10  HAVING
11      COUNT(1) > 1
12
```

Messages **Results** ▦ Open in Excel ◷ Explore this data (preview) ∨

	12L SupplierCategoryID	ABC SupplierCategoryName ↑	123 TotalRecords
1	6	Courier Services Supplier	2

FIGURE 2-95 Identifying the existence of duplicates using SQL

There are a few different methods to deal with the identified duplicates. In the dataflow editor, if the entire record is duplicated (as shown in the example) you can use the **Remove duplicates** option (Figure 2-96).

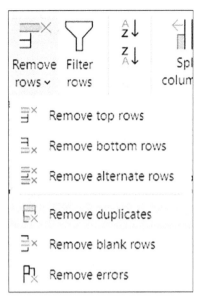

FIGURE 2-96 Remove Duplicates option in the dataflow editor

In SQL, the equivalent of this would be to use a DISTINCT() function in your SELECT statement, as shown here:

```
SELECT DISTINCT
    *
FROM
    SupplierCategories
```

In PySpark there is both a distinct() and a dropDuplicates() function available for manipulating dataframes, which could be used as following:

```
df = spark.sql("SELECT * FROM SupplierCategories")
df = df.dropDuplicates()

df = spark.sql("SELECT * FROM SupplierCategories")
df = df.distinct()
```

If the record is a duplicate across only some columns, a better approach would be to group the columns by the unique identifiers, and then use business logic to select the most appropriate values for the remaining columns, be that the minimum, maximum, first, or last value.

You can deal with missing data or null values a number of ways, as well. Empty values are another metric presented in the data profiling information in Dataflows. Again, with other transformation experiences it requires some analysis to uncover missing data.

One approach may be that you wish to exclude records where a null value is present. This would be a case of filtering the data. Filtering is covered later in this section.

However, you may wish to apply some other rules to deal with null values. In Dataflows you can use the **Replace values** feature, shown in Figure 2-97.

FIGURE 2-97 Dataflow editor's Replace values option

This will provide you with a dialog to specify which value you want to replace (blank, in this case) with the value you want instead.

When using SQL, the COALESCE() function is a great tool for dealing with null values. The COALESCE() function will accept a field as its first argument, and then a list of subsequent arguments that will be evaluated. The function will return the first argument that doesn't evaluate to NULL.

In the following example, null values are handled in column 1 by replacing a record with a null value with the value from column 2. If column 2 is also NULL, then it is replaced with the value from column 3, and if column 3 is also NULL it reverts to a default value of UNKNOWN.

```
SELECT
    COALESCE (column1, column2, column3, 'UNKNOWN')
FROM
    Table1
```

When using PySpark the function na.fill() can be used to replace NULLs. With na.fill() you can replace all NULLs in a DataFrame with a particular value, or you can target specific columns. The example below shows the syntax to do this for an entire DataFrame first and then the syntax for a specific column second.

```
df.na.fill("UNKNOWN")

df.na.fill("UNKNOWN", ["column1"])
```

Convert data types by using SQL or PySpark

Data types are essential for all calculations to work correctly. They also significantly affect the size of stored data and the ability to browse it. Therefore, users will often choose how the data will be stored; they need to know how to convert data formats.

> **NEED MORE REVIEW?** **DATA TYPES**
>
> For usable data types in Fabric warehouses or SQL endpoints, please visit *learn.microsoft.com/ fabric/data-warehouse/data-types*.

Convert data type by SQL

Within SQL, it is possible to use two functions to convert data types. Specifically, it's about functions CONVERT() and CAST():

- CONVERT (data_type [(length)] , expression [, style])
- CAST (expression AS data_type [(length)])

The CONVERT() function is SQL Server–specific, and the CAST() function is ANSI SQL. However, not all data types can be converted between each other without some loss of precision. For this reason, the user has a choice between these functions, and the following diagram helps. To download a copy of the diagram shown in Figure 2-98, visit *ww.microsoft.com/en-us/download/details.aspx?id=35834.*

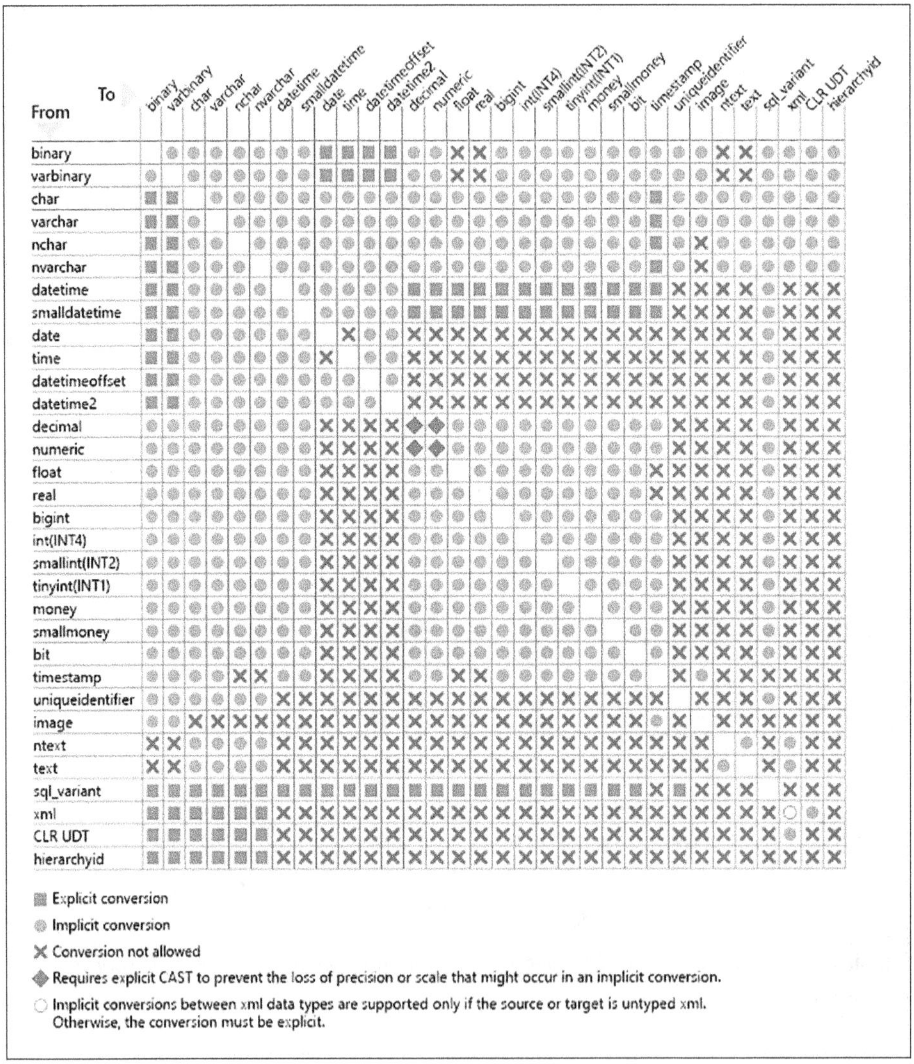

FIGURE 2-98 Data conversion diagram

Figure 2-99 shows an example of converting a date using both the two functions.

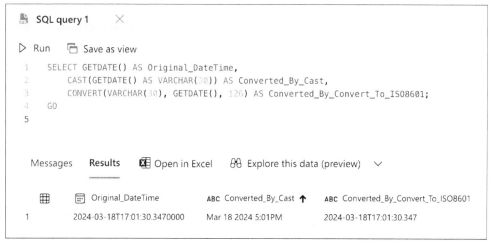

FIGURE 2-99 GETDATE() converted by CAST() and CONVERT()

Convert data type by PySpark

Data types can also be converted using PySpark. The usual ways to do this are the cast() and expr() functions:

- cast(data_type)
- expr(string)

   The cast() function is typically used in conjunction with the withColumn() function because it can create a new or overwrite an existing column. You can, however, also use it in conjunction with the select() function. Defining the required columns that should be included in the output is necessary. Making a mass select all columns using the * character is also possible. Still, you need to eliminate the duplicate column with a new data type or use the alias() function to create it with a different name as is shown in Figure 2-100.

> **NOTE   CSV FILE SAMPLE**
>
> The data in the following examples are created from the CSV found at *github.com/tirnovar/ dp-600/blob/main/data/sales*.

   The expr() function executes *SQL-like expressions* and uses an existing DataFrame column value as an expression argument to PySpark built-in functions. This allows users to use the same functions mentioned in the previous part of this section. Usage is shown in Figure 2-101.

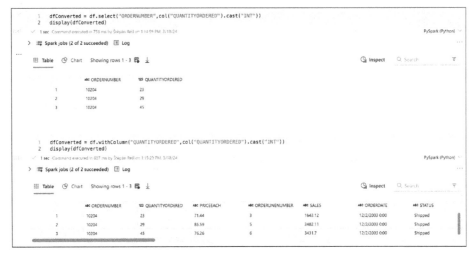

```
1  dfConverted = df.select("ORDERNUMBER",col("QUANTITYORDERED").cast("INT"))
2  display(dfConverted)
```

FIGURE 2-100 Data types converted by `cast()` function in `withColumn()`

```
1  dfConverted = df.select("ORDERNUMBER",expr("cast(QUANTITYORDERED as int) as QUANTITYORDERED"))
2  display(dfConverted)
```

FIGURE 2-101 Converted data types by function `expr()`

Filter data

When working with data, filtering only the relevant data that meets certain conditions is sometimes necessary, such as during transformations, during data analysis, or when compiling subsequent outputs. Individual filtering functions differ depending on the Microsoft Fabric item used. You might want to filter data using **T-SQL**, **PySpark**, **KQL**, the **Power Query Online** interface (**M formula language**), but of course, also using **DAX** and so on. Filtering has a slightly different impact on the data within all of the aforementioned. From this chapter's point of view, you need to know how to filter data using T-SQL, M, and PySpark.

Filter data by T-SQL

With T-SQL, you use the WHERE clause to filter data. It returns only those data that meet the defined condition to the user. Because WHERE is a general filtering clause, you can perform various second filtering. With the help of AND, OR, and NOT logical operands, you can filter for several individual conditions. You can also use any of the following common comparing operands in a WHERE clause:

- = Equals
- <> Not equal to
- > Greater than
- >= Greater than or equal to
- < Less than
- <= Less than or equal to

Figure 2-102 illustrates how to filter data by two operands.

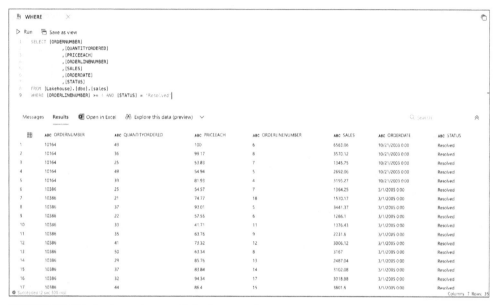

FIGURE 2-102 Filtering two columns with basic operands

In addition, you can use four other operands:

- IS NULL   Specifies a search for null values.
- IN   Specifies the search for an expression based on whether that expression is included in or excluded from a list.
- BETWEEN   Specifies an inclusive range of values. Use AND to separate the starting and ending values.
- LIKE   Indicates that the subsequent character string will be used with pattern matching. A pattern can use wildcards also, as shown in Figure 2-103:
  - %   Any string or more characters; for example, %WORD%

- ▪ _   Any single character; for example, W_RD
- ▪ []   Any single character within the defined range; for example, W[ao]RD
- ▪ [^]   Any single character not within the range; for example, W[^b-t]RD

FIGURE 2-103 Filtering data with LIKE operand

NEED MORE REVIEW? **SEARCH CONDITIONS (T-SQL)**

For more details about how to set search conditions, please visit *learn.microsoft.com/sql/t-sql/ queries/search-condition-transact-sql?view=sql-server-ver16.*

Filter data by M formula language

Using the M language, you can perform data filtering using a function, such as:

```
Table.SelectRows(table as table, condition as function) as table
```

The example function validates a condition specified as a function and returns rows from the browsed table. Both ()=> and each notations can be used within a function definition. As with T-SQL, you can build multiple conditional filtering; for example, you can use the same and, or, and not operators, but you must write them in lowercase.

In addition, you can perform filtering within **Power Query** and **Power Query Online**. Each column has a dropdown that offers specific filtering options depending on its data type. These options are always located above the preview window (Figure 2-104), and you can use them to filter a specific value.

All filters are translated into code so you can find exactly what is being executed in the step script. You can combine filters in the same way as with T-SQL through different columns at once and with different filter types. Power Query usually distinguishes what type of filtering is performed and for what type of data, and it merges filtering with operands into one step. If you select CONTAINS, this filter will be placed in a separate step; however, you can modify the code and add or copy the necessary filters into a single step (Figure 2-105) to reduce the number of **Applied steps**.

FIGURE 2-104 Filtering by Power Query Online

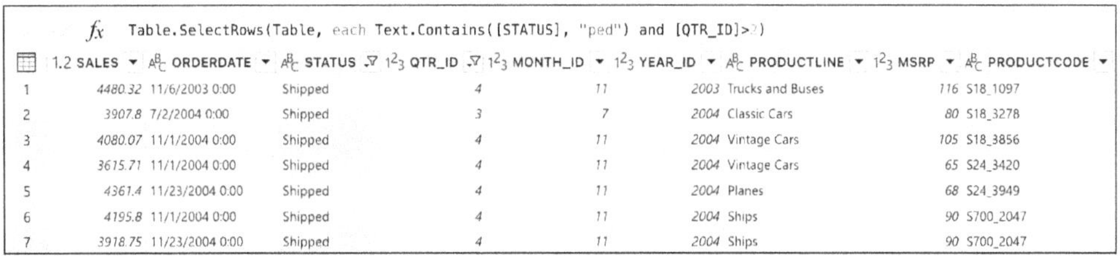

FIGURE 2-105 Concatenated filtering expressions

Filter data by PySpark

Within PySpark, you can use `spark.sql()` and, thanks to that, the `WHERE` clause to filter data. Everything is subject to the same laws as it was within the T-SQL variants. If you want to perform filtering not directly from the source, however, the `filter()` function is a better choice.

The `filter()` function is often confused with the `where()` function because the two functions work the same way. Note that `where()` is the sugar syntax (or alias) of the `filter()` function, so you can use both in the same cases. The function syntax looks like this:

`DataFrame.filter(condition: ColumnOrName)`

In general, these functions support two kinds of condition notation:

- **Filter by column instances** For example, `df.filter(df.STATUS == "Shipped")`
- **Filter by SQL expression in a string** For example, `df.filter("STATUS == 'Shipped'")`

Because SQL notation can also be used, the same operands can be used, and searching using the `LIKE` operand is also possible, as shown in Figure 2-106.

```
1  df.filter("STATUS LIKE '%ped'")
2  display(df)
```

1 sec -Command executed in 1 sec 29 ms by Štěpán Rešl on 10:51:59 AM, 3/19/24

> ⇛ Spark jobs (2 of 2 succeeded)

···

⊞ Table   ⏱ Chart   Showing rows 1 - 1000 🔛 ↓

ᴬᴮᶜ ORDERLINENUMBER	ᴬᴮᶜ SALES	ᴬᴮᶜ ORDERDATE	ᴬᴮᶜ STATUS	ᴬᴮᶜ QTR_ID
3	1643.12	12/2/2003 0:00	Shipped	4
5	2482.11	12/2/2003 0:00	Shipped	4
6	3431.7	12/2/2003 0:00	Shipped	4
10	1249.4	12/2/2003 0:00	Shipped	4
12	2241.45	12/2/2003 0:00	Shipped	4
8	4527.04	12/2/2003 0:00	Shipped	4
9	3184.8	12/2/2003 0:00	Shipped	4
11	4368.96	12/2/2003 0:00	Shipped	4
2	1295.97	12/2/2003 0:00	Shipped	4
1	2719.8	7/7/2004 0:00	Shipped	3
5	3204	7/7/2004 0:00	Shipped	3
8	1213.8	6/3/2003 0:00	Shipped	2
4	2275.2	12/1/2004 0:00	Shipped	4
3	3315.12	7/7/2004 0:00	Shipped	3
12	1489.41	6/3/2003 0:00	Shipped	2
3	1336.68	12/1/2004 0:00	Shipped	4

FIGURE 2-106 Filtering by PySpark and using LIKE operand

Skill 2.4: Optimize performance

This skill covers how you can identify areas of your solution that require optimization, as well as some of the concepts and best practices you should take into account to ensure that your Fabric capacity is operating as efficiently as possible.

> **This skill covers how to:**
> - Identify and resolve data loading performance bottlenecks in dataflows, notebooks, and SQL queries
> - Implement performance improvements in dataflows, notebooks, and SQL queries
> - Identify and resolve issues with the structure or size of Delta table files (including V-Order and optimized writes)

Identify and resolve data loading performance bottlenecks in dataflows, notebooks, and SQL queries

There is a running joke amongst the data community, that when it comes to answering nearly any question about how to approach a task, the answer will be "It depends." Bottlenecks related to data loading performance can have many causes, and so this section does not intend to be particularly detailed or exhaustive.

The first obvious indication of a performance bottleneck is that everything becomes slow. Be it a pipeline, dataflow, notebook, or SQL query, things are taking longer than you (or your stakeholders) might expect, and the worst case is that tasks may even fail with error messages.

The second signal is to look at the **Fabric Capacity Metrics** app for spikes in CU usage. You may find you are hitting the limits of your CU allocation and tasks are therefore waiting for available capacity due to throttling. You can set up notifications in the **Capacity settings** section of the admin portal to alert you when you exceed a configurable capacity utilization threshold.

You have a few options available to address bottlenecks. Perhaps the most brute force way is to throw more power at the problem. You could look to either scale up or scale out the compute available to your tasks, by upgrading to a SKU with a higher CU allocation or by taking out additional SKUs and spreading workloads across those SKUs.

But it's also highly likely that you can do additional performance tuning on your tasks to make sure they are as efficient as they can be. The following section covers some general concepts for you to optimize your data transformation work.

Implement performance improvements in dataflows, notebooks, and SQL queries

Again, there are far too many variables at play to be able to consider addressing every single possible performance tweak available to your data processing tasks. Each workload will be unique depending on the types of data you're dealing with, the volume of that data, and the transformations you need to carry out. Across the various data transformation options, however, a set of guidelines and best practices can help you to build efficient dataflows, notebooks, and SQL queries.

For dataflows, the following guidelines are recommended:

- **Don't break the fold.** This advice refers to query folding. *Query folding* allows transformations to data to be passed back to the data source. Query folding helps to reduce the volume of data that needs to be passed to Fabric and processed. Once query folding is broken for a dataflow query, all data is loaded into memory and subsequent transformations happen locally in Fabric, which can be inefficient. You should understand which operations break query folding. If some of these operations are unavoidable, at least make sure they take place in the later steps of your query to minimize the impact.

- **Avoid inefficient transformations where possible.** Transforms such as Sorting might be useful whilst you are developing and debugging a dataflow, but they are expensive and don't necessarily benefit the data once loading to your final destination.

- **Switch off the Staging option where possible.** The Staging option loads all your data to a hidden lakehouse in the background as an intermittent step. Whilst for some complex transformations this can benefit performance, for small volumes and for more simple transformations this extra hop is an additional overhead.

NEED MORE REVIEW? **QUERY FOLDING**

For a more in-depth look at query folding, visit *learn.microsoft.com/en-us/power-query/query-folding-basics*.

Notebooks best practices are as follows:

- **Write efficient Spark code.** For example, choose the appropriate data abstraction, use the cache, and use effective joins and shuffles.

- **Configure your Spark compute effectively.** Your Spark pool may be configured to reduce the max nodes and max executors in order to free up resources to allow other operations to happen in parallel.

- **End active Spark sessions.** Make sure not to leave these active longer than necessary, as they will continue to consume CUs. To end scheduled notebooks, for example, use `spark.stop()`.

NEED MORE REVIEW? **OPTIMIZE APACHE SPARK JOBS**

For a more in-depth look at writing efficient Spark code, visit *learn.microsoft.com/en-us/azure/synapse-analytics/spark/apache-spark-performance*.

For SQL queries, the following is recommended:

- **Use optimal SQL.** This means things like only selecting the columns required for the query, filtering data early perhaps with CTEs or subqueries, and trying to keep calculation and aggregations simple.

- **Make sure statistics are gathered on your warehouse tables**. Statistics help to optimize query plans, and whilst they should be created automatically, it's also worthwhile running periodic updates, or supplementing with the FULLSCAN hint.

- **Structure your data in a star schema.** This will help with writing more efficient queries. (For more discussion of using star schemas, see "Skill 2.3: Transform data.") For warehouses, you can use the query insights schema that contains views that allow you to see frequently run and long-running queries, which can help you identify bottlenecks as well as potential areas for performance tuning.

NEED MORE REVIEW? **STATISTICS**

For a more in-depth look at statistics for warehouses, visit *learn.microsoft.com/en-us/fabric/data-warehouse/statistics#manual-statistics-for-all-tables*.

Across all of the transformation experiences, the following is also sound advice:

- **Consider append only or incremental loads.** This will allow you to process a smaller volume of data, taking into consideration only new records or records that have changed since the previous load.

- **Give thought to how often you need to process your data.** If the data source is only updated once a day, does it make sense to do a full load every hour? Only refresh your data on a cadence that makes sense.

Identify and resolve issues with the structure or size of Delta table files (including V-Order and optimized writes)

The concept of a Delta table can be a little misleading. A *Delta table* itself is actually a collection of Parquet files, which is supplemented with additional log files in order to make the format ACID compliant. The metadata defined for this collection of files and logs allows the data to be queried as though it is a table in a database.

As data is inserted, updated, and deleted over time in a Delta table, the number of files captured in the logs as well as the number of Parquet files grows. This is because Parquet files are immutable: When data is altered for a particular file, the data doesn't actually get changed. Instead, it is superseded by a new version of the file. The files can also become fragmented. This is due to the parallel processing nature of some workloads, which means that when data is written down to Delta, it will ordinarily split the writing of data into at least one file per compute node.

Generating hundreds of small files over a period leads to increased storage costs and also affects performance as querying your data now needs to interrogate a large number of files.

You can observe the amount of storage you are using either by looking at the **System Storage** tab in **Workspace Settings**, or by looking at the Storage tab of the **Fabric Capacity Metrics** app.

Luckily there are methods available to reduce file volumes. The OPTIMIZE command will consolidate lots of small files into sets of larger ones, meaning fewer files to scan when querying data, whilst the VACUUM command will remove files that are no longer needed having been superseded by newer versions of the data. Lakehouse Explorer offers a maintenance option (Figure 2-107) that enables you to run these commands easily.

Selecting the **Maintenance** option opens the **Run maintenance commands** dialog (Figure 2-108).

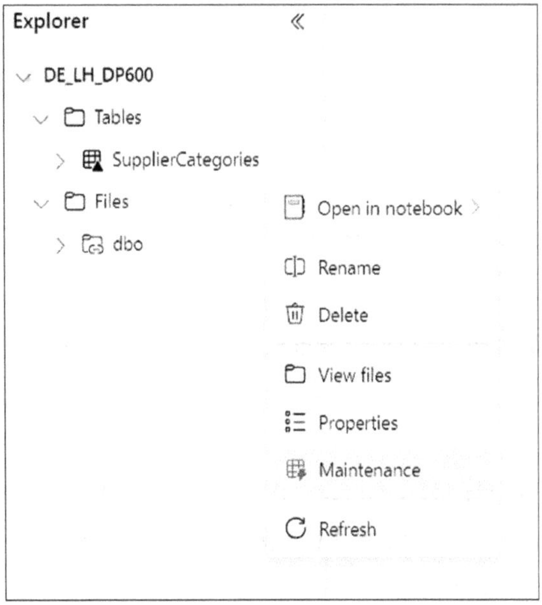

FIGURE 2-107 The Maintenance option in Lakehouse Explorer

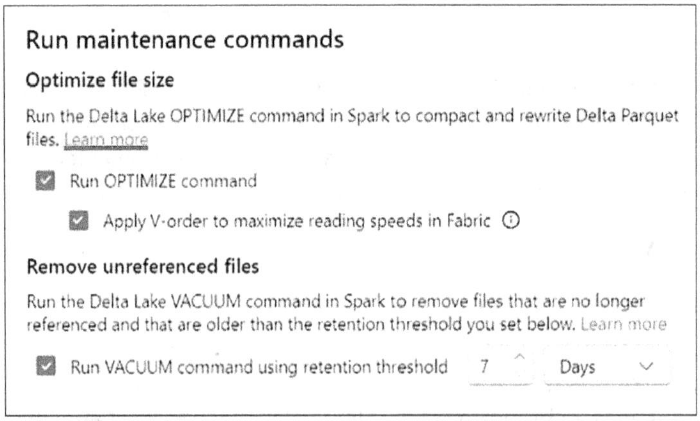

FIGURE 2-108 The **Run maintenance commands** dialog

The **V-Order** option applies a sorting algorithm on the data to help give optimal compression on files as well as making them optimized for queries in Fabric.

The method outlined above can be performed on an ad-hoc basis. You may wish to perform these maintenance tasks on a regular basis, however. To do so, create a notebook or Spark Job definition containing the OPTIMIZE and VACUUM commands for the tables you want to manage, and then execute it using a schedule that suits.

The optimize method outlined above is very much a reactive approach that alters the structure and size of the data stored after the event. You can take a more proactive approach instead by using **Optimized Write**.

Optimized Write is a feature in Apache Spark that reduces the number of files created and writes down larger file sizes. It best used for the following data processing scenarios:

- Delta Lake–partitioned tables subject to write patterns that generate suboptimal (less than 128 MB) or nonstandardized file sizes (files whose sizes differ depending on circumstance)
- Repartitioned data frames that will be written to disk with suboptimal file size
- Delta Lake–partitioned tables targeted by small batch SQL commands like UPDATE, DELETE, MERGE, CREATE TABLE AS SELECT, INSERT INTO, and so on
- Streaming ingestion scenarios with append data patterns to Delta Lake–partitioned tables where the extra write latency is tolerable

The feature is available for Apache Spark version 3.1 upwards and is turned on by default from version 3.3 upwards for partitioned tables. If you need to switch on the feature for older versions of Spark, you can do so.

To do this using SQL, use the following command:

```
SET `spark.microsoft.delta.optimizeWrite.enabled` = true
```

The equivalent command in PySpark is:

```
spark.conf.set("spark.microsoft.delta.optimizeWrite.enabled", "true")
```

By default, Optimized Write aims to create file sizes of 128 MB. You can, however, change this through configuration, either using the following SQL command:

```
SET `spark.microsoft.delta.optimizeWrite.binSize` = 134217728
```

or using PySpark:

```
spark.conf.set("spark.microsoft.delta.optimizeWrite.binSize", "134217728")
```

The number provided in each command represents the target file size in bytes.

NEED MORE REVIEW? **OPTIMIZED WRITE**

For a more in-depth look at Optimized Write, visit *learn.microsoft.com/en-us/azure/synapse-analytics/spark/optimize-write-for-apache-spark*.

Chapter summary

- Data can be ingested within the pipeline using the **Copy Activity**. The **Data Movement Service** has both its canvas activity and a **Copy data** wizard, which allows you to retrieve data using a wizard.
- **DataFlow Gen2** uses lakehouses with warehouses during staging to work with a larger volume of data and perform heavier transformations more efficiently. However, turning off staging is a good idea if you want to get data or perform light transformations.

- Notebooks allow you to use many pre-installed libraries and their functions. You can extend these libraries with custom or public libraries using the **Environment** item or **Workspace Runtime** settings.

- Shortcuts allow you to use data already in OneLake in another place, such as Azure Data Lake Storage Gen2, Amazon S3, or Dataverse, without duplicating it.

- Shortcuts are supported within **Lakehouse** and **KQL** databases.

- Partitions can be made using one or more different columns found in the data when partitions have the pattern `<partition-name>=<value>`, and if there is an empty value, then the name `__HIVE_DEFAULT_PARTITION__` is substituted.

- Partitions can be made for any files as well as Delta tables. They can be created using **Copy Activity** and notebooks.

- Views can be created using the **SQL query editor** and **visual query**, and in both cases, the view can be created even from part of the prepared query.

- Warehouse has ready-made templates for creating views and stored procedures. You can use these by selecting the **ellipsis** icon for the folders that group them or using the extended menu within the **New SQL query**.

- Expanding with new columns requires changing the schema of the existing table. This can be done using notebook, where the `write()` function can be extended with the option `overwriteSchema` or `mergeSchema`, depending on the desired change. When a column is removed from the schema and the original data is preserved, the column is not removed from the data but only from the schema.

- Columns can be added within notebooks using the `select()` function or the `withColumn() function.Summary`.

- Add data transform item types to a pipeline for orchestration. When choosing a data copying method, consider the team that will work with or manage the solution. Choose a manageable method that also takes into account CU(s) consumption. The resulting solution should use no more capacity than necessary.

- If it is possible to use data from its current location within OneLake rather than duplicate it, then use shortcuts as a best practice.

- If an item is directly created from a lakehouse via **Get data**, its outputs will be set to store data in that lakehouse.

- Data can be copied using the **Copy Activity** between lakehouses, and the lakehouse connector can be directly used if all lakehouses are in the same workspace. To copy data located in another workspace, you need to connect to the SQL endpoint using **Azure SQL Database** to copy the Delta table.

- In a notebook, `spark.sql()` can be used to get data within the same workspace, and `spark.read.load()` can also be used to refer to the Azure Blob File System (ABFS) to get data both from the same workspace and from other workspaces.

- Configure a schedule for a data pipeline.

- Create schedules for dataflows and notebooks.

- Structure data in a star schema including how to treat attributes that change over time.
- Create a bridge table to help resolve many-to-many relationships.
- Denormalize data into entities suitable for analytics.
- Transform data to a more aggregated or de-aggregated view.
- Join tables together using different join types.
- Identify and deal with duplicate values and/or missing data.
- Data types can be converted using **T-SQL**, **PySpark**, **M within DataFlow Gen2**, and **Copy Activity**. However, T-SQL and PySpark allow the exact type setting, so the system does not need to remap.
- Both CONVERT() and CAST() functions can be used within T-SQL. You can find a complete overview of data types that can be converted to and how at *www.microsoft.com/en-us/download/details.aspx?id=35834*.
- T-SQL syntax for converting data types can also be used within PySpark using the expr() function. Another conversion option uses the cast() function.
- The WHERE clause is used to filter data within T-SQL. It allows you to have one or more conditions that will be used for filtering, and you can filter using both simple operands and others such as IN, BETWEEN, or LIKE.
- The Table.SelectRows() function is used to filter within the M language. This feature is automatically applied even when the user filters the data using the UI. If the individual conditions are simple filters, they are folded into each other, but if they are more complex filter conditions, such as Text.Contains(), a new step is created when the UI is used.
- PySpark has two filtering functions: where() and filter(). The where() function is the sugar syntax of the filter() function and can be used in SQL-like notation, including more complex operands.
- Identify where you have data loading performance bottlenecks.
- Apply best practices for dataflow, notebook, and SQL query performance.
- Improve performance through optimizing Delta table sizes.

Thought experiment

In this thought experiment, demonstrate your skills and knowledge of the topics covered in this chapter. You can find the answers in the section that follows.

You are an analytics engineer at Contoso, where they are using Microsoft Fabric to build a new unified analytics platform. You are responsible for ingesting data into the platform, cleaning the data, and then reshaping it so it is suitable to have analytics and reporting built on top of it.

Based on these areas of responsibility, answer the following questions:

1. Which of the following will filter the data in the DataFrame to include only rows where the values in the Note column contain the word "INVOICE" somewhere in the text?

   A. `df.filter("Note LIKE '%INVOICE%'")`

   B. `df.filter("Note IN '%INVOICE%'")`

   C. `df.where("Note LIKE 'INVOICE%'")`

   D. `df.where("Note == '%INVOICE%'")`

2. Which of the following will create partitions for written files, and when are the partitions supposed to represent which date the data comes from and will be easily usable for following transformations?

   A. `df.write.partitionBy("year","month").save("Files/Sales")`

   B. `df.write.partitionBy("month","day").save("Files/Sales")`

   C. `df.write.partitionBy("year","month","day").save("Files/Sales")`

   D. `df.write.partitionBy("day","month","year").save("Files/Sales")`

3. What will you use to copy data between individual lakehouses that does not require structure or storage format modification? Assume that users have excellent knowledge of all items.

   A. Notebook

   B. Pipeline

   C. DataFlow Gen2

   D. Shortcut

4. If colleagues are to have access to the SQL queries that you often use within the warehouse, in which folder do you have to place these queries?

   A. My queries

   B. Shared queries

   C. Team queries

   D. Personal queries

5. You need to be able to track changes over time of the region in your customer dimension. What type of slowly changing dimension should you use?

   A. Type 0

   B. Type 1

   C. Type 2

   D. Type 12

6. In which scenario would you use a bridge table?

   A. In order to store calculated metrics

   B. To resolve many-to-many cardinality of entities

C. As a table to store descriptive attributes

D. For auditing purposes

7. You need to join two tables together, but only want to keep records where there is a matching common key in both tables, filtering out records where no match exists. What type of join should you use?

A. Left inner join

B. Inner join

C. Left outer join

D. Right outer join

8. Which T-SQL function can you use to evaluate a field and replace it with an alternative if it is NULL?

A. COALESCE

B. ISNULL

C. REPLACE

D. CONCAT

Thought experiment answers

1. The answer is **A**. Text content can be searched using the LIKE operand. However, to say that the given characters can be found anywhere in the text, the wildcard characters % must be used on both sides of the search term. If the % characters were only at the end, then the text would have to start with "INVOICE" always.

2. The answer is **C**. A partition created as Year, Month, Day will allow straightforward browsing for the following transformations, as it will be possible to query all months in a specific year, all days in a specific year and month, and it will also be possible to read data from precisely one day.

3. The answer is **D**. If the data does not need any modification, not even in its storage format, then the best option is not to copy or duplicate it! Shortcuts are the best option because they refer to the data storage location only, allowing subsequent items to access this data through the given lakehouse.

4. The answer is **B**. There are only two folders: My queries and Shared queries. My queries are used for all our private queries (SQL and Visual). Shared queries is a shared folder that contains all queries that can be used by anyone with appropriate permissions.

5. The answer is **C**, Type 2. A Type 0 dimension never changes, a Type 1 dimension would overwrite the old region so you would not be able to track historical change, whilst Type 12 is not a real dimension type. Type 2 slowly changing dimensions allow you to track changes over time by creating a new record for each change with a relevant valid from and to date.

6. The answer is **B**, to resolve many-to-many cardinality between entities. If two related entities, such as bank transactions and account holders, cannot be resolved with a one-to-many relationship, then introducing a bridge will help semantic models return the correct aggregation and filtering behaviors for the relationship.

7. The answer is **B**, inner join. A left inner join is not a real join type. A left outer join would keep all records on the left side of the join but still return records with no match in the right side of the join. A right outer join would keep all records on the right side of the join and still return records with no match on the left side of the join. An inner join only returns records where both sides of the join match.

8. The answer is **A**, COALESCE. This function will evaluate a field and if it is NULL replace it with a value from a list of alternatives. Those alternatives might be a different field or some kind of placeholder value. The first non-null value in the listed alternatives is returned.

CHAPTER 3

Implement and manage semantic models

The previous chapter reviewed the skills necessary to prepare data. This chapter covers data modeling skills. In Power BI, a *data model* is a collection of one or more tables connected by relationships. Apart from the M language, which is used for data shaping, Power BI uses DAX, which is its native formula and query language. Power BI possesses rich data modeling capabilities, which include creating relationships as well as enriching a data model with hierarchies, measures, calculated columns, calculated tables, and calculation groups.

> *NOTE* **COMPANION FILES**
>
> You can find the companion files for this chapter at *github.com/DaniilMaslyuk/DP-600*.

Skills covered in this chapter:

- Skill 3.1: Design and build semantic models
- Skill 3.2: Optimize enterprise-scale semantic models

Skill 3.1: Design and build semantic models

In this skill, you'll learn the different ways of building an enterprise-scale data model, including composite models, row- and object-level security, DAX, and external tools. DAX, being a language that deserves a separate book, takes up the vast majority of this skill.

> **This skill covers how to:**
>
> - Choose a storage mode, including Direct Lake
> - Identify use cases for DAX Studio and Tabular Editor 2
> - Implement a star schema for a semantic model
> - Implement relationships, such as bridge tables and many-to-many relationships
> - Write calculations that use DAX variables and functions, such as iterators, table filtering, windowing, and information functions
> - Implement calculation groups, dynamic strings, and field parameters

- Design and build a large-format semantic model
- Design and build composite models that include aggregations
- Implement dynamic row-level security and object-level security
- Validate row-level security and object-level security

Choose a storage mode, including Direct Lake

The most common way to consume data in Power BI is to import it into the data model. When you import data in Power BI, you create a copy of it that is kept static until you refresh your semantic model. Data from files and folders can only be imported in Power BI. In Microsoft Fabric, you can create data connections in three ways.

First, you can import your data, which makes the Power BI data model cache it. This method offers you the greatest flexibility when you model your data because you can use all the available modeling features in Power BI.

Second, you can connect to your data directly in its original source. This method is known as *DirectQuery*. With DirectQuery, data is not cached in Power BI. Instead, the original data source is queried every time you interact with Power BI visuals. Not all data sources support DirectQuery.

Third, with Fabric lakehouses and warehouses, you can use the Direct Lake connectivity method and query OneLake directly. This method should be used instead of Import mode only in specific cases, such as models that are hundreds of gigabytes in size.

DirectQuery

When you use the DirectQuery connectivity mode, you are not caching any data in Power BI. All data remains in the data source, except for metadata, which Power BI caches. Metadata includes column and table names, data types, and relationships.

For most data sources supporting DirectQuery, when connecting to a data source, you select the entities you want to connect to, such as tables or views. Each entity becomes a table in your data model. Data from DirectQuery tables cannot be seen in the **Table** view of Power BI Desktop; if all tables in a data model are in DirectQuery mode, the **Table view** button will not be visible, though you can still use the **Model** view.

ADVANTAGES
The main advantage of this method is that you are not limited by the hardware of your development machine or the capacity of the server to which you will publish your report. All data is kept in the data source, and all the calculations are done in the source as well.

Another advantage of using DirectQuery is that your reports will always use the latest available data, which means you won't have to worry about the discrepancy between the data in the database and the figures that your report is showing.

If you only use DirectQuery in your data model, the Power BI file size will be negligible compared to a file with imported data, so you won't be affected by the file size limits when publishing to the Power BI service.

DISADVANTAGES

When you're working in DirectQuery mode, it's unlikely that your visuals will be displayed as quickly as if you were using Import mode. Data sources that are too slow may result in an unacceptable user experience.

There's a limit on the number of rows that a single query in DirectQuery mode can return. The default is one million rows, which is relevant when you're trying to display data that hasn't been summarized.

Not all data transformations are supported in DirectQuery mode. In case your data needs to be transformed, it's best to create the necessary views in the database and connect to the new views in Power BI.

Direct Lake

The Direct Lake connectivity method combines some elements of importing data and Direct-Query. On the one hand, you don't import data. On the other hand, you get the performance that's not too far from Import mode.

ADVANTAGES

The advantage of Direct Lake over Import mode is that with Direct Lake, you don't need to refresh data in your semantic models, because you're querying the latest data available in OneLake, similar to DirectQuery. Therefore, you reduce the risk of showing stale data, and you save resources on scheduled refreshes.

The advantage of Direct Lake over DirectQuery is that you're querying OneLake, which is better optimized for DAX calculations, and Direct Lake performance is similar to Import mode. Additionally, your semantic models can use more data than the usual Import mode models.

DISADVANTAGES

A significant limitation of Direct Lake is that you cannot use calculated columns and calculated tables in your semantic model. Furthermore, all your semantic model tables need to be backed by physical tables, otherwise you may not get the best performance.

Direct Lake can be used for near real-time scenarios, though not for real-time scenarios, which are better suited for DirectQuery.

Identify use cases for DAX Studio and Tabular Editor 2

Some Power BI features aren't available in Power BI Desktop, and you may want to use an external tool to perform some operations. External tools connect to the underlying data model and allow you to query and make changes to your model. This section discusses some of the reasons to use DAX Studio and Tabular Editor 2.

DAX Studio

DAX Studio is an open source tool for querying tabular data models, including Power BI and Analysis Services.

> **NOTE** **DOWNLOADING DAX STUDIO**
>
> You can download DAX Studio from *daxstudio.org*.

After you install DAX Studio, you can launch it from Power BI Desktop by selecting **External tools** > **DAX Studio**. You can see the DAX Studio interface in Figure 3-1.

FIGURE 3-1 DAX Studio interface

While the full functionality of DAX Studio is outside of scope of this book, here are some features that can be useful to many users of Power BI:

- **Writing and analyzing queries** The primary function of DAX Studio is to query data models. "Skill 4.2: Query data by using SQL" reviews DAX queries in detail. If you don't want to write your own queries, you can use **Query Builder**, which will write DAX queries for you.

- **Clearing the cache** In many cases, Power BI caches the query results to improve the report viewing experience. When analyzing queries, you'll find it useful to clear this cache to ensure that your timings aren't tainted by caching. To do so, in DAX Studio select **Clear Cache**.

- **Viewing model metrics** You can see the relative size of tables and columns in your data model (see "Skill 3.2: Optimize enterprise-scale semantic models" for details).

Tabular Editor 2

Tabular Editor 2 is an open source tool for development of tabular data models. In addition to the open source version, a paid version called Tabular Editor 3 is available. This book covers only Tabular Editor 2.

NOTE **DOWNLOADING TABULAR EDITOR 2**

You can download Tabular Editor 2 from *github.com/TabularEditor/TabularEditor/releases/latest*.

Figure 3-2 shows Tabular Editor 2 connected to a local Power BI data model.

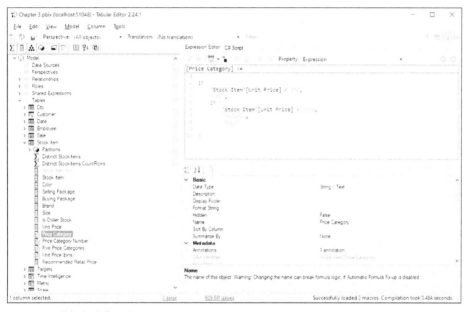

FIGURE 3-2 Tabular Editor 2

You can use Tabular Editor 2 to edit the data model metadata, including but not limited to adding or editing measures. Most actions in Tabular Editor 2 can be scripted and automated. For example, the following C# script will format the selected measures:

```
Selected.Measures.FormatDax();
```

To execute the script, select some measures in Tabular Editor, select **C# Script**, enter the script, and select **Run script**.

NEED MORE REVIEW? **USEFUL SCRIPT SNIPPETS**

For more examples of scripts you can run in Tabular Editor 2, see "Useful script snippets" at *docs.tabulareditor.com/te2/Useful-script-snippets.html*.

One of the standout features of Tabular Editor 2 is the Best Practice Analyzer (BPA), which you'll learn more about in "Skill 3.2: Optimize enterprise-scale semantic models." You can also create calculation groups in Tabular Editor 2 (see "Implement calculation groups, dynamic strings, and field parameters" for more details).

Implement a star schema for a semantic model

While Power BI can work with a variety of schemas, it works best with star schemas. Therefore, you should strive to denormalize snowflake schemas into star schemas. The closer to the source you get denormalized data, the better performance you get in most cases.

Note that in some cases a flat table will deliver better performance than snowflake schema. The price you may pay in this case is reduced user-friendliness for report builders, since all fields are going to be in the same table. Additionally, for some you may need to write more complex DAX, especially if you used to have more than one fact.

For more details on star schema and slowly changing dimensions, refer to "Skill 2.3: Transform data."

Implement relationships, such as bridge tables and many-to-many relationships

There are three main types of physical relationships in Power BI semantic models:

- One-to-one
- One-to-many (also many-to-one)
- Many-to-many

One-to-many relationships are most common, and one-to-one relationships are relatively rare, because they mean that one or more tables potentially could be combined in one. There are two ways to implement physical many-to-many relationships: directly or by using a bridge table.

Direct many-to-many relationships

To implement a many-to-many relationship, you can select **Many to many** from the **Cardinality** dropdown when creating a relationship (Figure 3-3).

When using many-to-many cardinality between tables A and B, you have three options for cross filter direction:

- Single (A filters B)
- Single (B filters A)
- Both

After you create a direct many-to-many relationship, it'll look like Figure 3-4.

FIGURE 3-3 Relationship creation

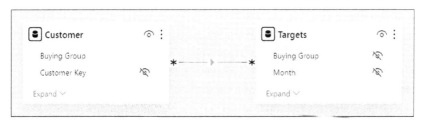

FIGURE 3-4 Direct many-to-many relationship

When using direct many-to-many relationships, keep a few things in mind:

- Values related to the blank row due to an invalid relationship won't be shown.
- When using REMOVEFILTERS or the ALL* family of functions on one table, it won't be applied to the other table.
- You cannot use the RELATED function in either table.

Direct many-to-many relationships work well only when the number of distinct values in columns participating in relationships is less than about 100,000, and when you're working with higher cardinalities, you may get better performance by using bridge tables.

Bridge tables

A *bridge table* is a table that sits between two tables that you want to relate and is related to both by using one-to-many relationships. Figure 3-5 shows the Customer and Targets tables related by using a bridge table called Buying Group.

FIGURE 3-5 Buying Group bridge table

Note that the cross filter direction between the Customer and Buying Group tables is set to **Both**; if it wasn't, filters from the Customer table wouldn't reach the Targets table by default. If you set the cross filter direction between Customer and Buying Group tables to **Single**, you can still make Customer filter Targets by using the CROSSFILTER function in DAX, for example.

You can create a table by using DAX or Power Query, or you can connect to a bridge table from your data source, if available.

Write calculations that use DAX variables and functions, such as iterators, table filtering, windowing, and information functions

While in some cases you can create insightful visuals without writing DAX, for more sophisticated analysis, you might need to enrich your model with calculated columns, calculated tables, and measures.

With DAX, you can derive many more insights from your data compared to using just the existing fields. For example, DAX allows you to dynamically calculate period-over-period figures, as well as percentages, such as weighted averages. This section reviews the skills that are needed to perform calculations and query with DAX.

DAX is a functional language that resembles the Excel formula language, and there are many functions that appear in both. Unlike the M language, DAX is not case-sensitive in most cases. At the same time, there are some important differences:

- In DAX, there is no concept of a cell in a data table. If you need to get a value from a table, you will need to filter a specific column down to that value.

- DAX is strongly typed; it is not possible to mix values of different data types in the same column.

DAX data types

Every column in a Power BI data model has exactly one data type. Currently, DAX supports the following eight data types:

- **Decimal Number** This is the most popular numeric data type. It is designed to hold fractional numbers, and it can handle whole numbers as well.
- **Fixed Decimal Number** This data type is similar to Decimal Number, but the number of decimal places is fixed at four. Internally, numbers of this type are stored as integers divided by 10,000.
- **Whole Number** This data type stores integers.
- **datetime** This data type stores dates and times together. Internally, values are stored as decimal numbers.
- **Date** This type enables you to store dates without time. If you convert a datetime value to Date, the time portion is truncated, not rounded.
- **Time** This data type stores time only, without dates.
- **Text** This type stores text strings in Unicode format.
- **True/False** Also known as Boolean, this data type stores True and False values, which, if converted to a number, will be 1 and 0, respectively.

DAX can perform implicit type conversions if needed. For example, you can add TRUE to a text string, "2", and the result will be 3:

```
3 = "2" + TRUE
```

On the other hand, if you concatenate two numbers, you will get a text string as a result:

```
23 = 2 & 3
```

You can perform explicit type conversion with functions such as INT and VALUE, which convert values to integers. For example, the following expression results in 45435:

```
45435 = INT("2024-05-23")
```

Dates in the form of text strings can be converted to dates using the DATEVALUE function:

```
23 May 2024 = DATEVALUE("2024-05-23")
```

Alternatively, you can prefix date strings with dt like so:

```
23 May 2024 = dt"2024-05-23"
```

You can convert numeric and datetime values to text using the FORMAT function, which takes two arguments: an expression to convert and a format string. FORMAT is an example of a function that is case-sensitive. The following two expressions provide different results:

```
// AM or PM, depending on time of the day
Upper = FORMAT(NOW (), "AM/PM")
```

```
// am or pm, depending on time of the day
Lower = FORMAT(NOW (), "am/pm")
```

NEED MORE REVIEW?   **DAX** FORMAT **FUNCTION**

To learn more about the FORMAT function in DAX, including information on which format
it accepts, see "FORMAT Function (DAX)" at *learn.microsoft.com/en-us/dax/format-
function-dax.*

Blank or null values in DAX act like zeros in many cases; this behavior is very different from
SQL nulls and Excel empty cells. For example, a sum of two blanks is blank, whereas in Excel
you would get 0; the sum of 1 and blank is 1, whereas in SQL, the sum is NULL. You can generate
a blank value using the BLANK function. You can check whether an expression is blank with the
ISBLANK function.

NEED MORE REVIEW?   **DATA TYPES IN POWER BI**

For a more detailed overview of data types supported in Power BI, including a table of implicit
type conversions and BLANK behavior, see "Data types in Power BI Desktop" at *learn.microsoft.
com/en-us/power-bi/connect-data/desktop-data-types.*

DAX operators

In DAX, you can use the following operators, as shown in Table 3-1.

TABLE 3-1 DAX operators

Type	Operator	Meaning	Example	Result
Arithmetic	+	Addition	2 + 3	5
	–	Subtraction or sign	2 – 3	–1
	*	Multiplication	2 * 3	6
	/	Division	3 / 2	1.5
	^	Exponentiation	2 ^ 3	8
Comparison	=	Equal to	0 = BLANK()	TRUE
	==	Strictly equal to	0 == BLANK()	FALSE
	>	Greater than	2 > 3	FALSE
	<	Less than	2 < 3	TRUE
	>=	Greater than or equal to	2 >= 3	FALSE
	<=	Less than or equal to	2 <= 3	TRUE
	<>	Not equal to	2 <> 3	TRUE

Type	Operator	Meaning	Example	Result
Text concatenation	&	Concatenates two text values	"2" & "3"	23
Logical	&&	AND condition between two Boolean expressions	(2 = 3) && (1 = 1)	FALSE
	||	OR condition between two Boolean expressions	(2 = 3) || (1 = 1)	TRUE
	IN	Belongness in a list	2 IN { 1, 2, 3 }	TRUE
	NOT	Negation	NOT 2 = 3	TRUE

Some logical operators are also available as functions. Instead of the double ampersand, you can use the AND function:

AND(2 = 3, 1 = 1)

Instead of a double pipe, you can use the OR function:

OR(2 = 3, 1 = 1)

Both functions, AND and OR, take exactly two arguments. If you need to evaluate more than two conditions, you can nest your functions:

AND(2 = 3, AND(1 = 1, 5 = 5))

The NOT operator can be used as a function as well:

NOT(2 = 3)

NEED MORE REVIEW? **DAX OPERATOR REFERENCE**

For more examples and details on DAX operators, including operator precedence, see "DAX operators" at *learn.microsoft.com/en-us/dax/dax-operator-reference*.

Create DAX formulas for calculated columns

A *calculated column* is an additional column in a table that you define with a DAX formula. The difference between a custom column created with M and a calculated column created with DAX is that the latter is based on data that has already been loaded into your model. Furthermore, calculated columns do not appear in Power Query Editor.

You can create a calculated column in several ways, for example, by selecting **Modeling** > **Calculations** > **New column** in the Report view. This will create a calculated column in the table that is selected in the Data pane. Alternatively, you can right-click a table in the **Data** pane and select **New Column**. Power BI will then open a formula bar (Figure 3-6) where you can write your DAX formula, then select the check mark or press Enter to validate the formula. Power BI will also create a new field in the Data pane, and this new field will have a column icon next to it.

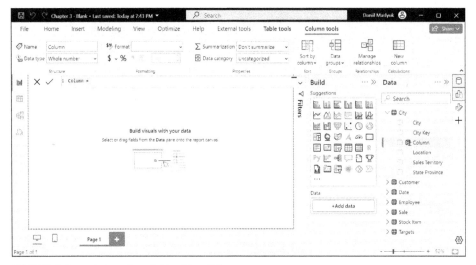

FIGURE 3-6 Formula bar after clicking New Column

The formula that you write is automatically applied to each row in the new column. You can reference another column in the following way:

```
'Table name'[Column name]
```

For example, calculate Unit Price Including Tax by creating a calculated column in the Sale table with the following formula:

```
Unit Price Including Tax = Sale[Unit Price] *(1 + Sale[Tax Rate] / 100)
```

Note that the formula includes both the column name, which precedes the equals operator, and the column formula itself, which follows the equals operator.

The Power BI Desktop formula bar has IntelliSense enabled, and it helps you with selecting tables, columns, and functions after you type a few characters, and it also highlights syntax. Instead of copying the previous formula, you can start by specifying the column name, followed by the equals operator, then start typing **uni**. At this stage, IntelliSense will give you a list of all columns and functions that have "uni" appear as part of their names (Figure 3-7). If you select a function from the list, it will also display the function's description.

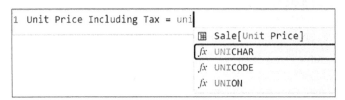

FIGURE 3-7 IntelliSense-suggested values

You can navigate in this list with the arrow keys on your keyboard and press Tab to autocomplete the statement. Alternatively, you can click a value, which has the same effect as pressing the Tab key.

In general, columns should always be referenced using a fully qualified syntax, which is a table name in single quotation marks followed by a column name in brackets. If a table name does not contain spaces, does not start with a number, and is not a reserved keyword such as `Calendar`, then you can safely omit the single quotation marks. If IntelliSense highlights a word, then it is likely a reserved keyword.

When you are referencing a column in the same table, you can use just a column name in brackets. Although this is syntactically correct, it might be difficult to read, especially because it is best practice to reference measures without table names. Measures are discussed in more detail in the "Measures" section later in this chapter.

If you want to reference a column from a table that is on the one side of a one-to-many relationship with the current table, you need to use the RELATED function. For example, you could add a Customer column to the Sale table with the following formula:

```
Customer = RELATED(Customer[Customer])
```

RELATED has a companion function, RELATEDTABLE, which can work in the opposite direction. For example, you could add a calculated column to the Date table that counts the number of rows in the Sale table. Because it is not possible to store a multi-row table in one row, you would also need to apply an aggregation function to RELATEDTABLE. In this case, you can use COUNTROWS, which counts the number of rows in a table:

```
Sales # = COUNTROWS(RELATEDTABLE(Sale))
```

Note that RELATEDTABLE only works in one direction by default. If you have not enabled bidirectional relationships, the following calculated column in the Date table will contain the same value for each row of the column, which is the same as the number of rows in the City table:

```
Cities # = COUNTROWS(RELATEDTABLE(City))
```

If this column is defined in the Date table, changing the cross-filter direction between the Sale and City tables from Single to Both ensures that each row shows the number of cities to which the company sold on a particular date.

USING DAX FUNCTIONS IN CALCULATED COLUMNS

DAX has hundreds of functions. Some functions return scalar values, whereas others return tables. If a function results in a one-column, one-row table, it can be implicitly converted to a scalar value.

There are many functions that perform the same tasks as some M functions. For example, the LOWER, UPPER, LEN, and TRIM functions transform text values in the same way as the M `Text.Lower`, `Text.Upper`, `Text.Length`, and `Text.Trim` functions, respectively.

Unlike M functions, DAX functions can perform implicit type conversion. For instance, in M, the following expression results in the error shown in Figure 3-8:

```
Text.Length(100)
```

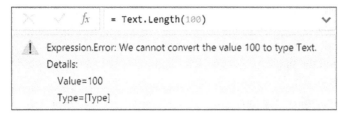

FIGURE 3-8 Error message

In DAX, on the other hand, LEN(100) returns 3. Using LEN on nontext values, however, is somewhat unpredictable, and it should be combined with the FORMAT function. For example, if the 'Date'[Date] column contains a date value of 1 January 2024, then a corresponding value in the following calculated column will result in 9:

```DAX
Length = LEN('Date'[Date])
```

If you format values explicitly inside the LEN function, however, then you can control the results. The following calculated column returns 10:

```DAX
Formatted Length = LEN(FORMAT('Date'[Date], "dd-MM-yyyy"))
```

The LEN function, as well as FIND and SEARCH, can be useful when you want to extract substrings of a variable length. For instance, in the Customer table, the column called Buying Group has three distinct values:

- N/A
- Tailspin Toys
- Wingtip Toys

Suppose you want to extract the first word only, so you are looking to create a column with the following three values:

- N/A
- Tailspin
- Wingtip

Note that each word has a different length. If the number of characters you wanted to extract were fixed, you could use the LEFT function, which gives you the first N characters. This function, along with RIGHT, MID, and LEN, also exists in Excel. To create a calculated column with the first three characters from Buying Group, you would write the following formula:

```
Buying Group First Three Characters = LEFT(Customer[Buying Group], 3)
```

To extract the first word, first calculate the length of the first word. For this, you need to find the position of the space symbol in a string. In this case, use the FIND or SEARCH function. Both functions have two required arguments: text to find and where to search. The only difference between them is that FIND is case-sensitive, whereas SEARCH is not. Because you are looking for a space symbol, you can use either function. First try the following formula:

```
Buying Group First Space Position = FIND(" ", Customer[Buying Group])
```

Because there is no space in "N/A," you get an error that propagates to the entire column, even though there is only one row in which the space was not found. You can see the error in Figure 3-9.

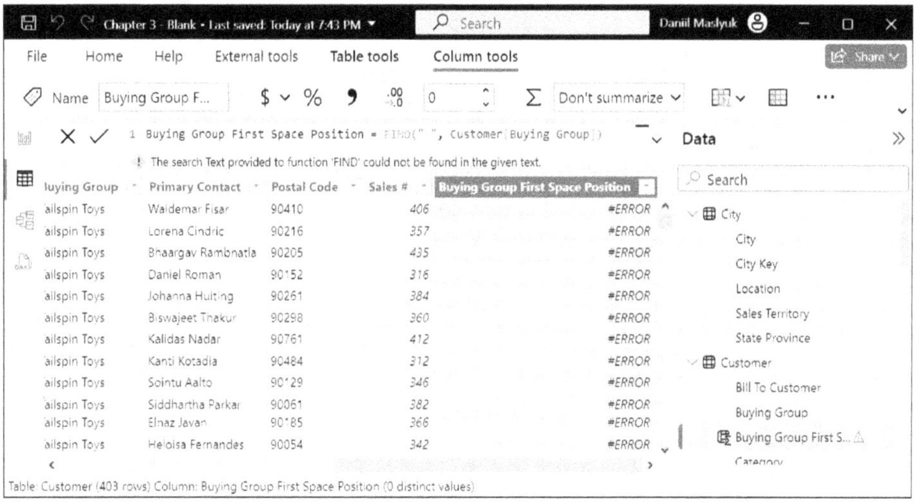

FIGURE 3-9 DAX error message in the whole column

This behavior is typical for DAX calculated columns. One way to solve this problem is to use the optional parameters in FIND. The third parameter specifies the number of character to start the search from; if omitted, it is 1. The fourth parameter specifies the value to return in case nothing is found. For example, return 0 if nothing is found:

```
Buying Group First Space Position No Error = FIND(" ", Customer[Buying Group], , 0)
```

In this case, you get no error. An alternative way to solve the same problem is to use the IFERROR function, which takes two arguments: an expression to evaluate and a value to return in case of an error. The following calculated column returns the same result as the previous one:

```
Buying Group First Space Position No Error = IFERROR(FIND(" ", Customer[Buying Group]), 0)
```

To extract the first word from Buying Group, use the following formula:

```
Buying Group First Word = IFERROR(LEFT(Customer[Buying Group], FIND(" ",
Customer[Buying Group]) - 1), Customer[Buying Group])
```

There are two things to note about this formula. First, it subtracts 1 from the result of the FIND, because DAX starts counting from 1, which is different from M. Second, this formula is quite long and could benefit from formatting to make the code easier to read. To help you make your code cleaner and easier to read, SQLBI offers a tool called **DAX Formatter** (daxformatter.com), which you can call from DAX Studio and Tabular Editor 2.

The following code was formatted with DAX Formatter:

```
Buying Group First Word =
IFERROR (
    LEFT ( Customer[Buying Group], FIND ( " ", Customer[Buying Group] ) - 1 ),
    Customer[Buying Group]
)
```

The DAX Query view in Power BI Desktop also has some code formatting capabilities.

The LEN function can be useful when you want to calculate how many times a text string appears in another text string. For this, use the SUBSTITUTE function. The SUBSTITUTE function, which is case-sensitive, has three required parameters: text, old text, and new text. For instance, replace all instances of "a" with the letter "o" in "Alabama," you would use the following code:

```
Alobomo = SUBSTITUTE("Alabama", "a", "o")
```

As a result, you get "Alobomo." Because SUBSTITUTE is case-sensitive, the first "A" is not affected. To count the number of times a character appears in a string, substitute the character with an empty string and calculate the difference in lengths of the old and the new strings. The following expression counts the number of times the capital letter "T" appears in the Buying Group column values:

```
Number of T's = LEN(Customer[Buying Group]) - LEN(SUBSTITUTE(Customer[Buying Group],
"T", ""))
```

To count the number of times the letter "T" appears regardless of case, you can either use another SUBSTITUTE function or use LOWER or UPPER. The following three formulas provide identical results, demonstrating that in DAX there is often more than one way to solve the same problem:

```
// Using second SUBSTITUTE
Number of all T's SUBSTITUTE =
LEN(Customer[Buying Group]) - LEN(SUBSTITUTE(SUBSTITUTE(Customer[Buying Group],
"t", ""), "T", ""))
```

```
// Using LOWER
Number of all T's LOWER =
LEN(Customer[Buying Group]) - LEN(SUBSTITUTE(LOWER(Customer[Buying Group]), "t", ""))
```

```
// Using UPPER
Number of all T's UPPER =
LEN(Customer[Buying Group]) - LEN(SUBSTITUTE(UPPER(Customer[Buying Group]), "T", ""))
```

The Number of T's and Number of all T's columns provide the following results, shown in Table 3-2.

TABLE 3-2 Comparison of the Number of T's and Number of all T's columns

Buying Group	Number of T's	Number of all T's LOWER
N/A	0	0
Tailspin Toys	2	2
Wingtip Toys	1	2

NEED MORE REVIEW?   TEXT DAX FUNCTIONS

For more information on the available text functions in DAX, see "Text Functions (DAX)" at *learn.microsoft.com/en-us/dax/text-functions-dax.*

DAX has several mathematical functions available, many of which are similar to the Excel functions with which they share their names. In the following list, you can see how some of the most common mathematical DAX functions work:

- `ABS(Number)`   Returns the absolute value of a number.
- `DIVIDE(Numerator, Denominator, AlternateResult)`   Safe division function that can handle division by 0.
- `EXP(Number)`   Returns e raised to the power of a number.
- `EVEN(Number)`   Returns a number rounded up to the nearest even number. You can check if a number is even using the `ISEVEN` function.
- `ODD(Number)`   Returns a number rounded up to the nearest odd number. You can check if a number is odd using the `ISODD` function.
- `FACT(Number)`   Returns the factorial of a number.
- `LN(Number)`   Returns the natural logarithm of a number.
- `LOG(Number, Base)`   Returns the logarithm of a number to the base you specify.
- `MOD(Number, Divisor)`   Returns the remainder of a number divided by a divisor.
- `PI()`   Returns the number Pi, accurate to 15 digits.
- `POWER(Number, Power)`   Returns the result of a number raised to a power. This is the function equivalent of the exponentiation (^) operator.
- `QUOTIENT(Numerator, Denominator)`   Returns the integer portion of a division.
- `SIGN(Number)`   Returns −1 if a number is negative, 1 if it is positive, and 0 if it is zero.
- `ROUNDDOWN(Number, NumberOfDigits)`   Rounds a number toward 0 to a specified number of decimal places.
- `FLOOR(Number, Significance)`   Rounds a number toward 0 to the nearest multiple of significance.
- `TRUNC(Number, NumberOfDigits)`   Truncates a number, keeping the specified number of decimal places.

- ROUND(Number, NumberOfDigits) Rounds a number to a specified number of decimal places.

- MROUND(Number, Multiple) Rounds a number to the nearest multiple.

- ROUNDUP(Number, NumberOfDigits) Rounds a number away from 0 to a specified number of decimal places.

- CEILING(Number, Significance) Rounds a number up to the nearest multiple of significance.

- INT(Number) Rounds a number down to the nearest integer.

- RAND() Returns a random number greater than or equal to 0 and less than 1.

- RANDBETWEEN(Bottom, Top) Returns a random integer between two specified numbers.

- SQRT(Number) Returns the square root of a number.

NEED MORE REVIEW? **MATHEMATICAL DAX FUNCTIONS**

For more information on the available mathematical and trigonometric functions in DAX, see "Math and Trig Functions (DAX)" at *learn.microsoft.com/en-us/dax/ math-and-trig-functions-dax*.

The date and time functions in DAX help you create calculations based on dates and time. The following list shows some of the most common date and time functions:

- TODAY() Returns the current system date in datetime format.

- NOW() Returns the current system date and time in datetime format.

- DATE(Year, Month, Day) Returns the specified date in datetime format.

- DATEVALUE(TextDate) Converts a text date to a date in datetime format.

- YEAR(Date) Returns the year portion of a date.

- MONTH(Date) Returns the month number of a date.

- DAY(Date) Returns the day number of a date.

- TIME(Hour, Minute, Second) Returns the specified time in datetime format.

- TIMEVALUE(TextTime) Converts a text time to time in datetime format.

- HOUR(Date/time) Returns the hour of a date and time.

- MINUTE(Date/time) Returns the minute of a date and time.

- SECOND(Date/time) Returns the second of a date and time.

- DATEDIFF(StartDate, EndDate, Interval) Returns the number of intervals between two dates. The interval can be any of the following: SECOND, MINUTE, HOUR, DAY, WEEK, MONTH, QUARTER, or YEAR.

- EDATE(Date, Months) Shifts a date back or forward by a specified number of months.

- EOMONTH(Date, Months)   Returns the end of month date of a specified date, shifted by a specified number of months.

- WEEKDAY(Date, ReturnType)   Returns the number of the day of the week according to the specified ReturnType.

- WEEKNUM(Date, ReturnType)   Returns the week number in the year according to the specified ReturnType.

NEED MORE REVIEW? **DATE AND TIME DAX FUNCTIONS**

For more information on the available date and time functions in DAX, see "Date and Time Functions (DAX)" at *learn.microsoft.com/en-us/dax/date-and-time-functions-dax*.

USING LOOKUPVALUE

If there is a many-to-one relationship between two tables, you can bring a related value from the one side to the many side with RELATED, as discussed earlier. With LOOKUPVALUE, you can look up values from another table based on one or more conditions. This is especially useful when you need to look up two or more conditions, because DAX allows creating physical relationships based on one column only.

LOOKUPVALUE uses the following syntax: column to retrieve values from, followed by pairs of arguments, in which the first item is a column to search and the second item is a scalar expression to look for. If there is no match, a blank value is returned. If there are multiple values that match the same condition, an error is returned.

For review purposes, consider the following example. In the Sale table, you can insert values from the Targets table using the following formula:

```
Target Excluding Tax =
LOOKUPVALUE (
    Targets[Target Excluding Tax],
    Targets[Month], EOMONTH(Sale[Invoice Date Key], -1) + 1,
    Targets[Buying Group], RELATED(Customer[Buying Group])
)
```

Note that this particular calculated column does not provide useful results because the granularity of the Sale and Targets tables is different, but LOOKUPVALUE can nonetheless be useful in situations where the granularity of tables is the same or does not matter. Also note that the following formula, which is not specific enough, does not work, and results in an error, as shown in Figure 3-10:

```
Target Excluding Tax Wrong =
LOOKUPVALUE (
    Targets[Target Excluding Tax],
    Targets[Buying Group], RELATED(Customer[Buying Group])
)
```

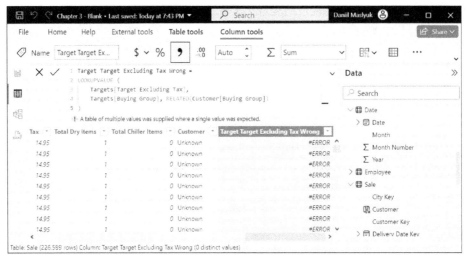

FIGURE 3-10 LOOKUPVALUE that results in an error

GROUPING VALUES

Calculated columns can be very useful for grouping values. For instance, if you have a column with unit prices, such as `'Stock Item'[Unit Price]`, you may want to put them into Low, Medium, and High categories based on business requirements. The column contains 58 distinct values. Suppose that items under $100 can be placed in the Low category, items from $100 to $1,000 can be placed into the Medium category, and the rest can be placed into the High category.

One way to do it would be by using the IF function. IF, like many other DAX functions, can be nested. The following calculated column produces the necessary grouping:

```
Price Category =
IF (
    'Stock Item'[Unit Price] < 100,
    "Low",
    IF (
        'Stock Item'[Unit Price] < 1000,
        "Medium",
        "High"
    )
)
```

If you use this calculated column in a visual, you will notice that the values are sorted in alphabetic order: High, Low, Medium. To solve this problem, try the following code:

```
Price Category Number =
IF (
    'Stock Item'[Price Category] = "Low",
    1,
    IF (
```

```
        'Stock Item'[Price Category] = "Medium",
        2,
        3
    )
)
```

An alternative way to produce the same column is to use the SWITCH function. The first parameter in this function is an expression to be evaluated multiple times. The other parameters come in pairs: a value to evaluate against the expression, and a result to return in case the value and the expression match. The last argument, which is optional, is the result to return if no value matched the expression.

The following formula returns the same results as the previous formula:

```
Price Category Number SWITCH = SWITCH('Stock Item'[Price Category], "Low", 1,
"Medium", 2, 3)
```

After you create the column using either approach and try to sort the Price Category column by Price Category Number, you will get the error shown in Figure 3-11.

FIGURE 3-11 Sort by another column error

This error message appears because you are trying to sort the Price Category column by a column that derives its values from Price Category. Note that you can sort Price Category Number by Price Category. This problem can be fixed in at least two ways. One way is to create the two calculated columns in reverse order:

// First, create Price Category Number
```
Price Category Number =
IF (
    'Stock Item'[Unit Price] < 100,
    1,
    IF (
        'Stock Item'[Unit Price] < 1000,
        2,
        3
    )
)
```

// Second, create Price Category
```
Price Category = SWITCH('Stock Item'[Price Category Number], 1, "Low", 2, "Medium", "High")
```

Now the Price Category column can be sorted by the Price Category Number column without any errors. An alternative approach is to write the two calculated columns in the same way so that both of them reference the Unit Price column without referencing each other:

```
// The order of creation does not matter in this case
Price Category =
IF (
    'Stock Item'[Unit Price] < 100,
    "Low",
    IF (
        'Stock Item'[Unit Price] < 1000,
        "Medium",
        "High"
    )
)
Price Category Number =
IF (
    'Stock Item'[Unit Price] < 100,
    1,
    IF (
        'Stock Item'[Unit Price] < 1000,
        2,
        3
    )
)
```

In this way, you can also sort the Price Category column by the Price Category Number column without any problem.

The SWITCH function is especially useful when you have many conditions you want to check. For instance, if you decide to group unit prices into five categories, use four IF statements:

```
Five Price Categories =
IF (
    'Stock Item'[Unit Price] < 10,
    "Very Low",
    IF (
        'Stock Item'[Unit Price] < 100,
        "Low",
        IF (
            'Stock Item'[Unit Price] < 200,
            "Medium",
            IF (
                'Stock Item'[Unit Price] < 1000,
                "High",
                "Very High"
            )
        )
    )
)
```

With SWITCH, you can use the SWITCH TRUE pattern to check Boolean statements:

```
Five Price Categories SWITCH =
SWITCH (
    TRUE (),
    'Stock Item'[Unit Price] < 10, "Very Low",
    'Stock Item'[Unit Price] < 100, "Low",
    'Stock Item'[Unit Price] < 200, "Medium",
    'Stock Item'[Unit Price] < 1000, "High",
    "Very High"
)
```

You can also group values with the user interface. To group the Unit Price values, right-click the column in the **Data** pane, then select **New Group**. The Groups window (Figure 3-12) will then open, where you can specify the settings for grouping, also called *binning*.

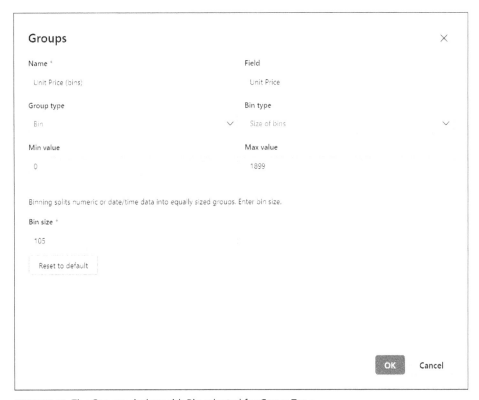

FIGURE 3-12 The Groups window with Bin selected for Group Type

Power BI analyzes the values in the column and chooses the group type that it deems best for the selected column. Because you have numeric values in Unit Price, Power BI decided that it's best to group the values into bins. Power BI gave the new column a default name, Unit Price (bins), which you can change.

Two bin type settings are available: **Size of bins** and **Number of bins**. For Size of bins, Power BI determines the best **Bin size** value, which can be adjusted. For the example, Power BI deemed 105 to be the best bin size. If necessary, you can reset the bin size to its default. If you select OK with default settings, Power BI will create a calculated column in which unit prices are rounded down to the nearest multiple of 105.

In this specific case, the new column will contain five distinct values:

- 0
- 105
- 210
- 315
- 1890

Internally, Power BI uses the following formula:

```
Unit Price (bins) =
IF(
 ISBLANK('Stock Item'[Unit Price]),
 BLANK(),
 INT('Stock Item'[Unit Price] / 105) * 105
)
```

Note that this calculated column has a special icon next to it: squares inside a rounded square. This is different from the icons shown with other calculated columns that you have created so far. You can see the Unit Price (bins) icon in Figure 3-13.

FIGURE 3-13 The Unit Price (bins) column in the fields list

The other calculated columns have one of two icons:

- When a column is of a numeric data type, such as the Price Category Number column, it has a calculated column icon with a capital sigma.

- When a column is of other data type text, like the Price Category column, it has a calculated column icon with *fx* written on it.

Even though technically Unit Price (bins) is a calculated column, it is not possible to see and modify its formula with Power BI Desktop. Instead, you can edit the group by right-clicking the column and selecting **Edit groups**. The Groups window will then open where you make changes, but you will not be able to change the group type.

If you choose to change the bin type to **Number of bins**, you will need to specify the number of bins, which, for the Unit Price column, Power BI set to 18 by default. When you edit the **Bin Count** field, Power BI will show you the approximate bin size; for the default 18 bins, the bin size is 105.5. You can see the Groups dialog box in Figure 3-14.

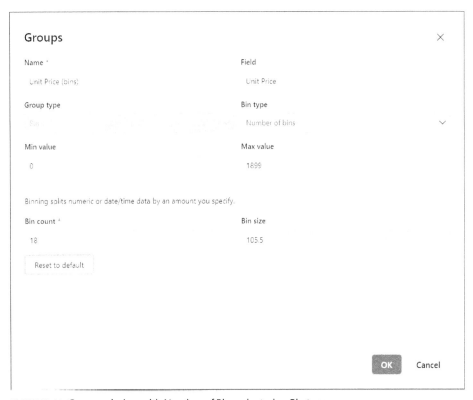

FIGURE 3-14 Groups window with Number of Bins selected as Bin type

Grouping Unit Price by number of bins results in the following five distinct values, which are different from groups based on bin size:

- 0
- 105.50

- 211
- 316.50
- 1793.50

When you create a new group, you can also choose the List group type. If you choose **List** in the **Group type** dropdown list, the Groups window interface will change, allowing you to pick values and group them. The Groups dialog with List selected as Group type can be seen in Figure 3-15.

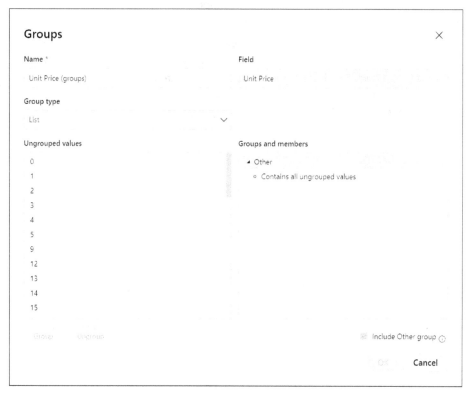

FIGURE 3-15 Groups window with List group type

In this dialog, you can either group items individually, resulting in single-item groups, or you can select multiple values at once by holding the Ctrl key. Holding the Shift key allows you to select a range of values. Once you select some values and click the **Group** button, the values are transferred to the list on the right, **Groups and members**, and you can specify a new name for each group. By default, every group is given a name that is the list of values separated by ampersands. Below the **Groups and members** list, the **Include Other group** checkbox enables you to create the Other group, which contains all ungrouped values. If you choose not to include the Other group, ungrouped values will be left as is.

USING VARIABLES

By using variables in DAX, you can write more readable and concise code. For example, suppose you want to define a discounted unit price that includes tax, but if the new price is less than $20, then you keep the old price, including tax. The discount rate is 20 percent. One way to write this formula is as follows:

```
New Price =
IF (
    Sale[Unit Price]
        *(1 + Sale[Tax Rate] / 100)
        * 0.8
        < 20,
    Sale[Unit Price]
        *(1 + Sale[Tax Rate] / 100),
    Sale[Unit Price]
        *(1 + Sale[Tax Rate] / 100)
        * 0.8
)
```

Note that the formula contains repeated code. If you rewrite the formula with variables, it will become easier to read. The general pattern for using variables is as follows:

```
Measure name =
VAR FirstVariable = … // DAX expression
VAR NthVariable = … // DAX expression
RETURN = … // DAX expression
```

The names of variables cannot include spaces or be reserved keywords, such as `Measure`. You can reference previously declared variables inside variables. The variables can only be accessed in the expression they are defined in; you cannot access variables defined in column A from column B, for example.

Here's the New Price formula rewritten with variables:

```
New Price =
VAR TaxPct = Sale[Tax Rate] / 100
VAR PriceInclTax = Sale[Unit Price] *(1 + TaxPct)
VAR DiscountedPriceInclTax = PriceInclTax * 0.8
RETURN
    IF (
        DiscountedPriceInclTax < 20,
        PriceInclTax,
        DiscountedPriceInclTax
    )
```

Another way to solve the problem of repetitive code in calculated columns is to split intermediate calculations in different columns. For instance, you can instead create four calculated columns as follows:

```
TaxPct = Sale[Tax Rate] / 100
PriceInclTax = Sale[Unit Price] *(1 + Sale[TaxPct])
DiscountedPriceInclTax = Sale[PriceInclTax] * 0.8
New Price =
```

```
IF (
    Sale[DiscountedPriceInclTax] < 20,
    Sale[PriceInclTax],
    Sale[DiscountedPriceInclTax]
)
```

Although this approach results in the same values as the previous New Price formulas, it has an important drawback: increased data model size. Every calculated column is materialized, resulting in greater file size. Because Power BI uses VertiPaq, an in-memory engine, calculated columns also occupy RAM space. The size of a calculated column depends on the number of its distinct values, so some columns may take more space than others.

EVALUATION CONTEXT

Most functions discussed so far were executed in row context. *Row context* can be thought of as the current row. When you define a calculated column, its formula is evaluated for each row of a table to which the column is added. Some table and aggregation functions, such as FILTER and SUMX, iterate over tables and, as a result, also use row context.

Some functions ignore row context, and they use filter context instead. You can think of *Filter context* as all the filters that are applied to a calculation. Filters can come from several places: visual-, page-, and report-level filters; axes in a visual; slicers; rows and columns in the Matrix visual; and more. For example, when you create a bar chart with Calendar Year Label on the axis and Profit in values, then each Calendar Year Label provides filter context for its Profit values, and as a result, each bar is different. Filters can also be applied programmatically with DAX.

> **IMPORTANT   SORT BY COLUMN AND FILTER CONTEXT**
>
> Columns used for sorting are part of filter context. For example, if you show Profit by Month, and you sort Month by Month Number, then Month Number is also part of filter context.

The two contexts always coexist at the same time, though either of them can be empty at certain times. For instance, when you define a calculated column in a physical table with a formula that uses no functions, the filter context is empty.

Functions that ignore row context include, but are not limited to, SUM, AVERAGE, and COUNTROWS. To see the effect of using a formula that ignores the row context, imagine you have a table called Scale with the following values:

- 1
- 1000
- 1000000

You can create a calculated column in the Scale table with the following formula:

```
Sum of Scale = SUM(Scale[Scale])
```

Figure 3-16 shows the resulting column.

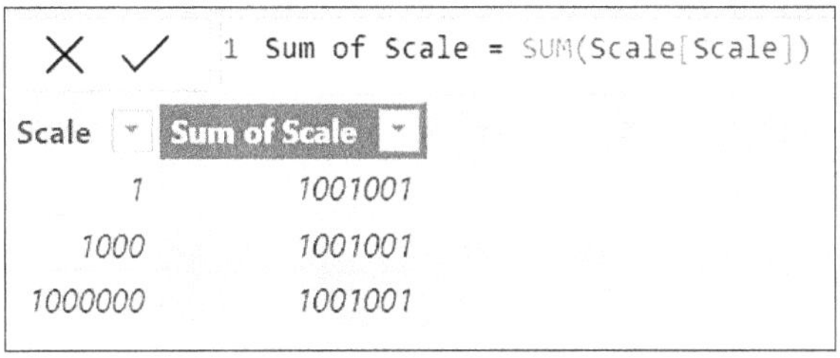

FIGURE 3-16 Sum of Scale calculated column

Note that the new column has the same value for each row because SUM works in filter context and ignores row context. In other words, SUM calculates its values irrespective of what the current row's value in the Scale[Scale] column is.

By default, row context ignores any relationships that are in place unless you use the RELATED or RELATEDTABLE function. You can leverage the effect of relationships between tables using filter context only. You can, however, transform row context into equivalent filter context with the help of the CALCULATE function, which has one required parameter: an expression that works in filter context. This function can also take optional filter arguments, which are discussed later in the "Using CALCULATE in Measures" section. For now, focus on the context transition capability of CALCULATE. To see the effect of context transition, create the following calculated column:

```
Sum of Scale Calculate = CALCULATE(SUM(Scale[Scale]))
```

Note that writing CALCULATE(Scale[Scale]) results in an error because Scale[Scale] can work in row context only. The reason why you cannot use Scale[Scale] in filter context is that DAX does not know what you want to do with values in the column. Do you want to sum the values, take an average of them, or something else? Figure 3-17 shows the Sum of Scale Calculate column.

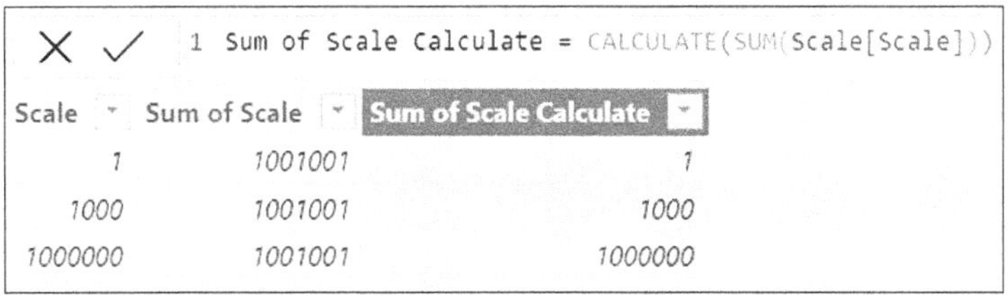

FIGURE 3-17 Sum of Scale Calculate column

When context transition happens, the row context is transformed into equivalent filter context. This means that for each row, a table is filtered to contain only those rows where the values are the same as in the current row. For example, when you define the Sum of Scale Calculate calculated column with CALCULATE and context transition happens, in the first row the following filter context is applied: Scale[Scale] = 1 and Scale[Sum of Scale] = 1001001. For the Scale rows that remain after filtering, SUM(Scale[Scale]) is performed. Therefore, every row contains a different value in the Sum of Scale Calculate column.

It's important to remember that the current row and the equivalent filter context are not the same thing. For an example that highlights the difference, add a duplicate row to the Scale table. To do that, follow these steps:

1. In the **Model** view, select the **Scale** table.

2. In **Properties**, ensure no column is selected as **Key column**.

3. Right-click the **Scale** table in the **Data** pane and select **Edit query**.

4. In Power Query Editor, click the **gear** icon next to the **Source** step.

5. Type **1** in the fourth row, and select **OK**.

6. Select **Close & Apply**.

You can see the results in Figure 3-18.

		1 Sum of Scale Calculate = CALCULATE(SUM(Scale[Scale]))
Scale	Sum of Scale	**Sum of Scale Calculate**
1	1001002	2
1000	1001002	1000
1000000	1001002	1000000
1	1001002	2

FIGURE 3-18 Resulting Sum of Scale Calculate values with duplicate rows

Note that the rows in which Scale = 1 has the Sum of Scale Calculate value of 2. For these rows, here are the steps that DAX followed to arrive at these figures:

1. Identify the row context: Scale = 1, Sum of Scale = 1001002.

2. Convert the row context into the equivalent filter context: Filter the Scale table and keep only those rows where Scale = 1 and Sum of Scale = 1001002.

3. For the two rows that remain, sum the values in the Scale column: 1 + 1 = 2.

4. Return the result of the summation, which is 2.

Because there are two identical rows, DAX follows the same procedure twice. The filter context cannot distinguish between identical rows, and as a result, the Sum of Scale Calculate values are not the same as the Scale column values.

Earlier in this chapter, you defined the following two columns in the Date table:

```
// Returns different values for each row
Sales # = COUNTROWS(RELATEDTABLE(Sale))
```

```
// Returns different values only with bidirectional filtering enabled
Cities # = COUNTROWS(RELATEDTABLE(City))
```

The reason why these calculated columns returned different values is that RELATEDTABLE is an alias for CALCULATETABLE, a sister function of CALCULATE, which works similarly, but receives a table expression as the first parameter instead of a scalar expression. Therefore, for each row in the Date table, context transition occurred, which filtered the Sale and City tables to only those rows that were related to the current row.

CIRCULAR DEPENDENCIES IN CALCULATED COLUMNS

DAX evaluates every expression and does so in the order that respects every dependency of one expression on another. To understand circular dependencies, first review with the following calculated column in the Stock Item table:

```
Profit $ = 'Stock Item'[Recommended Retail Price] - 'Stock Item'[Unit Price]
Profit % = DIVIDE('Stock Item'[Profit $], 'Stock Item'[Unit Price])
```

Note that the Profit % column references and depends on the Profit $ column. At this point, attempt to change the Profit $ column formula to the following one:

```
Profit $ = 'Stock Item'[Profit %] * 'Stock Item'[Unit Price]
```

Using this formula results in a circular dependency error: "A circular dependency was detected: Stock Item[Profit %], Stock Item[Profit $], Stock Item[Profit %]." This is because Profit % depends on Profit $, which also depends on Profit % to calculate its value. As a result, neither column can be calculated.

You can now remove both columns and go to the Scale table, where you have previously added the following column:

```
Sum of Scale Calculate = CALCULATE(SUM(Scale[Scale]))
```

For clarity purposes, rename it to Calculate1 and remove the Sum of Scale column, keeping only the Scale and Calculate1 columns. Now, try to add the following column to the Scale table:

```
Calculate2 = CALCULATE(SUM(Scale[Scale]))
```

Note that this formula is the same as the Calculate1 column formula, and neither column references the other. At the same time, you get the circular dependency error: "A circular dependency was detected: Scale[Column], Scale[Calculate1], Scale[Column]."

The reason this happens lies in context transition. When DAX evaluates Calculate1, it converts the row context into equivalent filter context: It filters the Scale table to those rows where Scale and Calculate2 column values are the same as the values of the current row. For Calculate2, it keeps those Scale rows where Scale and Calculate1 column values are the same as current row values. Therefore, Calculate1 implicitly depends on Calculate2, and vice versa.

This situation happens in tables in which there is no column that is used as a primary key. In the example's case, the Scale column can be used as a *primary key*, because it contains unique values only. When a column is used as a primary key, DAX performs context transition differently: Because it knows it can rely on the column having unique values, it uses this column to filter the table during context transition, without using values from other columns. For the Scale table, it means that during context transition DAX will only look at the Scale column values to filter the table. To fix the error, follow these steps:

1. Go to the **Model view**.
2. Select the **Scale table**.

3. In the **Properties** pane, select **Scale** from the **Key column** dropdown (if necessary, remove the duplicate row that you added previously).

4. If prompted to refresh a calculated column, select **Refresh now**.

5. If necessary, go to the Calculate2 formula and press Enter, prompting Power BI to reevaluate the column.

At this stage, you can see that the Calculate2 column can be evaluated with no errors.

Calculated tables

As previously mentioned, some DAX functions return tables. Table expressions can be used inside formulas of calculated columns and measures, as well as by themselves to materialize calculated tables. There are a few ways to create a calculated table; for example, you can create a calculated table by selecting **Modeling** > **Calculations** > **New table** in the Report view. You will then need to write a DAX formula for a table in the formula bar.

One way to create a calculated table is to duplicate an existing one. For example, you can duplicate the Date table:

```
Date Duplicate = 'Date'
```

Because Date is a reserved keyword, you need to enclose it in single quotation marks.

The technique of duplicating tables can be useful if you want to separate multiple relationships between two tables—for example, between Sale and Date.

FILTER

By using FILTER, you can filter a table based on specified condition. The FILTER function takes two arguments: a table expression and a filter condition. The filter condition is evaluated in row context for each row of the table. For example, to create a calculated table for stock items in which unit price is greater than $300, use the following formula:

```
Expensive Stock Items =
FILTER (
    'Stock Item',
    'Stock Item'[Unit Price] > 300
)
```

This formula creates a table with six rows. Note that if you had calculated columns in the Stock Item table, those columns would appear as native columns in the Expensive Stock Items table.

Although FILTER takes only one condition, you can combine the conditions into a single Boolean condition with AND or OR logic. For instance, if you want to select only those stock items that are more expensive than $300 or are gray, you can write the following formula:

```
Expensive or Gray Stock Items =
FILTER (
    'Stock Item',
    OR (
        'Stock Item'[Unit Price] > 300,
        'Stock Item'[Color] = "Gray"
    )
)
```

You would get 15 rows in this case.

Unlike CALCULATETABLE, FILTER does not trigger context transition. The following two calculated columns, created in the Date table, produce different results:

// Different value for each row
```
Countrows Calculatetable = COUNTROWS(CALCULATETABLE(Sale))
```

// Same number for each row
```
Countrows Filter = COUNTROWS(FILTER(Sale, TRUE))
```

Note that while CALCULATETABLE has only one mandatory parameter, FILTER always uses two parameters.

When you use FILTER in context transition—for example, in a calculated column—it generates new row context. This means that in each row of the table where you create a calculated column, DAX iterates over each row in the table used inside FILTER. It is possible to access the original row context from the new one with the EARLIER function. Doing so allows you to perform calculations in a way similar to SUMIF in Excel. For instance, you can count the number of rows in the Date table for each year in the following calculated column formula:

```
Days in Year EARLIER =
COUNTROWS (
    FILTER (
        'Date',
        'Date'[Year] = EARLIER('Date'[Year])
    )
)
```

You can achieve the same effect by using a variable instead of EARLIER. Because variables always stay constant after being evaluated, they are not affected by the new context. In a way, variables behave like constants. This behavior will be reviewed in the "Using variables in calculated tables" section. You can see an example of using a variable in the following formula:

```
Days in Year VAR =
VAR CurrentMonth = 'Date'[Year]
RETURN
    COUNTROWS (
        FILTER (
            'Date',
            'Date'[Year] = CurrentMonth
        )
    )
```

If needed, you can perform context transition inside FILTER. For example, you can create a calculated table for salespeople who have made over 5,000 sales:

```
Productive Salespeople =
FILTER (
    Employee,
    CALCULATE(COUNTROWS(Sale)) > 5000
)
```

> **IMPORTANT** **CONTEXT TRANSITION AND FILTERING**
>
> Remember that when you perform context transition in large tables, the operation is much slower than filtering column values. Therefore, instead of filtering a table and doing context transition, precalculate the results in a calculated column and then filter by the column.

ALL

The ALL function removes any filters that were placed on a table or columns. You can use this function to create calculated tables, as well. When used to create a calculated table, the function can accept one or more columns from a table, or a whole table as a parameter. The ALL function cannot accept another function as an argument. When you use a table as an argument for ALL, every row, including duplicated rows, is returned in the new table. When you use one column in ALL, a one-column table containing distinct values from the column is returned. When you use multiple columns from the same table in ALL, a table containing all existing combinations of the column values is returned. It is not possible to use columns from different tables inside one ALL statement. Note that if a table contains duplicate rows, then ALL with a table as the only argument and ALL with all columns listed will return tables with a different number of rows.

For examples of using ALL to create calculated tables, create the following three tables:

```
All Stock Item = ALL('Stock Item')
All Color = ALL('Stock Item'[Color])
All Color, Buying Package = ALL('Stock Item'[Color], 'Stock Item'[Buying Package])
```

- The first table, All Stock Item, is a duplicate of the Stock Item table.

- The second table, All Color, contains distinct values from the Color column from the Stock Item table.

- The third table, All Color, Buying Package, contains all existing distinct combinations of the Color and Buying Package columns from the Stock Item table. This table is shown in Figure 3-19.

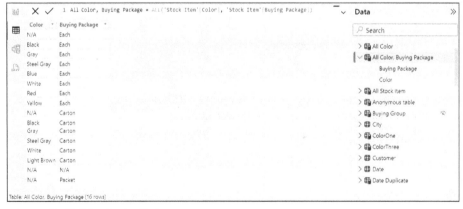

FIGURE 3-19 All Color, Buying Package

To see the difference that ALL makes in filter context, create the following calculated columns in the Customer table:

```
Customer Rows = COUNTROWS(Customer)
Customer Rows Calculate = CALCULATE(COUNTROWS(Customer))
Customer Rows Calculate All = CALCULATE(COUNTROWS(ALL(Customer)))
```

- The first calculated column, Customer Rows, returns the total number of rows in the Customer table. Because there is no context transition, you get the same value, the total number of rows, for every row in the calculated column.

- The second calculated column, Customer Rows Calculate, includes CALCULATE, which triggers context transition. This means that for every row of the table, DAX counts only those rows that have the same column values as the current row. Because there is a primary key in this table, the result is always 1.

- The third calculated column, Customer Rows Calculate All, also includes CALCULATE, but it has Customer wrapped in ALL. Here's what happens: First, context transition transforms the row context into equivalent filter context. Because the Customer table contains a primary key, the Customer table for each row is filtered to include that row only. Next, the changes produced by the filter placed on the Customer table are undone with ALL.

Note that the calculated columns, Customer Rows and Customer Rows Calculate All, return the same value, 403, which is the total number of rows in the Customer table. These two values are not always equivalent. Remember, when a table on the many side of a relationship includes some values that are not present in the table on the one side of a relationship, DAX adds a virtual row to the table on the one side. This row is blank and not visible by default. To review this effect on the example formulas, follow these steps:

1. In the **Data** pane, right-click the **Customer** table and select **Edit query**.
2. Select the **AutoFilter** button of the Customer Key column.
3. If necessary, click **Load More** in the bottom-right corner of the filter list.
4. Deselect values 1, 2, and 3, and click **OK**.
5. Click **Close & Apply**.

Once the Customer table is updated, you can see different values in the Customer Rows and Customer Rows Calculate All calculated columns: 400 and 401, respectively, as shown in Figure 3-20.

Note that the total number of rows in the Customer table is now 400, which can be seen at the bottom of the screen. The Customer Rows Calculate All, however, displays 401, which includes the virtual row that DAX included for those Customer Key values in the Sale table that do not have a corresponding value in the Customer table.

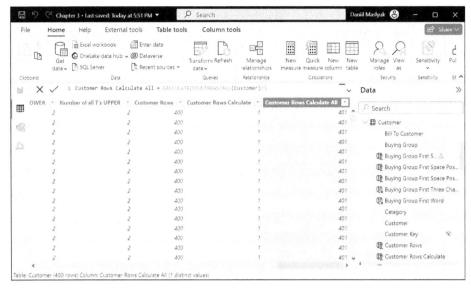

FIGURE 3-20 Customer Rows calculated columns

You can see this row materialized if you create the following calculated table:

```
All Customer = ALL(Customer)
```

Note that this table has 401 rows, which includes the special blank row. You can create a duplicate of the Customer table without the blank row in at least three ways. First, reference the original table without using any functions:

```
Duplicate Customer = Customer
```

Second, filter out the blank row:

```
Filter All Customer =
FILTER (
    ALL(Customer),
    NOT ISBLANK(Customer[Customer Key])
)
```

Third, use a variation of ALL–ALLNOBLANKROW:

```
AllNoBlankRow Customer = ALLNOBLANKROW(Customer)
```

The ALLNOBLANKROW function returns a table without the virtual blank row that is added in cases in which a table on the many side contains values that are not in the table on the one side. Note that if a table or a column contains a genuine blank row or value, the ALLNOBLANKROW function will not filter it out. This function, like ALL, also removes any filters on a specified table or column.

At this stage, go back to Power Query Editor and remove the Filtered Rows step from the Customer query.

The third variation of the ALL function, ALLEXCEPT, has a different syntax from ALL and ALLNOBLANKROW: It receives a table as the first argument, followed by at least one column to exclude. ALLEXCEPT returns all columns from a specified table except the excluded columns. This function can be useful when you want to include more columns than you want to exclude.

Another application of the ALLEXCEPT function can be inside calculated columns to calculate subtotals without using the combination of FILTER and EARLIER or VAR. Earlier in the "Filter" section, you created two calculated columns that calculated the number of rows in the Date table for each year. The following formula returns the equivalent results:

```
Days in Year ALLEXCEPT =
CALCULATE(
    COUNTROWS('Date'),
    ALLEXCEPT('Date', 'Date'[Year])
)
```

CALCULATETABLE

While learning about the RELATEDTABLE function, you encountered CALCULATETABLE. RELATEDTABLE is an alias for CALCULATETABLE when only one argument is used. In CALCULATETABLE, you can specify optional conditions, which are combined with AND logic. CALCULATETABLE accepts either tables or Boolean statements as filter conditions. Any table expression can be used in place of filters, including functions that return tables. The following is an example of a Boolean filter condition:

```
'Stock Item'[Color] = "Black"
```

The following example reduces the number of rows in the Stock Item table, keeping only those in which Unit Price is greater than $300:

```
Expensive Stock Items =
CALCULATETABLE (
    'Stock Item',
    'Stock Item'[Unit Price] > 300
)
```

As when using FILTER before, you will receive a table with six rows. Unlike FILTER, CALCULATETABLE can accept more than one filter parameter. The following calculated table contains stock items that are both black *and* priced higher than 300:

```
Expensive and Black Stock Items =
CALCULATETABLE (
    'Stock Item',
    'Stock Item'[Unit Price] > 300,
    'Stock Item'[Color] = "Black"
)
```

Similarly, you can combine filter conditions with OR logic using either the OR function or the double pipe operator. For example, the following calculated table will filter the Stock Item table to contain only those items that are priced either below 1 *or* above 1000, but not at 0:

```
Stock Items below $1 or above $1000 =
CALCULATETABLE (
    'Stock Item',
```

```
    OR (
        'Stock Item'[Unit Price] < 1,
        'Stock Item'[Unit Price] > 1000
    ),
    'Stock Item'[Unit Price] <> 0
)
```

When you combine filters using the OR logic, the filters that you specify must be applied to columns from one table only.

VALUES AND DISTINCT

The VALUES and DISTINCT functions work similarly: They return tables that contain only distinct rows. Both functions can receive a column reference as a parameter. For example, the following table returns 12 month names from the Date table:

```
Months = DISTINCT('Date'[Month])
```

Both functions can also receive a table as a parameter. While the VALUES function can receive only a physical table as a parameter, the DISTINCT function can also work with table expressions, which means that the table can be either a physical table or a table returned by another function.

Unlike the ALL function, which also returns a table with distinct rows, the VALUES and DISTINCT functions do not remove filters from their tables. In practice, this means that these two calculated columns in the Employee table return the same results:

```
Sale Rows Calculate = CALCULATE(COUNTROWS(Sale))
Sale Rows Calculate VALUES = CALCULATE(COUNTROWS(VALUES(Sale)))
```

As previously mentioned, if a table expression returns a table with one row and one column, it can be converted to a scalar value. The following calculated column in the Employee table works, too; it contains the same values as the Employee column:

```
Employee Calculate = CALCULATE(VALUES(Employee[Employee]))
```

Another major difference between the VALUES and DISTINCT functions is that the former might include a special blank row that is added when some values on the many side of a relationship do not have a matching value on the one side. The DISTINCT function never includes a blank row unless a blank row physically exists in the data. To illustrate this difference, use the Date table, which has an active relationship with the Sale table using the Delivery Date Key column. There are null values in the column, which causes a special blank row to be added. The following two tables return a different number of rows:

```
// 13 rows
Month Values = VALUES('Date'[Month])
```

```
// 12 rows
Month Distinct = DISTINCT('Date'[Month])
```

In this regard, the behavior of VALUES corresponds to ALL, while the behavior of DISTINCT corresponds to ALLNOBLANKROW.

SUMMARIZE AND SUMMARIZECOLUMNS

The SUMMARIZE function allows you to group a table by one or more columns and add new columns, if necessary. The general syntax is as follows:

```
SUMMARIZE(Table, OldColumns, NewColumns)
```

The new columns are defined by specifying a name and formula for each column. SUMMARIZE expects at least two arguments: a table to summarize and a column to group by.

The following formula produces a table with month names and numbers:

```
Month = SUMMARIZE('Date', 'Date'[Month], 'Date'[Month Number])
```

In this case, the table does not include the special blank row that results from null values being present in the Delivery Date Key column of the Sale table. If you decide to add a column that contains the number of rows in the Sale table for each month, the blank row will still not be included. You can see the summarized table in Figure 3-21.

```
Month Sale =
SUMMARIZE (
    'Date',
    'Date'[Month],
    'Date'[Month Number],
    "Sale Rows", COUNTROWS(Sale)
)
```

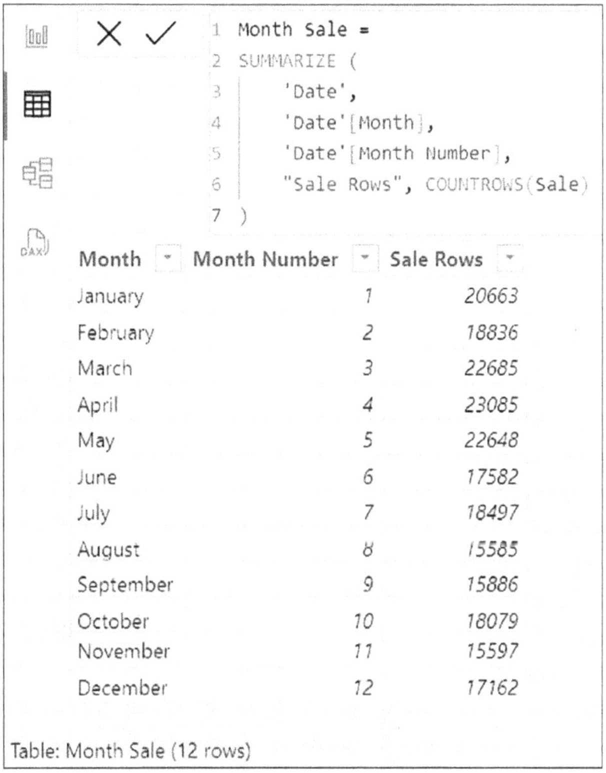

FIGURE 3-21 Date table summarized

Note that the example summarized the Date table. If instead you summarize the Sale table with the same columns, the blank row will appear, and it does not matter whether you include the Sale Rows column. The table can be seen in Figure 3-22.

```
Month Sale from Sale =
SUMMARIZE (
    Sale,
    'Date'[Month],
    'Date'[Month Number],
    "Sale Rows", COUNTROWS(Sale)
)
```

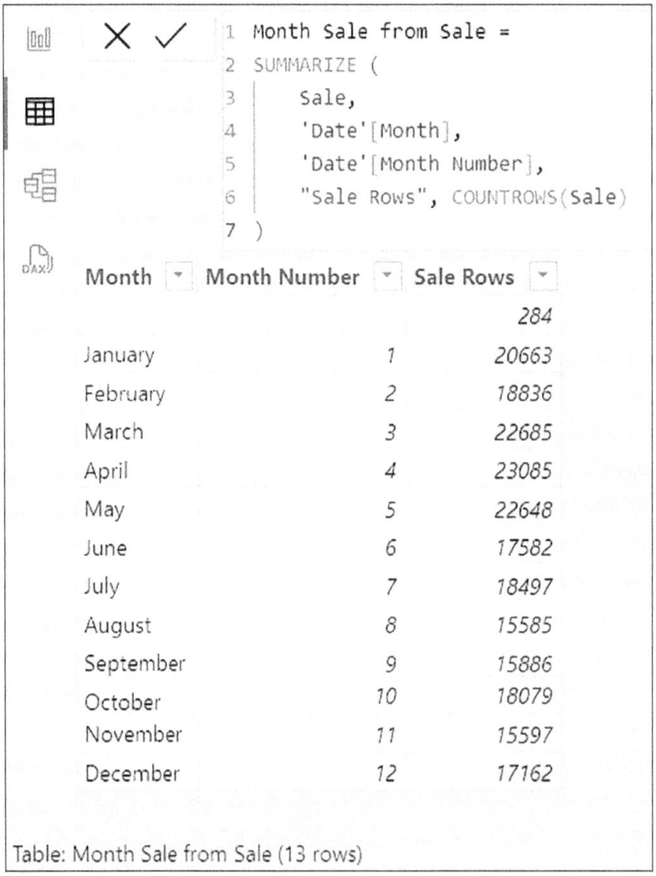

```
Month Sale from Sale =
SUMMARIZE (
    Sale,
    'Date'[Month],
    'Date'[Month Number],
    "Sale Rows", COUNTROWS(Sale)
)
```

Month	Month Number	Sale Rows
		284
January	1	20663
February	2	18836
March	3	22685
April	4	23085
May	5	22648
June	6	17582
July	7	18497
August	8	15585
September	9	15886
October	10	18079
November	11	15597
December	12	17162

Table: Month Sale from Sale (13 rows)

FIGURE 3-22 Sale table summarized

The columns to group by are optional. You can specify a table to summarize, new column names, and expressions. If you specify only one new column name and expression, it will result in a one-row and one-column table with a single value. As in the previous examples, the table you summarize can make a difference.

// Returns 196719256.02
```
Summarize Sale Single =
SUMMARIZE (
    Sale,
    "Total Sales", SUM(Sale[Total Including Tax])
)
```

// Returns 196452244.58
```
Summarize Date Single =
SUMMARIZE (
    'Date',
    "Total Sales", SUM(Sale[Total Including Tax])
)
```

Figure 3-23 offers an example of such a table.

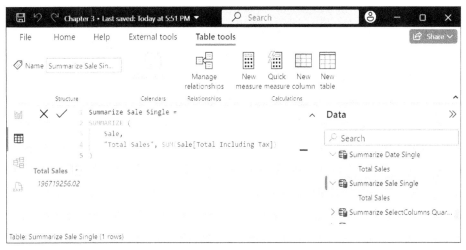

FIGURE 3-23 Sale table summarized to one row

SUMMARIZE returns only rows that have data. For example, if you summarize the Date table by Year and Month, you will get 72 rows. If you summarize the Sale table instead, you will get 43 rows: 42 Year and Month combinations when sales happened plus the special blank row.

// Returns 72 rows
```
Date Year Month =
SUMMARIZE (
    'Date',
    'Date'[Year],
    'Date'[Month],
    'Date'[Month Number]
)
```

```
// Returns 43 rows
Sale Year Month =
SUMMARIZE (
    Sale,
    'Date'[Year],
    'Date'[Month],
    'Date'[Month Number]
)
```

In SUMMARIZE, you do not have access to row context of the table you are summarizing. Instead, SUMMARIZE divides the table into parts, grouping them by the columns you select, with each part of the original table having its own filter context. This is why you don't need to wrap COUNTROWS(Sales) in CALCULATE to trigger context transition, as no context transition is necessary.

SUMMARIZECOLUMNS performs similar operations to SUMMARIZE, except you do not need to specify the table you want to summarize. It also works in a slightly different way from SUMMARIZE. For instance, if you use the function to create a table with Calendar Year and Month combinations, you will get a table with 73 rows: 72 existing Calendar Year and Month combinations, plus the special blank row. If you add a count of Sale rows, the table will have 43 rows, which is the same as using SUMMARIZE with the Sale table:

```
// 73 rows
Month Year = SUMMARIZECOLUMNS('Date'[Year], 'Date'[Month])
```

```
// 43 rows
Month Year =
SUMMARIZECOLUMNS (
    'Date'[Year],
    'Date'[Month],
    "Sale Rows", COUNTROWS(Sale)
)
```

ADDCOLUMNS AND SELECTCOLUMNS

The ADDCOLUMNS function adds new columns to a table, generating row context in the process. The new columns are also known as *extension columns*. The function expects at least three arguments: a table to add columns to, a new column name, and a new column expression. For example, the following calculated table is equivalent to the Month Sale from Sale table you created before:

```
AddColumns Month Sale =
ADDCOLUMNS (
    ALL('Date'[Month], 'Date'[Month Number]),
    "Sale Rows", CALCULATE(COUNTROWS(Sale))
)
```

The row context in ADDCOLUMNS makes this function different from SUMMARIZE in two ways:

- First, you need to perform context transition to get different values for each row (you can see it in the preceding formula). Without CALCULATE, you would get the same value for each row, which would be the total number of rows in the Sale table.

- Second, you can reference columns in the table to which you add columns. For instance, you can take all the Year and Month Number combinations from the Date table and create a column that puts them in a sequential order:

```
AddColumns YearMonthSequential =
ADDCOLUMNS (
    ALL (
        'Date'[Year],
        'Date'[Month Number]
    ),
    "Year Month Sequential",
    'Date'[Year] * 12 + 'Date'[Month Number]
)
```

To achieve the same effect using SUMMARIZE or SUMMARIZECOLUMNS, which use filter context, you must use VALUES to convert multiple column values into scalar values:

```
SummarizeColumns YearMonthSequential =
SUMMARIZECOLUMNS (
    'Date'[Year],
    'Date'[Month Number],
    "Year Month Sequential",
    VALUES('Date'[Year]) * 12
        + VALUES('Date'[Month Number])
)
```

The SELECTCOLUMNS function works like ADDCOLUMNS, except it does not keep the original columns. If you want to keep some of them using this function, you will have to create new columns that reference them. For example, you can take a table that contains all Calendar Year and Month combinations and keeps only the Calendar Year column:

```
SelectColumns Calendar Year =
SELECTCOLUMNS (
    ALL('Date'[Year], 'Date'[Month]),
    "Year", 'Date'[Year]
)
```

You can see the first few rows of the resulting table in Figure 3-24. Note that SELECTCOLUMNS does not produce distinct values in its columns.

Using SUMMARIZE, you can group the results by extension columns. For example, you can create an extension column that returns a quarter label for each date, and then get the distinct values of this column. The code follows, and the results can be seen in Figure 3-25.

```
Summarize SelectColumns Quarter =
SUMMARIZE (
    SELECTCOLUMNS (
        'Date',
        "Quarter", FORMAT('Date'[Date], "\QQ")
    ),
    [Quarter]
)
```

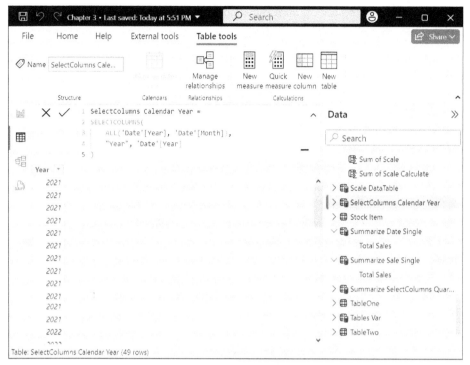

FIGURE 3-24 Partial results of the `SelectColumns` Calendar Year calculated table

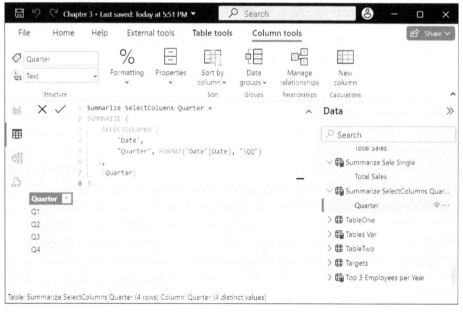

FIGURE 3-25 Date summarized by the extension column, Quarter

Note that you must reference the extension column without a table name because it is not a physical column.

TOPN

The TOPN function ranks table rows by specified criteria and takes the top N rows. There are three arguments, the first two of which are required: N number, table expression, and expression to order rows by. The fourth argument, which is optional, defines the order: ASC for ascending and DESC for descending. If omitted, the default value is DESC. The order of rows is not guaranteed.

For example, you can rank salespeople by sales amount and take the top three. The result is a subset of the original table and does not include the values you are ranking by.

```
Top 3 Employees by Sales =
TOPN (
    3,
    VALUES(Employee[Employee]),
    CALCULATE(SUM(Sale[Total Excluding Tax]))
)
```

Employee
Hudson Hollinworth
Anthony Grosse
Archer Lamble

Note that TOPN uses row context, so to rank employees properly you need to perform context transition. Without CALCULATE, you would get incorrect results. Because you can use row context, you can also get the first three employees alphabetically if you order them by name:

```
Top 3 Employees by Name =
TOPN (
    3,
    VALUES(Employee[Employee]),
    Employee[Employee],
    ASC
)
```

Employee
Archer Lamble
Anthony Grosse
Amy Trefl

In case of ties, you get more rows than expected. For instance, if you order Wide World Importers employees by sales in ascending order and take the top three, you end up with five rows because five employees did not sell anything. As a result, they all tie for the first place with zero (more precisely, blank) sales.

```
Bottom 3 Employees by Sales =
TOPN (
    3,
    VALUES(Employee[Employee]),
    CALCULATE(SUM(Sale[Total Excluding Tax])),
    ASC
)
```

Employee
Henry Forlonge
Unknown
Isabella Rupp
Jai Shand
Jack Potter

CROSSJOIN, GENERATE, AND GENERATEALL

The CROSSJOIN function allows you to create a Cartesian product between two or more tables. For example, you can create a table with all possible Brand and Buying Package combinations, not just those that exist in your data:

```
Buying Package, Brand =
CROSSJOIN (
    VALUES('Stock Item'[Buying Package]),
    VALUES('Stock Item'[Brand])
)
```

The resulting table has eight rows: four Buying Package values multiplied by two Brand values. If you wrote ALL('Stock Item'[Buying Package], 'Stock Item'[Brand]), you would get only five rows. All columns in the resulting tables must be unique. This means that if you want to create a Cartesian product of a table with itself, you must rename the columns of one of the tables in advance. For example, you could rename one of the columns using SELECTCOLUMNS:

```
Buying Package CrossJoin =
CROSSJOIN (
    VALUES('Stock Item'[Buying Package]),
    SELECTCOLUMNS (
        VALUES('Stock Item'[Buying Package]),
        "Buying Package 2", 'Stock Item'[Buying Package]
    )
)
```

With CROSSJOIN, there is no row context that you can use when writing the expression of the second and subsequent tables. The GENERATE function, which always receives two table expressions as parameters, allows you to reference the current row in the first table when writing the second table expression. For instance, create a table with calendar years and top three employees in each year:

```
Top 3 Employees per Year =
GENERATE (
    SUMMARIZE(Sale, 'Date'[Year]),
    TOPN (
        3,
        VALUES(Employee[Employee]),
        CALCULATE(SUM(Sale[Total Excluding Tax]))
    )
)
```

Year	Employee
	Archer Lamble
	Taj Shand
	Anthony Grosse
2020	Hudson Hollinworth
2020	Anthony Grosse
2020	Archer Lamble
2021	Hudson Hollinworth
2021	Anthony Grosse
2021	Archer Lamble
2022	Hudson Hollinworth
2022	Anthony Grosse
2022	Archer Lamble
2023	Sophia Hinton
2023	Anthony Grosse
2023	Archer Lamble

The resulting table includes only those years and employees that actually had sales, including the blank year. If you wanted to include all years and employees that meet the criteria, even those that did not make any sales, use the GENERATEALL function. It works in the same way as GENERATE, except it includes all possible combinations:

```
// Returns 123 rows
Top 3 Employees per Calendar Year Month =
GENERATE (
    ALLNOBLANKROW('Date'[Year], 'Date'[Month]),
```

```
    TOPN (
        3,
        SUMMARIZE(RELATEDTABLE(Sale), Employee[Employee]),
        CALCULATE(SUM(Sale[Total Excluding Tax]))
    )
)


// Returns 130 rows
Top 3 Employees per Calendar Year Month =
GENERATEALL (
    ALLNOBLANKROW('Date'[Year], 'Date'[Month]),
    TOPN (
        3,
        SUMMARIZE(RELATEDTABLE(Sale), Employee[Employee]),
        CALCULATE(SUM(Sale[Total Excluding Tax]))
    )
)
```

In these expressions, the seven-row difference comes from months that have no deliveries, yet you have these combinations in your Date table.

GENERATESERIES

With GENERATESERIES, you can generate a table with one column, called Value, containing a list of numbers with predefined increment. These values need not exist in the data model. The function expects at least two arguments: the start value and the end value. If the start value is greater than the end value, the result will be a table with no rows. The optional third parameter specifies the increment; if omitted, it is 1 by default. The following expression outputs a list of numbers from 1 to 5:

```
1 to 5 = GENERATESERIES(1, 5)
```

Value
1
2
3
4
5

Using the optional third parameter, you can create consecutive lists that increment by a number other than 1. For example, generate a list of odd numbers from 1 to 9 inclusive:

```
Odd 1 to 9 = GENERATESERIES(1, 10, 2)
```

Value
1
3
5
7
9

Note that even though you specified 10 as the end value, the table goes up to only 9 because the next value in the sequence, 11, falls outside of the specified range.

The GENERATESERIES function automatically detects the data type. The only column in the previous table has the Whole Number data type. In the following expression, the data type is set as Decimal Number:

```
0.1 to 0.5 Decimal = GENERATESERIES(0.1, 0.5, 0.1)
```

Value
0.1
0.2
0.3
0.4
0.5

It is also possible to specify data types explicitly. For instance, you can use the CURRENCY function to convert values to the Fixed Decimal Number type:

```
1 to 5 Fixed Decimal = GENERATESERIES(CURRENCY(1), CURRENCY(5))
```

GENERATESERIES can be used to generate lists of datetime values as well. The following table expression creates a one-column table of datetime data type that starts at 12 a.m. on May 1, 2024, and finishes at 12 a.m. on May 3, 2024, incrementing by 12 hours:

```
1 to 3 May 2024 at 12-hour intervals =
GENERATESERIES (
    DATE(2024, 5, 1),
    DATE(2024, 5, 3),
    TIME(12, 0, 0)
)
```

Value
1/05/2024 12:00:00 AM
1/05/2024 12:00:00 PM

Value
2/05/2024 12:00:00 AM
2/05/2024 12:00:00 PM
3/05/2024 12:00:00 AM

Though GENERATESERIES can generate only numeric or datetime value lists, it is possible to generate lists of letters by combining SELECTCOLUMNS and UNICHAR:

```
Uppercase Latin alphabet: =
SELECTCOLUMNS (
    GENERATESERIES(65, 90),
    "Letter", UNICHAR([Value])
)
```

Letter
A
B
C
...
Z

CALENDAR AND CALENDARAUTO

The CALENDAR function works like GENERATESERIES when you work with dates only: It generates a one-column table of datetime data type called Date. This function can be especially useful when your data model does not have a Date table and you want to create your own calendar.

CALENDAR has two required parameters: the start date and the end date. By default, the values increment by one day. The following expression generates a table with 365 rows, starting with January 1, 2024, and ending with December 31, 2024:

```
Year 2024 = CALENDAR(DATE(2024, 1, 1), DATE(2024, 12, 31))
```

Date
1/01/2024 12:00:00 AM
2/01/2024 12:00:00 AM
3/01/2024 12:00:00 AM
...
29/12/2024 12:00:00 AM

Date
30/12/2024 12:00:00 AM
31/12/2024 12:00:00 AM

The CALENDARAUTO function generates a list of dates, taking into account all date and date-time type columns in the data model; it takes the minimum and maximum of all dates found and extracts years and then generates a list of dates starting with January 1 of the minimum year and ending with December 31 of the maximum year.

CALENDARAUTO has one optional parameter, which is the fiscal year end month. If omitted, the default value is 12, which corresponds to the year ending on December 31. If your data model contains only dates from January 1, 2024, to December 31, 2024, then the following calculated table returns all dates from July 1, 2023, to June 30, 2025:

```
Fiscal Date = CALENDARAUTO(6)
```

Because CALENDARAUTO considers all the Date and datetime columns in a data model, some-times this can lead to tables having more rows than necessary. For example, data warehouses often use the date December 31, 9999, to denote the currently valid value. If your Power BI data model contains such a date, then creating the following calculated table will result in a table with close to 3 million rows:

```
All Dates = CALENDARAUTO ()
```

Unless your data model contains many meaningful Date or datetime columns, it is prefer-able to use the CALENDAR function, referencing the relevant Date columns. If you did not have the Date table in your data model, and the only Date column you had was the Invoice Date Key column in the Sale table, you could create the following date table:

```
Calendar = CALENDAR(MIN(Sale[Invoice Date Key]), MAX(Sale[Invoice Date Key]))
```

Because you also have the Delivery Date Key column in the data model, you can use the alternative MIN and MAX syntax, which allows the comparison of two scalar values:

```
Calendar =
CALENDAR (
    MIN (
        MIN(Sale[Delivery Date Key]),
        MIN(Sale[Invoice Date Key])
    ),
    MAX (
        MAX(Sale[Delivery Date Key]),
        MAX(Sale[Invoice Date Key])
    )
)
```

If you prefer having complete years in your calendar table, you can use the DATE/YEAR combination:

```
Calendar =
CALENDAR (
    DATE (
        YEAR (
            MIN (
                MIN(Sale[Delivery Date Key]),
                MIN(Sale[Invoice Date Key])
            )
        ),
        1,
        1
    ),
    DATE (
        YEAR (
            MAX (
                MAX(Sale[Delivery Date Key]),
                MAX(Sale[Invoice Date Key])
            )
        ),
        12,
        31
    )
)
```

You can then add calculated columns, such as month name and calendar year number, to the newly created table to make it a proper calendar table.

ROW

With the ROW function, you can create one-row tables with several columns at once. The arguments come in pairs: a column name goes first, then an expression. Only one pair of arguments is required. For example, you can create a one-row table with two columns: the number of rows in the Sale table and the number of rows in the Date table:

```
One Row =
ROW (
    "Sale Rows", COUNTROWS(Sale),
    "Date Rows", COUNTROWS('Date')
)
```

Sale Rows	Date Rows
226589	1461

The ROW function can be useful when you want to add a row to another table using the UNION function, covered next.

UNION

The UNION function works similarly to the **Append** feature in Power Query Editor: It combines two or more tables vertically. If the tables you are combining have the same rows among them, duplicate rows will be retained. The names of the columns do not have to match, but the number of columns in tables must be the same because tables are combined by the position of columns, not the names. The output table will have the same column names as the first table. If tables have different data types, they will be combined in accordance with DAX data type coercion. The following is an example of using UNION:

```
Table1 =
UNION (
    ROW("Color", "Red", "Value 1", 1),
    ROW("Color", "Red", "Value 1", 2),
    ROW("Color", "Green", "Value 1", 3),
    ROW("Color", "Blue", "Value 1", CURRENCY(1))
)
```

Color	Value 1
Red	1.00
Red	2.00
Green	3.00
Blue	1.00

Note that in this case, the second column will have the Fixed Decimal Number data type.

UNION can be used to create common dimensions from several different tables. For instance, the Buying Group column is in both the Targets and Customer tables. To create a bridge table to pass filters from the Customer table to the Targets table, you can create the following calculated table:

```
// Bridging table between Customer and Targets
Buying Group =
DISTINCT (
    UNION (
        ALLNOBLANKROW(Targets[Buying Group]),
        ALLNOBLANKROW(Customer[Buying Group])
    )
)
```

You can then hide the bridging table and create the following relationships:

- From 'Targets'[Buying Group] to 'Buying Group'[Buying Group]
- Bidirectional from 'Customer'[Buying Group] to 'Buying Group'[Buying Group]

At this point, if you go to the relationships view, your data model, excluding tables created for illustration purposes, should look similar to Figure 3-26.

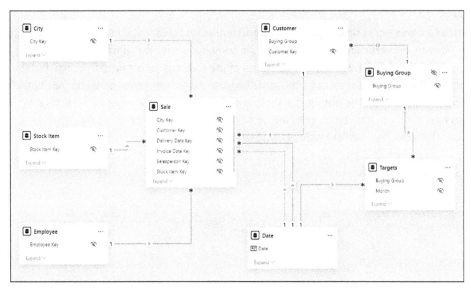

FIGURE 3-26 Relationships view after adding and relating bridge tables

INTERSECT

The INTERSECT function creates a table that consists of rows that are present in both tables that are used as arguments in INTERSECT. In the following examples, you will practice using the function on these two tables, called TableOne and TableTwo, as shown in Table 3-3 and Table 3-4, respectively.

TABLE 3-3 TableOne

Color	Value 1
Red	1
Red	2
Green	3
Blue	1

TABLE 3-4 TableTwo

Color	Value 2
Green	3
Blue	1
Blue	1
Yellow	2

Note that there is a common column name, Color, which differs from the name of the second column. Also, these tables have common rows. INTERSECT has the same requirements for tables as UNION: Both tables must have the same number of columns, and the tables are combined based on the position of columns. The result of the following expression is a two-row table that has the same column names as TableOne:

```
IntersectOneTwo =
INTERSECT (
    UNION (
        ROW("Color", "Red", "Value 1", 1),
        ROW("Color", "Red", "Value 1", 2),
        ROW("Color", "Green", "Value 1", 3),
        ROW("Color", "Blue", "Value 1", 1)
    ),
    UNION (
        ROW("Color", "Green", "Value 2", 3),
        ROW("Color", "Blue", "Value 2", 1),
        ROW("Color", "Blue", "Value 2", 1),
        ROW("Color", "Yellow", "Value 2", 2)
    )
)
```

Color	Value 1
Green	3
Blue	1

The order in which two tables are used in INTERSECT matters. The following calculated table also uses TableOne and TableTwo, but in reverse order:

```
IntersectTwoOne =
INTERSECT (
    UNION (
        ROW("Color", "Green", "Value 2", 3),
        ROW("Color", "Blue", "Value 2", 1),
        ROW("Color", "Blue", "Value 2", 1),
        ROW("Color", "Yellow", "Value 2", 2)
    ),
    UNION (
        ROW("Color", "Red", "Value 1", 1),
        ROW("Color", "Red", "Value 1", 2),
        ROW("Color", "Green", "Value 1", 3),
        ROW("Color", "Blue", "Value 1", 1)
    )
)
```

Color	Value 2
Green	3
Blue	1
Blue	1

Note that the second column name is now Value 2 instead of Value 1. Also, the output table retains duplicate rows from the first table but not from the second table.

EXCEPT

The EXCEPT function takes two tables as arguments and outputs all rows that are in the first table but not in the second table. Columns are compared based on their positions, so the number of columns in both tables must be the same, which is the same behavior as with the UNION and INTERSECT functions.

As with INTERSECT, the order of tables used as arguments influences the results. Note the difference in the results when EXCEPT is used with TableOne and TableTwo versus TableTwo and TableOne:

```
ExceptOneTwo =
EXCEPT (
    UNION (
        ROW("Color", "Red", "Value 1", 1),
        ROW("Color", "Red", "Value 1", 2),
        ROW("Color", "Green", "Value 1", 3),
        ROW("Color", "Blue", "Value 1", 1)
    ),
    UNION (
        ROW("Color", "Green", "Value 2", 3),
        ROW("Color", "Blue", "Value 2", 1),
        ROW("Color", "Blue", "Value 2", 1),
        ROW("Color", "Yellow", "Value 2", 2)
    )
)
```

Color	Value 1
Red	1
Red	2

```
ExceptTwoOne =
EXCEPT (
    UNION (
        ROW("Color", "Green", "Value 2", 3),
        ROW("Color", "Blue", "Value 2", 1),
        ROW("Color", "Blue", "Value 2", 1),
        ROW("Color", "Yellow", "Value 2", 2)
    ),
    UNION (
        ROW("Color", "Red", "Value 1", 1),
        ROW("Color", "Red", "Value 1", 2),
        ROW("Color", "Green", "Value 1", 3),
        ROW("Color", "Blue", "Value 1", 1)
    )
)
```

Color	Value 2
Yellow	2

Like with INTERSECT, the output table has the same column names as the first table. Duplicate rows from the first table, if any, are retained.

NATURALINNERJOIN

The NATURALINNERJOIN function works like the **Merge** feature in Power Query Editor: It receives two tables as arguments and joins them based on common column names. The columns that are used for joining must have the same data types. NATURALINNERJOIN joins two tables and outputs a table that has the same values present in join columns of both tables.

The following examples again use TableOne and TableTwo:

```
NaturalInnerJoinOneTwo =
NATURALINNERJOIN (
    UNION (
        ROW("Color", "Red", "Value 1", 1),
        ROW("Color", "Red", "Value 1", 2),
        ROW("Color", "Green", "Value 1", 3),
        ROW("Color", "Blue", "Value 1", 1)
    ),
    UNION (
        ROW("Color", "Green", "Value 2", 3),
        ROW("Color", "Blue", "Value 2", 1),
        ROW("Color", "Blue", "Value 2", 1),
        ROW("Color", "Yellow", "Value 2", 2)
    )
)
```

Color	Value 1	Value 2
Green	3	3
Blue	1	1
Blue	1	1

Note that in this case, the order in which you join tables matters only when considering the order of columns:

```
NaturalInnerJoinTwoOne =
NATURALINNERJOIN (
    UNION (
        ROW("Color", "Green", "Value 2", 3),
        ROW("Color", "Blue", "Value 2", 1),
        ROW("Color", "Blue", "Value 2", 1),
        ROW("Color", "Yellow", "Value 2", 2)
    ),
    UNION (
        ROW("Color", "Red", "Value 1", 1),
        ROW("Color", "Red", "Value 1", 2),
        ROW("Color", "Green", "Value 1", 3),
        ROW("Color", "Blue", "Value 1", 1)
    )
)
```

Color	Value 2	Value 1
Green	3	3
Blue	1	1
Blue	1	1

NATURALINNERJOIN can also join physical tables that have a relationship between them. For instance, create the following two calculated tables:

```
// Many side of a relationship
ColorOne =
UNION (
    ROW("ColorOne", "Red", "Value 1", 1),
    ROW("ColorOne", "Red", "Value 1", 2),
    ROW("ColorOne", "Green", "Value 1", 3),
    ROW("ColorOne", "Blue", "Value 1", 1)
)
```

ColorOne	Value 1
Red	1
Red	2
Green	3
Blue	1

```
// One side of a relationship
ColorThree =
UNION (
    ROW("ColorThree", "Green", "Value 3", 3),
    ROW("ColorThree", "Blue", "Value 3", 1),
    ROW("ColorThree", "Yellow", "Value 3", 2)
)
```

ColorThree	Value 3
Green	3
Blue	1
Yellow	2

Once you create a relationship between ColorOne and ColorThree, you can create the following calculated table:

```
NaturalInnerJoin One Three = NATURALINNERJOIN(ColorOne, ColorThree)
```

ColorThree	Value 3	ColorOne	Value 1
Blue	1	Blue	1
Green	3	Green	3

In this case, the order of arguments makes no difference. Note that you are able to create this calculated table only because there are no columns that have the same name and there is a relationship between these tables. Without a relationship, you would get the error: "No common join columns detected. The join function 'NATURALINNERJOIN' requires at-least one common join column."

If you were joining two related tables that had columns that shared names, you would get an error like this one: "The Column with the name of 'ColorOne' already exists in the 'Table' Table." This limitation is not unique to NATURALINNERJOIN—in general, all column names in materialized tables must be unique in DAX. Virtual tables can have the same column names in some cases. The following calculated table works even if TableOne and TableThree have common column names:

```
Aggregated Virtual Table =
ROW (
    "NumRows",
    COUNTROWS(NATURALINNERJOIN(ColorOne, ColorThree))
)
```

NumRows
2

The ability to join tables with common names can be useful when passing filters to CALCULATE or CALCULATETABLE.

NATURALLEFTOUTERJOIN

The NATURALLEFTOUTERJOIN function is similar to NATURALINNERJOIN, but it performs the left outer join instead of the inner join. NATURALLEFTOUTERJOIN returns a table with all rows from the first table and extra columns from the second table where values in the join columns of the right table are present in the join columns of the first table:

```
NaturalLeftOuterJoinOneTwo =
NATURALLEFTOUTERJOIN (
    UNION (
        ROW("Color", "Red", "Value 1", 1),
        ROW("Color", "Red", "Value 1", 2),
        ROW("Color", "Green", "Value 1", 3),
        ROW("Color", "Blue", "Value 1", 1)
    ),
    UNION (
        ROW("Color", "Green", "Value 2", 3),
        ROW("Color", "Blue", "Value 2", 1),
        ROW("Color", "Blue", "Value 2", 1),
        ROW("Color", "Yellow", "Value 2", 2)
    )
)
```

Color	Value 1	Value 2
Red	1	
Red	2	
Green	3	3
Blue	1	1
Blue	1	1

Because NATURALLEFTOUTERJOIN performs a left outer join, the order of tables used as parameters is very important. The following table not only has a different order of columns, but the rows are also different:

```
NaturalLeftOuterJoinTwoOne =
NATURALLEFTOUTERJOIN (
    UNION (
        ROW("Color", "Green", "Value 2", 3),
        ROW("Color", "Blue", "Value 2", 1),
        ROW("Color", "Blue", "Value 2", 1),
        ROW("Color", "Yellow", "Value 2", 2)
    ),
    UNION (
        ROW("Color", "Red", "Value 1", 1),
        ROW("Color", "Red", "Value 1", 2),
        ROW("Color", "Green", "Value 1", 3),
        ROW("Color", "Blue", "Value 1", 1)
    )
)
```

Color	Value 2	Value 1
Green	3	3
Blue	1	1
Blue	1	1
Yellow	2	

Same as NATURALINNERJOIN, NATURALLEFTOUTERJOIN can be used with tables that have a relationship and no common column names.

DATATABLE

The DATATABLE function allows you to create calculated tables with data that you enter manually. The **Enter Data** feature of Power BI allows you to enter data manually—DATATABLE provides an alternative.

At a minimum, DATATABLE takes three arguments: column name, data type, and list of values. The data types that you can choose are as follows:

- **BOOLEAN** True/False
- **CURRENCY** Fixed Decimal Number
- **DATETIME** datetime
- **DOUBLE** Decimal Number
- **INTEGER** Whole Number
- **STRING** Text

The final argument is a list of values in braces that resembles what you would type in M inside the #table construct. Create the Scale table using the DATATABLE function as follows:

```
Scale DataTable =
DATATABLE (
    "Scale", INTEGER,
    {
        {1},
        {1000},
        {1000000}
    }
)
```

Scale
1
1000
1000000

You can create a table with more than one column by listing all column names and data types in pairs:

```
Enriched Scale =
DATATABLE (
    "Scale", INTEGER,
    "Description", STRING,
    {
        {1, "Normal"},
        {1000, "Thousands"},
        {1000000, "Millions"}
    }
)
```

Scale	Description
1	Normal
1000	Thousands
1000000	Millions

Note that all values in braces must be constants. You cannot use expressions inside DATATABLE. For instance, the following calculated table cannot be created:

```
Scale Wrong =
DATATABLE (
    "Scale", INTEGER,
    {
        {1 + 0},
        {1000},
        {1000000}
    }
)
```

The error message you'd get in this case is: "The tuple at index '1' from the table definition of the DATATABLE function does not have a constant expression in the column at index '1'."

DAX also allows you to create anonymous tables without defining column names, though the syntax is slightly different from the DATATABLE syntax. After the equation operator, you also use braces, but inside them, you do not use braces again. If you define a one-column table, you list your values separated by a comma, and DAX will call the new column Value. You can also define multicolumn tables by listing values of each row in parentheses; the parenthesis sets should be separated by commas as well. In this case, DAX will give the new columns names like Value1, Value2, and so on. Data types will also be defined automatically. For instance, you can create the following table:

```
Single-column table = {1, 2}
```

Value
1
2

The following is an example of an anonymous table with three columns:

```
Anonymous table =
{
    (1, "a", DATE(2024, 5, 1)),
    (2, "b", DATE(2024, 5, 23))
}
```

Value1	Value2	Value3
1	a	1/05/2024 12:00:00 AM
2	b	23/05/2024 12:00:00 AM

USING VARIABLES IN CALCULATED TABLES

DAX variables can store scalar values, as well as tables. For example, rewrite one of the previous table expressions as follows:

```
Tables Var =
VAR Table1 =
```

```
    UNION (
        ROW("Color", "Red", "Value 1", 1),
        ROW("Color", "Red", "Value 1", 2),
        ROW("Color", "Green", "Value 1", 3),
        ROW("Color", "Blue", "Value 1", 1)
    )
VAR Table2 =
    UNION (
        ROW("Color", "Green", "Value 2", 3),
        ROW("Color", "Blue", "Value 2", 1),
        ROW("Color", "Blue", "Value 2", 1),
        ROW("Color", "Yellow", "Value 2", 2)
    )
RETURN
    NATURALINNERJOIN(Table1, Table2)
```

While variables improve the readability of your code and potentially increase performance, it is important to understand that variables are evaluated only once in the context in which they are defined, and they become immutable. This means that using CALCULATE or CALCULATETABLE on a variable has no effect.

Variables in calculated tables can be used to create more readable code that is still complex. This allows you to save the time spent on creating calculated columns one by one; instead, you can define them in one calculated table expression. For instance, you can create a full calendar table in one expression using the GENERATE/ROW pattern developed by Marco Russo:

```
Calendar =
VAR Days =
    CALENDAR("2024-1-1", "2025-12-31")
RETURN
    GENERATE (
        Days,
        VAR BaseDate = [Date]
        VAR MonthName = FORMAT(BaseDate, "MMM")
        VAR MonthNumber = MONTH(BaseDate)
        VAR BaseYear = YEAR(BaseDate)
        RETURN
            ROW (
                "Month", MonthName,
                "MonthNo", MonthNumber,
                "Year", BaseYear
            )
    )
```

Date	Month	MonthNo	Year
1/01/2024 12:00:00 AM	Jan	1	2024
2/01/2024 12:00:00 AM	Jan	1	2024
3/01/2024 12:00:00 AM	Jan	1	2024
...	...	...	...
31/12/2025 12:00:00 AM	Dec	12	2025

Note that in this case, you have multiple levels of VAR/RETURN constructs. At the top level, you are defining the Days variable, which stores the table returned by the CALENDAR function. Use the Days variable in the outer RETURN expression. You have another VAR/RETURN construct, where you define more variables; this time, the variables hold scalar values, because GENERATE enables you to access the row context. The variables defined in the inner VAR/RETURN construct are not accessible in the outer construct.

Measures

An important limitation of calculated columns is that not all values can be calculated with them. For example, if you need to calculate the profit percentage, the calculated column formula might look as follows:

```
Net Profit % = DIVIDE(Example[Net Profit], Example[Gross Profit])
```

While this formula calculates the profit percentage for each row of the table, it would be incorrect to use the values from this column in a visual, because they would show an arithmetic average at best. To illustrate the problem, consider Table 3-5, a two-row table called Example.

TABLE 3-5 Sample profit values in the Example table

Product	Gross Profit	Net Profit	Net Profit %
A	3,000	300	10%
B	2,000	1,000	50%

If you use the Net Profit % column from this table in a visual, you can only show 30%, the average of 10% and 50%. This is not correct; a correct value would be (300 + 1,000) / (3,000 + 2,000) = 26%. In other words, you need to sum all Net Profit values first, then divide the result by the sum of all Gross Profit values. While displaying this value in a calculated column is possible, this value will be incorrect as soon as you filter by Product.

In this case, you need to create a measure. To create a measure in the currently selected table, select **Modeling** > **Calculations** > **New measure** in the Report view. Alternatively, you can right-click a table in which you want to create a measure and select **New Measure**. Either option will open the formula bar where you can write your DAX formula. When finished, you can either click the **check** icon to the left of the formula bar or press **Enter**. If you create a measure in the wrong table, you can move it by selecting the correct table by selecting **Modeling** > **Properties** > **Home Table**.

Measures aggregate columns and tables, and they always work in filter context. For this reason, there is no concept of current row in measures by default. A measure with the following formula cannot be created:

```
Net Profit % = DIVIDE(Example[Net Profit], Example[Gross Profit])
```

Note that this is the same formula that works for a calculated column. This formula does not work in a measure because DAX does not know what it should do with the columns that you used.

Because of this, any table or column used in a measure must be aggregated. The following functions are the most popular aggregation functions:

- SUM
- AVERAGE
- MIN
- MAX

For instance, you can create a measure that sums all Net Profit column values as follows:

```
Total Net Profit = SUM(Example[Net Profit])
```

The functions listed here always take one argument: column reference. If you want to reference two columns in an aggregation function, you need to use the iterator functions, which usually have an x suffix. These are the most commonly used ones:

- SUMX
- AVERAGEX
- MINX
- MAXX

These functions always take two arguments: a table to iterate over and an expression to evaluate for each row in row context. The aggregation functions without an x suffix are often syntactic sugar for their x-suffixed counterparts. The following two expressions are equivalent:

```
Total Net Profit = SUM(Example[Net Profit])
Total Net Profit = SUMX(Example, Example[Net Profit])
```

As mentioned earlier, the iterator functions can reference more than one column at a time. For example, the following expression iterates over the Sale table and, for each row, multiplies Quantity by Unit Price. Finally, it sums all of the resulting values:

```
Gross Sales = SUMX(Sale, Sale[Quantity] * Sale[Unit Price])
```

Because iterators generate row context, all row functions, such as RELATED, can be used:

```
Full Price Sales =
SUMX (
    Sale,
    Sale[Quantity] * RELATED('Stock Item'[Recommended Retail Price])
)
```

In the Example table, you can create the weighted profit percentage measure with the following code:

```
Net Profit % =
DIVIDE (
    SUM(Example[Net Profit]),
    SUM(Example[Gross Profit])
)
```

While this measure works and displays the correct values, you can make the code more readable and easier to maintain by splitting the calculation into three measures: Total Net

Profit, Total Gross Profit, and Net Profit %. Because you can reference other measures when you create a measure, you can first create the Total Net Profit and Total Gross Profit measures, then the Net Profit % one:

```
// Create these two measures first
Total Net Profit = SUM(Example[Net Profit])
Total Gross Profit = SUM(Example[Gross Profit])

// Create this measure last
Net Profit % = DIVIDE([Total Net Profit], [Total Gross Profit])
```

At this stage, the Net Profit and Gross Profit columns can be hidden. This practice is called *fixing implicit measures*; when you use a column in the values field well in a visual, an implicit measure is created using the default aggregation. When you write measures with DAX, you are creating *explicit measures*. Hiding the columns you aggregate in explicit measures is usually a good practice because it prevents user confusion over which field should be used.

MEASURES VS. CALCULATED COLUMNS

In many cases, the same values can be computed by using either a measure or a calculated column. Calculated columns are computed when they are defined and at data refresh time. Because they are materialized in a data model, they consume RAM and disk space. Measures, on the other hand, are calculated at query time, which means every time you interact with a visual, a measure recalculates its value. For this reason, measures consume CPU resources.

As you have seen, some values, such as weighted averages, cannot be computed in a calculated column, which leaves creating measures as the only option. At the same time, there are situations in which you should create a calculated column instead of a measure:

- **Slicing or filtering by values** It is currently impossible to put a measure into a slicer. If you want to slice by newly created values, such as Price Category in the example, you must create a calculated column and not a measure.

- **Writing CPU-intensive formulas** If your formula is very complex and it takes many seconds to compute its values, this may result in a poor user experience. In this case, it might be a good idea to precompute results in a calculated column or a calculated table, and then aggregate the results with a measure.

COUNTING VALUES IN DAX

There are several functions in DAX with which you can count values:

- COUNT
- COUNTA
- COUNTAX
- COUNTBLANK
- COUNTROWS
- COUNTX

- DISTINCTCOUNT

- DISTINCTCOUNTNOBLANK

One of the most frequently used functions is COUNTROWS, which you have already used a few times in the chapter. The function takes one parameter: a table expression. The following measure counts the number of rows in the Sale table in the current filter context:

```
Sale Rows = COUNTROWS(Sale)
```

Because you are not limited to physical tables, you can also count rows in tables calculated dynamically. The following measure returns the number of Calendar Year and Month combinations that had sales:

```
Years and Months with Sales =
COUNTROWS (
    SUMMARIZE (
        Sale,
        'Date'[Year],
        'Date'[Month]
    )
)
```

The COUNT function takes a column reference as the only argument and counts the number of non-blank values in a column. For example, the following measure counts the number of non-blank Delivery Date Key values in the Sale table:

```
Count DeliveryDate = COUNT(Sale[Delivery Date Key])
```

The limitation of the COUNT function is that it cannot count Boolean values. To count the number of non-blank values regardless of data type, you can use the COUNTA function.

The COUNTX and COUNTAX functions, the behavior of which corresponds to COUNT and COUNTA, respectively, allow you to count non-blank expressions when iterating over a table. Both tables take two arguments: a table to iterate over and an expression to be evaluated in row context. For instance, the following measure counts the number of rows in the Sale table where either Invoice Date Key or Delivery Date Key is not blank:

```
CountX Invoice Delivery =
COUNTX (
    Sale,
    Sale[Invoice Date Key] + Sale[Delivery Date Key]
)
```

This measure returns the same results as COUNTROWS because in the data model, either Invoice Date Key or Delivery Date Key will always be not blank for any row.

To count blank values in a column, you can use the COUNTBLANK function, which always receives a column reference as its only parameter. You can count the number of blank Delivery Date Key values with the following measure:

```
CountBlank DeliveryDate = COUNTBLANK(Sale[Delivery Date Key])
```

Note that COUNTBLANK doesn't count the special blank row. The sum of COUNT (and its equivalent COUNTA, COUNTX, and COUNTAX expressions) and COUNTBLANK will always give you the same result as COUNTROWS, unless the special blank row is involved. In Table 3-6, you can see that the sum of Count DeliveryDate and CountBlank DeliveryDate is equal to Sale Rows:

TABLE 3-6 Sale Rows, Count DeliveryDate, and CountBlank DeliveryDate sliced by Calendar Year Label

Year	Sale Rows	Count DeliveryDate	CountBlank DeliveryDate
	284		284
2020	36907	36907	
2021	63760	63760	
2022	69845	69845	
2023	57469	57469	
Total	228265	227981	284

If you want to count the number of distinct values in a column, you can either use a combination of COUNTROWS and DISTINCT, or you can use DISTINCTCOUNT, which takes a column reference as its only parameter. For instance, the following measure returns the number of Stock Item Key values that have been sold at least once:

```
Sold StockItems = DISTINCTCOUNT(Sale[Stock Item Key])
```

Note that this measure returns different results compared to a measure that counts the distinct Stock Item Key values in the Stock Item table when sliced by Calendar Year Label or Brand. Note also that when a column contains unique values only, you can safely use COUNTROWS instead. The following two measures produce equivalent results, as shown in Table 3-7:

```
Distinct StockItems = DISTINCTCOUNT( 'Stock Item'[Stock Item Key])
Distinct StockItems = COUNTROWS('Stock Item')
```

TABLE 3-7 Sold StockItems and Distinct StockItems sliced by Calendar Year Label

Calendar Year Label	Sold StockItems	Distinct StockItems
	164	672
2019		672
2020	219	672
2021	219	672
2022	219	672
2023	227	672

Calendar Year Label	Sold StockItems	Distinct StockItems
2024		672
Total	227	672

The Distinct StockItems value is the same in this table because filter context from the Date table does not pass to the Stock Item table. Note that because of the nature of distinct counts, the results might not always be additive.

In Table 3-8, the difference between Sold StockItems and Distinct StockItems is that some stock items do not sell at all, even though they are in the data model.

TABLE 3-8 Sold StockItems and Distinct StockItems sliced by Brand

Brand	Sold StockItems	Distinct StockItems
N/A	209	605
Northwind	18	67
Total	227	672

USING CALCULATE IN MEASURES

The CALCULATE function, covered earlier in the chapter, is most often used in measures. Its syntax is identical to CALCULATETABLE except it received a scalar expression as the first parameter instead of a table expression. Using CALCULATE in a measure without filters is useless because every measure has an implicit CALCULATE wrapped around it. To illustrate this effect, look at the Scale table and create the following calculated column and measure in it:

```
// Calculated column
Sum Column = SUM(Scale[Scale])
```

```
// Measure
Sum Measure = SUM(Scale[Scale])
```

Note that the formula used in the two expressions is the same. As expected, Sum Column shows the same value for each row. Now, create the following calculated column in the Scale table:

```
Sum Measure Column = [Sum Measure]
```

In this calculated column, you are referencing Sum Measure only. Note the brackets around the measure name; this is the standard way to reference measures in DAX. Now, the Scale table should look like the one in Figure 3-27.

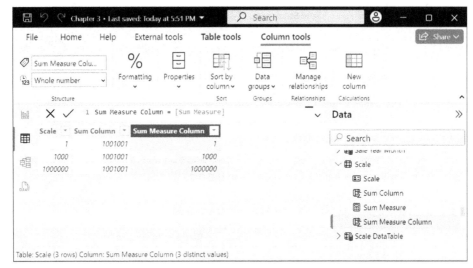

FIGURE 3-27 The Scale table with `Sum Column` and `Sum Measure Column` created

Even though the formulas of `Sum Measure` and `Sum Column` are identical, the values in the `Sum Measure Column` calculated column are different because each measure has an implicit `CALCULATE` wrapped around it. In other words, you can rewrite the `Sum Measure Column` expression as follows:

```
Sum Measure Column = CALCULATE(SUM(Scale[Scale]))
```

For this reason, `CALCULATE` becomes useful inside measures when you want to change the filter context. As with `CALCULATETABLE`, you can pass Boolean expressions or tables as filter parameters in `CALCULATE`. For example, you can create the `All-time Profit` measure, which displays the all-time profit made, regardless of the selections made in the Date table:

// Create the Total Profit measure first
```
Total Profit = SUM(Sale[Profit])
```

// Create the All-time Profit measure that references Total Profit
```
All-time Profit = CALCULATE([Total Profit], ALL('Date'))
```

If you use this measure in a table visual alongside Total Profit, you will see results similar to Figure 3-28.

As expected, the measure shows the same value for each row, which is the same as the grand total of `Total Profit`. While `ALL` removes the filter, you can also set the new filter context at the same time. For example, Figure 3-29 shows profit made in January regardless of the selected Month.

Month	Total Profit	All-time Profit
	119,456.90	85,139,717.75
January	7,793,690.40	85,139,717.75
February	7,126,200.70	85,139,717.75
March	8,458,476.40	85,139,717.75
April	8,841,635.80	85,139,717.75
May	8,598,731.45	85,139,717.75
June	6,543,944.65	85,139,717.75
July	6,984,320.65	85,139,717.75
August	5,866,417.85	85,139,717.75
September	5,919,840.05	85,139,717.75
October	6,658,632.25	85,139,717.75
November	5,883,737.80	85,139,717.75
December	6,344,632.85	85,139,717.75
Total	**85,139,717.75**	**85,139,717.75**

FIGURE 3-28 All-time Profit alongside Total Profit sliced by Month

Month	Total Profit	January Profit
	119,456.90	7,793,690.40
January	7,793,690.40	7,793,690.40
February	7,126,200.70	7,793,690.40
March	8,458,476.40	7,793,690.40
April	8,841,635.80	7,793,690.40
May	8,598,731.45	7,793,690.40
June	6,543,944.65	7,793,690.40
July	6,984,320.65	7,793,690.40
August	5,866,417.85	7,793,690.40
September	5,919,840.05	7,793,690.40
October	6,658,632.25	7,793,690.40
November	5,883,737.80	7,793,690.40
December	6,344,632.85	7,793,690.40
Total	**85,139,717.75**	**7,793,690.40**

FIGURE 3-29 January Profit measure alongside Total Profit sliced by Month

When you pass Boolean expressions as filters in CALCULATE, they are transformed into table filters with FILTER and ALL combined. Because you only have the Month column visible, and you sort it by the Calendar Month Number column, the following formula will not work correctly. You can see the values it returns in Figure 3-30.

```
January Profit Wrong = CALCULATE([Total Profit], 'Date'[Month] = "January")
```

Month	Total Profit	January Profit Wrong
	119,456.90	
January	7,793,690.40	7,793,690.40
February	7,126,200.70	
March	8,458,476.40	
April	8,841,635.80	
May	8,598,731.45	
June	6,543,944.65	
July	6,984,320.65	
August	5,866,417.85	
September	5,919,840.05	
October	6,658,632.25	
November	5,883,737.80	
December	6,344,632.85	
Total	**85,139,717.75**	**7,793,690.40**

FIGURE 3-30 January Profit Wrong visualized

The formula does not return the expected results because when slicing by Month, Calendar Month Number is also part of filter context because it sorts Month. To make the formula work correctly, either list conditions for both columns or iterate over a table that includes both columns. Each of the following expressions returns the expected result:

// Including conditions for both columns
```
January Profit =
CALCULATE (
    [Total Profit],
    'Date'[Month] = "January",
    'Date'[Month Number] = 1
)
```

// Boolean expressions internally converted to table filters
```
January Profit =
CALCULATE (
    [Total Profit],
    FILTER (
        ALL('Date'[Month]),
        'Date'[Month] = "January"
    ),
```

```
    FILTER (
        ALL('Date'[Month Number]),
        'Date'[Month Number] = 1
    )
)

// Alternative approach: iterating over a table that includes both columns
January Profit =
CALCULATE (
    [Total Profit],
    FILTER (
        ALL('Date'[Month], 'Date'[Month Number]),
        'Date'[Month] = "January"
    )
)
```

There is another function in the ALL family of functions that you have not yet explored: ALLSELECTED. This function receives one optional argument: either a table or one or more columns from one table. According to the official documentation, this function removes filter context from rows and columns of a table, while retaining all other context filters or explicit filters. In Power BI, rows and columns of a table can be extended to mean axes, legends, and so on. To review the effect of ALLSELECTED, follow these steps:

1. Create a new measure with the following formula:

```
Profit AllSelected = CALCULATE([Total Profit], ALLSELECTED('Date'))
```

2. Create a table visual with the following fields:

   - **Year**

   - **Total Profit**

   - **Profit AllSelected**

3. Create a slicer with **Year** as its field.

4. Select years 2022–2023, inclusive.

At this stage, you should see figures like those shown in Figure 3-31.

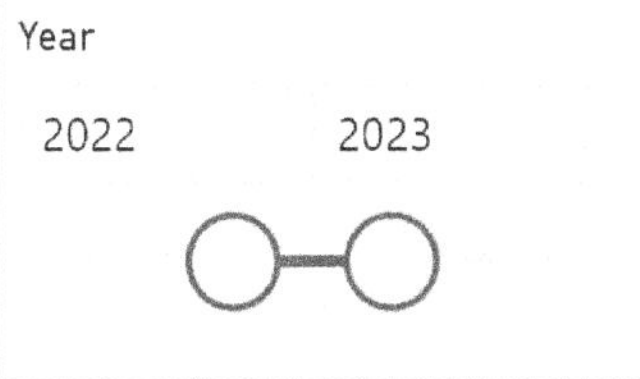

Year	Total Profit	Profit AllSelected
2022	24,920,540.35	52,058,214.50
2023	27,137,674.15	52,058,214.50
Total	**52,058,214.50**	**52,058,214.50**

Year: 2022, 2023

FIGURE 3-31 Profit AllSelected used in a table

Note the values displayed by the Profit AllSelected measure; they are the same as the grand total of Total Profit in this table. If you change the year selection, the values will change to the new grand total.

Because the only parameter of ALLSELECTED is optional, you can use it with no parameters as follows:

```
Profit AllSelected = CALCULATE([Total Profit], ALLSELECTED ())
```

Used in this way, ALLSELECTED will consider filters from the entire data model, not just one table or column.

TIME INTELLIGENCE

Time Intelligence in DAX is an umbrella term that often refers to calculations that span over predefined periods of time. DAX has more than 30 built-in functions to handle Time Intelligence. An example of using Time Intelligence is the comparison of different periods—this year versus last year, for instance.

Most Time Intelligence functions receive a date column as a parameter and return a table that can be used as a filter in CALCULATE, while a small group of functions return scalar values. The functions that return scalar values are all shorthand and can be rewritten using CALCULATE and one of the functions that return a table.

For the Time Intelligence functions to work correctly, you must have a date table, which is also known as a calendar table. The table should be similar to the Date table from the Wide World Importers data model, where you have a row for each date between the earliest and latest dates in your data model with no gaps. If your data source does not contain such a table, you can create one yourself using the CALENDAR and CALENDARAUTO functions.

Another requirement for the calendar table is either to be part of a one-to-many relationship with a column of type Date or be marked as Date table. This way, the Time Intelligence functions will work without needing modifications.

Once your calendar table satisfies the requirements, you can use the Time Intelligence functions correctly. For example, to calculate year-to-date profit, you can use the DATESYTD function and write the following formula:

```
Profit YTD = CALCULATE([Total Profit], DATESYTD('Date'[Date]))
```

If you use this measure alongside the Total Profit measure in a matrix visual and add Year and Month on rows, you can see a visual like in Figure 3-32.

Note how the profit amount is being added month by month from January to December 2021, and then it starts at January 2022 again. DATESYTD has an optional second parameter, which is the year-end date. With this parameter, you can specify a custom year-end date such as **30-6** or **6-30**, depending on your locale. This option is often used for calculations involving fiscal or financial years. When omitted, the default option is December 31. For instance, the following measure calculates year-to-date profit for the year ending on June 30. You can see the values it returns in Figure 3-33.

```
Profit FYTD = CALCULATE([Total Profit], DATESYTD('Date'[Date], "30-6"))
```

Year	Total Profit	Profit YTD
⊟ **2021**	**22,460,592.70**	**22,460,592.70**
January	1,500,134.40	1,500,134.40
February	1,360,102.55	2,860,236.95
March	2,009,662.35	4,869,899.30
April	1,986,178.65	6,856,077.95
May	2,161,421.95	9,017,499.90
June	2,148,420.70	11,165,920.60
July	2,097,517.75	13,263,438.35
August	1,743,965.90	15,007,404.25
September	1,893,954.45	16,901,358.70
October	1,820,979.55	18,722,338.25
November	1,937,131.40	20,659,469.65
December	1,801,123.05	22,460,592.70
⊟ **2022**	**24,920,540.35**	**24,920,540.35**
January	1,950,025.25	1,950,025.25
February	1,736,023.65	3,686,048.90
Total	**85,139,717.75**	**10,501,453.65**

FIGURE 3-32 Profit YTD shown alongside Total Profit and sliced by Year and Month

Year	Total Profit	Profit YTD	Profit FYTD
⊟ **2021**	**22,460,592.70**	**22,460,592.70**	**11,294,672.10**
January	1,500,134.40	1,500,134.40	1,500,134.40
February	1,360,102.55	2,860,236.95	2,860,236.95
March	2,009,662.35	4,869,899.30	4,869,899.30
April	1,986,178.65	6,856,077.95	6,856,077.95
May	2,161,421.95	9,017,499.90	9,017,499.90
June	2,148,420.70	11,165,920.60	11,165,920.60
July	2,097,517.75	13,263,438.35	2,097,517.75
August	1,743,965.90	15,007,404.25	3,841,483.65
September	1,893,954.45	16,901,358.70	5,735,438.10
October	1,820,979.55	18,722,338.25	7,556,417.65
November	1,937,131.40	20,659,469.65	9,493,549.05
December	1,801,123.05	22,460,592.70	11,294,672.10
⊟ **2022**	**24,920,540.35**	**24,920,540.35**	**12,742,252.65**
January	1,950,025.25	1,950,025.25	13,244,697.35
February	1,736,023.65	3,686,048.90	14,980,721.00
Total	**85,139,717.75**	**10,501,453.65**	

FIGURE 3-33 Profit FYTD shown alongside Profit YTD and Total Profit

Note how the calculation of year-to-date profit now starts over in July instead of January.

DATESYTD also has two sister functions, DATESMTD and DATESQTD, which return month-to-date and quarter-to-date date tables, respectively. Both functions always receive one parameter only, with no optional parameters.

Because the DATESMTD, DATESQTD, and DATESYTD functions are almost always used as filters for CALCULATE expressions, there are three functions that simplify writing formulas with these functions: TOTALMTD, TOTALQTD, and TOTALYTD. For example, you can rewrite the Profit FYTD formula as follows:

```
Profit FYTD = TOTALYTD([Total Profit], 'Date'[Date], "30-6")
```

The three functions receive two mandatory arguments: a scalar expression and the calendar table date column. The optional third parameter can be used to pass an additional filter. TOTALYTD can also receive an optional fourth parameter, the year-end date. When no third parameter is specified, the year-end date can be used as the third parameter.

With DAX, it is possible to calculate semi-additive measures such as opening and closing balances. For these purposes, there are monthly, quarterly, and yearly functions for both opening and closing balances:

- OPENINGBALANCEMONTH
- OPENINGBALANCEQUARTER
- OPENINGBALANCEYEAR
- CLOSINGBALANCEMONTH
- CLOSINGBALANCEQUARTER
- CLOSINGBALANCEYEAR

Each of the six functions received two required parameters: a scalar expression and the date column of a calendar table. A filter can be passed as the optional third parameter. Also, the yearly functions can receive an optional fourth parameter specifying the year-end date.

For review purposes, calculate the opening and closing month balance of profit as follows, even if the measures make no sense financially:

```
Opening Profit = OPENINGBALANCEMONTH([Total Profit], 'Date'[Date])
Closing Profit = CLOSINGBALANCEMONTH([Total Profit], 'Date'[Date])
```

The OPENINGBALANCEMONTH function calculates the scalar value used as the first parameter for the last day of the previous month. In general, the opening balance functions return the same values as closing balance functions for the previous month. For example, the opening monthly balance for June 2020 will be the same as the closing monthly balance for May 2020. Both measures are shown in Figure 3-34.

Year	Total Profit	Opening Profit	Closing Profit
2021-01-29	21,593.60		25,118.40
2021-01-30	18,608.00		25,118.40
2021-01-31	25,118.40		25,118.40
⊟ February	1,360,102.55	25,118.40	20,806.10
2021-02-01	21,863.65	25,118.40	20,806.10
2021-02-02	64,585.60	25,118.40	20,806.10
2021-02-03	51,783.85	25,118.40	20,806.10
2021-02-04	63,978.00	25,118.40	20,806.10
2021-02-05	66,731.20	25,118.40	20,806.10
2021-02-06	78,559.85	25,118.40	20,806.10
2021-02-07	81,113.30	25,118.40	20,806.10
2021-02-08	85,014.15	25,118.40	20,806.10
2021-02-09	60,854.60	25,118.40	20,806.10
2021-02-10	67,043.55	25,118.40	20,806.10
2021-02-11	35,546.85	25,118.40	20,806.10
2021-02-12	56,449.05	25,118.40	20,806.10
2021-02-13	59,901.60	25,118.40	20,806.10
2021-02-14	45,540.50	25,118.40	20,806.10
2021-02-15	56,827.45	25,118.40	20,806.10
2021-02-16	29,323.30	25,118.40	20,806.10
2021-02-17	34,499.95	25,118.40	20,806.10
2021-02-18	39,551.15	25,118.40	20,806.10
2021-02-19	37,594.85	25,118.40	20,806.10
2021-02-20	58,113.90	25,118.40	20,806.10
2021-02-21	49,456.95	25,118.40	20,806.10
2021-02-22	46,510.20	25,118.40	20,806.10
2021-02-23	47,305.75	25,118.40	20,806.10
2021-02-24	40,516.35	25,118.40	20,806.10
2021-02-25	47,624.95	25,118.40	20,806.10
2021-02-26	6,767.90	25,118.40	20,806.10
2021-02-27	6,238.00	25,118.40	20,806.10
2021-02-28	20,806.10	25,118.40	20,806.10
⊟ March	2,009,662.35	20,806.10	51,329.65
2021-03-01	38,292.90	20,806.10	51,329.65
2021-03-02	42,583.35	20,806.10	51,329.65
Total	85,139,717.75		

FIGURE 3-34 Opening Profit and Closing Profit shown alongside Total Profit

The opening and closing balance functions return scalar values. You can also use DAX functions to return table functions for the beginning and the end of periods:

- STARTOFMONTH
- STARTOFQUARTER
- STARTOFYEAR
- ENDOFMONTH
- ENDOFQUARTER
- ENDOFYEAR

Each function in this list receives one required parameter: the date column from a calendar table. As before, the yearly functions can also receive a year-end date as an optional parameter. For example, you can rewrite the Closing Profit measure using the ENDOFMONTH function as follows:

```
Closing Profit = CALCULATE([Total Profit], ENDOFMONTH('Date'[Date]))
```

The Opening Profit measure cannot be rewritten using only CALCULATE and STARTOFMONTH. Use a function that can shift dates because the opening balance of a measure is its closing balance for the previous month. The most often used function is DATEADD, which receives exactly three arguments: the dates column of a calendar table, the number of intervals, and the interval. The interval can be one of the following:

- DAY
- MONTH
- QUARTER
- YEAR

DATEADD is not the only function that can shift dates. There is a similar function, PARALLELPERIOD, that receives the same arguments as DATEADD. However, PARALLELPERIOD cannot receive DAY as the fourth parameter. The difference between the two functions is that DATEADD shifts dates for each date in the current filter context, while PARALLELPERIOD returns a full parallel period as a result. To illustrate the difference between the two functions, create the following two functions:

```
Profit Last Month DateAdd =
CALCULATE (
    [Total Profit],
    DATEADD('Date'[Date], -1, MONTH)
)
Profit Last Month ParallelPeriod =
CALCULATE (
    [Total Profit],
    PARALLELPERIOD('Date'[Date], -1, MONTH)
)
```

The two measures are shown side by side in Figure 3-35.

Note how the two measures display the same results at the month level, but the values are different at date level: DATEADD displays a different value for each date, whereas PARALLELPERIOD shows the same value for each date within one month. Also, note that the value of the DATEADD measure is the same from March 28 to March 31, 2022, because the last date in February 2022 is February 28, 2022, and dates from March 28 to March 31, 2022, are all treated as the last day of the month when compared to the previous month.

Year	Total Profit	Profit Last Month DateAdd	Profit Last Month ParallelPeriod
2021-02-28	20,806.10	6,632.15	1,500,134.40
⊟ **March**	**2,009,662.35**	**1,360,102.55**	**1,360,102.55**
2021-03-01	38,292.90	21,863.65	1,360,102.55
2021-03-02	42,583.35	64,585.60	1,360,102.55
2021-03-03	43,706.60	51,783.85	1,360,102.55
2021-03-04	59,354.60	63,978.00	1,360,102.55
2021-03-05	79,317.20	66,731.20	1,360,102.55
2021-03-06	127,517.95	78,559.85	1,360,102.55
2021-03-07	136,496.00	81,113.30	1,360,102.55
2021-03-08	143,253.50	85,014.15	1,360,102.55
2021-03-09	121,019.60	60,854.60	1,360,102.55
2021-03-10	95,154.80	67,043.55	1,360,102.55
2021-03-11	72,004.90	35,546.85	1,360,102.55
2021-03-12	56,028.15	56,449.05	1,360,102.55
2021-03-13	35,478.80	59,901.60	1,360,102.55
2021-03-14	57,721.50	45,540.50	1,360,102.55
2021-03-15	77,196.70	56,827.45	1,360,102.55
2021-03-16	71,642.70	29,323.30	1,360,102.55
2021-03-17	53,773.95	34,499.95	1,360,102.55
2021-03-18	45,766.65	39,551.15	1,360,102.55
2021-03-19	47,176.50	37,594.85	1,360,102.55
2021-03-20	47,808.65	58,113.90	1,360,102.55
2021-03-21	53,941.00	49,456.95	1,360,102.55
2021-03-22	84,807.25	46,510.20	1,360,102.55
2021-03-23	49,750.60	47,305.75	1,360,102.55
2021-03-24	54,631.70	40,516.35	1,360,102.55
2021-03-25	55,298.10	47,624.95	1,360,102.55
2021-03-26	42,462.15	6,767.90	1,360,102.55
2021-03-27	39,268.65	6,238.00	1,360,102.55
2021-03-28	55,145.25	20,806.10	1,360,102.55
2021-03-29	30,867.20	20,806.10	1,360,102.55
2021-03-30	40,865.80	20,806.10	1,360,102.55
2021-03-31	51,329.65	20,806.10	1,360,102.55
⊟ **April**	**1,986,178.65**	**2,009,662.35**	**2,009,662.35**
2021-04-01	46,282.60	38,292.90	2,009,662.35
Total	**85,139,717.75**	**85,020,260.85**	**85,020,260.85**

FIGURE 3-35 Profit Last Month DateAdd and Profit Last Month ParallelPeriod used in a matrix visual

In addition to DATEADD and PARALLELPERIOD, the following functions have descriptive names that shift by a predefined period:

- SAMEPERIODLASTYEAR: same as DATEADD(Dates, -1, YEAR)
- PREVIOUSDAY
- PREVIOUSMONTH
- PREVIOUSQUARTER

- PREVIOUSYEAR

- NEXTDAY

- NEXTMONTH

- NEXTQUARTER

- NEXTYEAR

This list of functions receives the date column of a calendar table as the only required parameter. PREVIOUSYEAR and NEXTYEAR can also receive the year-end date as the optional second parameter.

You can combine some Time Intelligence functions. For example, using either DATEADD or PARALLELPERIOD, you can rewrite the Opening Profit measure as follows:

```
Opening Profit DateAdd =
CALCULATE (
    [Total Profit],
    DATEADD(STARTOFMONTH('Date'[Date]), -1, DAY)
)
```

Note that the order in which you nest functions matters. While the following measure works, it returns incorrect results, as seen in Figure 3-36:

```
Opening Profit DateAdd Wrong =
CALCULATE (
    [Total Profit],
    STARTOFMONTH(DATEADD('Date'[Date], -1, DAY))
)
```

The reason why this is not correct is that the dates are shifted back first, then STARTOFMONTH returns the first date of the month of the shifted date.

If you need to calculate a value for the first or last date in the current filter context, you can use the FIRSTDATE or the LASTDATE function, respectively. Both functions can be used as filters in CALCULATE. The functions do not override the currently selected dates. More specifically, the two functions can be rewritten as follows:

// Same as FIRSTDATE
```
'Date'[Date] = MIN('Date'[Date])
```

// Same as LASTDATE
```
'Date'[Date] = MAX('Date'[Date])
```

Year	Total Profit	Opening Profit	Opening Profit DateAdd	Opening Profit DateAdd Wrong
2021-02-28	20,806.10	25,118.40	25,118.40	21,863.65
⊟ March	2,009,662.35	20,806.10	20,806.10	21,863.65
2021-03-01	38,292.90	20,806.10	20,806.10	21,863.65
2021-03-02	42,583.35	20,806.10	20,806.10	38,292.90
2021-03-03	43,706.60	20,806.10	20,806.10	38,292.90
2021-03-04	59,354.60	20,806.10	20,806.10	38,292.90
2021-03-05	79,317.20	20,806.10	20,806.10	38,292.90
2021-03-06	127,517.95	20,806.10	20,806.10	38,292.90
2021-03-07	136,496.00	20,806.10	20,806.10	38,292.90
2021-03-08	143,253.50	20,806.10	20,806.10	38,292.90
2021-03-09	121,019.60	20,806.10	20,806.10	38,292.90
2021-03-10	95,154.80	20,806.10	20,806.10	38,292.90
2021-03-11	72,004.90	20,806.10	20,806.10	38,292.90
2021-03-12	56,028.15	20,806.10	20,806.10	38,292.90
2021-03-13	35,478.80	20,806.10	20,806.10	38,292.90
2021-03-14	57,721.50	20,806.10	20,806.10	38,292.90
2021-03-15	77,196.70	20,806.10	20,806.10	38,292.90
2021-03-16	71,642.70	20,806.10	20,806.10	38,292.90
2021-03-17	53,773.95	20,806.10	20,806.10	38,292.90
2021-03-18	45,766.65	20,806.10	20,806.10	38,292.90
2021-03-19	47,176.50	20,806.10	20,806.10	38,292.90
2021-03-20	47,808.65	20,806.10	20,806.10	38,292.90
2021-03-21	53,941.00	20,806.10	20,806.10	38,292.90
2021-03-22	84,807.25	20,806.10	20,806.10	38,292.90
2021-03-23	49,750.60	20,806.10	20,806.10	38,292.90
2021-03-24	54,631.70	20,806.10	20,806.10	38,292.90
2021-03-25	55,298.10	20,806.10	20,806.10	38,292.90
2021-03-26	42,462.15	20,806.10	20,806.10	38,292.90
2021-03-27	39,268.65	20,806.10	20,806.10	38,292.90
2021-03-28	55,145.25	20,806.10	20,806.10	38,292.90
2021-03-29	30,867.20	20,806.10	20,806.10	38,292.90
2021-03-30	40,865.80	20,806.10	20,806.10	38,292.90
2021-03-31	51,329.65	20,806.10	20,806.10	38,292.90
⊟ April	1,986,178.65	51,329.65	51,329.65	38,292.90
Total	85,139,717.75			

FIGURE 3-36 Opening Profit DateAdd Wrong shown alongside the correct Opening Profit measure

If you need to filter by a custom date interval, you can use DATESBETWEEN. The function receives three arguments: the date column of a calendar table, a start date, and an end date. For example, calculate Total Profit between June 10, 2022, and April 5, 2025, inclusive, as follows:

```
Profit Custom Period =
CALCULATE (
    [Total Profit],
    DATESBETWEEN (
        'Date'[Date],
        DATE(2022, 10, 6),
        DATE(2025, 4, 5)
    )
)
```

The measure shows the same value regardless of the selected date.

If your custom time interval is based on days, months, quarters, or years, you can use the DATESINPERIOD function. The function receives exactly three arguments: the date column from a calendar table; a start date; the number of intervals; and the interval, which can be DAY, MONTH, QUARTER, or YEAR. For instance, you can calculate the rolling monthly profit with the following measure:

```
Rolling Monthly Profit =
CALCULATE (
    [Total Profit],
    DATESINPERIOD (
        'Date'[Date],
        MAX('Date'[Date]),
        -1,
        MONTH
    )
)
```

USING INACTIVE RELATIONSHIPS

As discussed earlier, there can be no more than one active physical relationship between two tables. Between the Sale and Date tables there are two active relationships:

- Active one from Sale (Delivery Date Key) to Date (Date)
- Inactive one from Sale (Invoice Date Key) to Date (Date)

By default, all values you aggregate in the Sale table are going to be filtered by Delivery Date Key. To use the inactive relationship, activate it programmatically with DAX using the USERELATIONSHIP function. This function receives two parameters, which are the columns used in a relationship. To calculate Total Profit by Invoice Date Key, you can write the following measure formula (results shown in Figure 3-37):

```
Total Profit by Invoice Date =
CALCULATE (
    [Total Profit],
    USERELATIONSHIP('Date'[Date], Sale[Invoice Date Key])
)
```

Year	Total Profit	Total Profit by Invoice Date
	119,456.90	
2021	22,460,592.70	22,712,120.80
2022	24,920,540.35	24,925,260.90
2023	27,137,674.15	27,100,682.55
2024	10,501,453.65	10,401,653.50
Total	**85,139,717.75**	**85,139,717.75**

FIGURE 3-37 Total Profit by Invoice Date used in a table visual

Note that the `Total Profit by Invoice Date` measure is blank when `Year` is blank. This is because no `Invoice Date Key` value is blank, which means there is no blank row automatically added to the Date table when filtering by `Invoice Date Key` instead of `Delivery Date Key`.

The order of the columns used as parameters does not matter, although a relationship must exist between two columns. Otherwise, you will get the error seen in Figure 3-38.

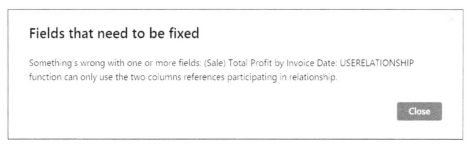

FIGURE 3-38 Error message when using USERELATIONSHIP without a relationship

USING SELECTEDVALUE

The SELECTEDVALUE function receives a column reference as the first parameter, which is required, and SELECTEDVALUE receives a default value as the optional second parameter. The function returns a column value if there is only one in the current filter context. Otherwise, it returns the default value. The function acts as a shortcut for the following syntax:

```
MyParameter Value =
IF (
    HASONEVALUE(MyParameter[MyParameter]),
    VALUES(MyParameter[MyParameter]),
    5
)
```

The HASONEVALUE function checks whether the input column has only one value in the current filter context. If it does, then the VALUES function, which returns a table, is converted into a scalar value because it has only one row and one column. If the input column has more than one value, the default value—in this case, 5—is returned. This function can be useful when you want to change a metric based on the selection. For instance, you can scale the `Total Profit` value based on the selected value in the Scale column of the Scale table with the following measure:

```
Profit Scaled = [Total Profit] / SELECTEDVALUE(Scale[Scale], 1)
```

If you put the Scale column values on rows in a matrix visual and `Total Profit` and `Profit Scaled` as values, you should see a visual similar to Figure 3-39.

Scale	Total Profit	Profit Scaled
1	85,139,717.75	85,139,717.75
1000	85,139,717.75	85,139.72
1000000	85,139,717.75	85.14
Total	**85,139,717.75**	**85,139,717.75**

FIGURE 3-39 Total Profit and Profit Scaled put against the Scale column

Note how Total Profit shows the same value for each Scale value because there is no relationship between Scale and any other table. However, Profit Scaled shows different values because it reads the currently selected value of Scale from the current filter context by using SELECTEDVALUE. Also, note two things:

- First, Total Profit and Profit Scaled have the same value when Scale is 1.
- Second, Profit Scaled at the total level shows the same value as when Scale is 1 because at the total level, there is no filter on Scale; therefore, the default value of 1 is used.

PASSING FILTERS FROM DISCONNECTED TABLES

In some cases, you may need to pass filters from disconnected tables. For example, it might be too expensive to create a column with concatenated keys to create a physical relationship. In this case, it might make sense to use virtual relationships.

One way you can pass filters from one table to another is by using INTERSECT. As discussed earlier, this table function returns a table with rows that exist in both tables.

To see the effect of using a virtual relationship, deactivate the relationship between Customer and Targets and create the following measures in the Targets table:

```
Total Target Amount = SUM(Targets[Target Excluding Tax])
Target Amount Intersect =
CALCULATE (
    [Total Target Quantity],
    INTERSECT (
        VALUES(Targets[Buying Group]),
        VALUES(Customer[Buying Group])
    )
)
```

If you create a matrix visual with Buying Group on rows and Total Target Amount and Target Amount Intersect as values, you will see a visual similar to Figure 3-40.

Buying Group	Total Target Amount	Target Amount Intersect
N/A	180400000	
Tailspin Toys	180400000	55400000
Wingtip Toys	180400000	55700000
Total	**180400000**	**111100000**

FIGURE 3-40 Year, Total Target Amount, and Target Amount Intersect in matrix visual

Note how Total Target Amount has the same value regardless of the Buying Group value. This is because you deactivated the relationship between the Targets and Buying Group table, meaning that filters from the Date table do not reach the Targets table. However, the Target Amount Intersect measure shows different values for each Buying Group because it is being filtered by a virtual relationship created with INTERSECT.

It is important to note that the order in which you pass the parameters to INTERSECT matters. The following measure returns the same values as Total Target Amount, which is the same value for each year:

```
Target Amount Intersect Wrong =
CALCULATE (
    [Total Target Amount],
    INTERSECT (
        VALUES(Customer[Buying Group]),
        VALUES(Targets[Buying Group])
    )
)
```

When you create virtual relationships with INTERSECT, the table you want to pass filters from should come first, and the table you want to filter should come second.

It's also possible to create virtual relationships by using the TREATAS function. The function receives at least two arguments: a table to pass filters from, and one or more columns to pass filters to. For instance, you can rewrite the preceding measures in the following way:

```
Target Amount TreatAs =
CALCULATE (
    [Total Target Amount],
    TREATAS (
        VALUES(Customer[Buying Group]),
        Targets[Buying Group]
    )
)
```

Figure 3-41 shows the INTERSECT and TREATAS measures compared.

Buying Group	Total Target Amount	Target Amount Intersect	Target Amount TreatAs
N/A	180400000		
Tailspin Toys	180400000	55400000	55400000
Wingtip Toys	180400000	55700000	55700000
Total	**180400000**	**111100000**	**111100000**

FIGURE 3-41 Measures with virtual relationships

Note how Total Target Amount still displays the same value for each row. At the beginning of this exercise, you purposefully deactivated relationships between Targets and Buying Group to highlight the effect that virtual relationships can have. Although virtual relationships can be very powerful, if you have an option to create physical relationships, as in this case, it is best to pass filters using physical relationships instead of virtual ones. Your code will be much shorter, and it will also perform much better. If at this point you activate the relationship between Buying Group and Targets again, the same matrix visual will look like the one shown in Figure 3-42.

Buying Group	Total Target Amount	Target Amount Intersect	Target Amount TreatAs
Tailspin Toys	55400000	55400000	55400000
Wingtip Toys	55700000	55700000	55700000
Total	**180400000**	**111100000**	**111100000**

FIGURE 3-42 The same matrix visual after activating relationships

When you are using activated relationships, the Total Target Amount measure displays the same values as the other two measures because the filters from the Customer table now reach the Targets table.

WINDOW FUNCTIONS

There are several window functions in DAX, including RANK, ROWNUMBER, INDEX, OFFSET, and WINDOW. There are also supporting window functions: ORDERBY, PARTITIONBY, and MATCHBY, which are used for ordering, partitioning, and matching rows that aren't unique, respectively. This section covers the scalar and window functions.

The RANK and ROWNUMBER functions return scalar values. The two functions work in a similar way, with the main difference being that RANK will return the same value in case of ties, while ROWNUMBER guarantees uniqueness of values. RANK also can accept DENSE or SKIP as the first parameter to handle ties. Here's an example of how the RANK and ROWNUMBER functions can be used:

```
Rank Example =
RANK(
    DENSE,
    ALLSELECTED(Customer[Buying Group]),
    ORDERBY([Total Target Amount], DESC BLANKS FIRST)
)

RowNumber Example =
ROWNUMBER(
    ALLSELECTED(Customer[Buying Group]),
    ORDERBY([Total Target Amount], DESC BLANKS FIRST)
)
```

You can see the result in Figure 3-43.

Year			
2021 ⌄			

Buying Group	Total Target Amount	Rank Example	RowNumber Example
N/A		1	3
Tailspin Toys	9000000	2	1
Wingtip Toys	9000000	2	2
Total	**27000000**		

FIGURE 3-43 RANK and ROWNUMBER examples

Note how even though the N/A buying group has no target, it still has a rank and row number. The other two buying groups have the same target amount, and while their rank is the same, the row number is different. Also note how you can handle blanks differently in the ORDERBY function.

The INDEX, OFFSET, and WINDOW functions are table functions that can be used as CALCULATE filters, for example.

INDEX returns a specified row from a specified table. For example, the function can be used to show the third-best-selling product in the following way:

```
EVALUATE
INDEX(
    3,
    'Stock Item',
    ORDERBY(
        [Total Revenue Excluding Tax],
        DESC
    )
)
```

OFFSET returns a row that was offset relative to the current row. For example, you can show daily sales and the previous day sales like so:

```
EVALUATE
ADDCOLUMNS(
    VALUES('Date'[Date]),
    "Sales", [Total Revenue Excluding Tax],
    "Previous Day Sales",
        CALCULATE(
            [Total Revenue Excluding Tax],
            OFFSET(
                -1,
                ORDERBY('Date'[Date], ASC BLANKS LAST)
            )
        )
)
```

WINDOW returns a set of rows relative to the current row, specified in either a relative or an absolute way. For example, you can calculate running all-time daily sales by using the following query:

```
EVALUATE
ADDCOLUMNS(
    VALUES('Date'[Date]),
    "Sales", [Total Revenue Excluding Tax],
    "Running Total Sales",
        CALCULATE(
            [Total Revenue Excluding Tax],
            WINDOW(
                0, ABS,
                0, REL,
                ORDERBY('Date'[Date], ASC BLANKS LAST)
            )
        )
)
```

Note that WINDOW can also be used instead of INDEX or OFFSET. For example, you can rewrite the INDEX and OFFSET examples above by using WINDOW:

```
// WINDOW used instead of INDEX
EVALUATE
WINDOW(
    3, ABS,
    3, ABS,
    'Stock Item',
    ORDERBY(
        [Total Revenue Excluding Tax],
        DESC
    )
)
// WINDOW used instead of OFFSET
EVALUATE
ADDCOLUMNS(
    VALUES('Date'[Date]),
    "Sales", [Total Revenue Excluding Tax],
    "Previous Day Sales",
        CALCULATE(
            [Total Revenue Excluding Tax],
            WINDOW(
                -1, REL,
                -1, REL,
                ORDERBY('Date'[Date], ASC BLANKS LAST)
            )
        )
)
```

Information functions

DAX has many information functions starting with INFO, which in many ways give you the same information as Dynamic Management Views (DMVs). For example, the following two queries return equivalent results, with the first one using an information function, and the last one using a DMV:

// Information function
```
EVALUATE INFO.MEASURES()
```

// DMV
```
select * from $SYSTEM.TMSCHEMA_MEASURES
```

There's also the COLUMNSTATISTICS function in DAX, which returns a table with the following columns:

- Table Name
- Column Name
- Min
- Max

- Cardinality
- Max Length

This function can be especially useful to perform data profiling for the entire model.

Implement calculation groups, dynamic strings, and field parameters

It's common for semantic models to apply the same filters in DAX to different calculations, and *calculation groups* can help avoid repeating the same code multiple times. Occasionally you may need to format the same measure differently depending on selection, and *dynamic format strings* can apply different formatting without converting values to text. *Field parameters* can be used to switch between different columns or measures to help analysts uncover more insights.

Calculation groups

Calculation groups are a feature of tabular models; the main use of calculation groups is to reduce the amount of code you need to write. For example, if you need to apply the same filters, such as month-to-date, year-to-date, and so on, to a set of measures, you can create a Time Intelligence calculation group instead of creating a separate measure for each calculation.

There are other reasons you may want to use calculation groups; for instance, you can create a calculation group to switch between different measures in a visual. A calculation group can apply measure formatting dynamically, unlike a solution based on the SWITCH function in DAX, and a calculation group will work when connecting from Excel, unlike a field parameter.

While it's possible to create calculation groups by using several tools, the best way is to use Tabular Editor 2.

> **IMPORTANT CALCULATION GROUPS AND IMPLICIT MEASURES**
>
> You should be aware that if you choose to use calculation groups in your data model, you won't be able to use implicit measures anymore. Power BI creates implicit measures when you add a summarized field to a visual. The implicit measures you created before creating a calculation group will continue to work, except they won't be affected by calculation groups.

To create a calculation group in Tabular Editor 2, select **Model** > **New Calculation Group**. You'll be prompted to enter a name for the new calculation group, and you'll see the calculation group properties (Figure 3-44).

An important property of a calculation group is the precedence, which becomes relevant when your data model contains more than one calculation group. The *precedence* determines the order in which calculation groups are applied: the higher the number, the earlier it will be applied.

FIGURE 3-44 New calculation group created in Tabular Editor

A calculation group contains one or more calculation items, and these become rows in a calculation group table. To create a calculation item, right-click a calculation group and select **Create New > Calculation Item**. You'll be prompted to enter a new calculation item name, and you'll see the calculation item properties (Figure 3-45).

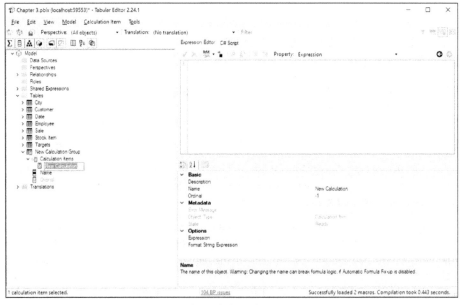

FIGURE 3-45 New calculation item created in Tabular Editor

Apart from Name, the following are the most important calculation item properties:

- **Ordinal** Because calculation items appear as rows in a calculation group, the Ordinal property determines the order of calculation items. You can edit this property manually, or you can drag and drop calculation items within a calculation group to adjust the order.

- **Expression** The expression determines which calculation applies to measures when you select a calculation item. While you see and can edit the calculation item expression in the properties section, it's easier to work in the Expression Editor section (more on the kinds of expressions you can apply soon).

- **Format String Expression** This property determines the format that'll be applied to measures when you select a calculation item. You can use a DAX formula to specify a format dynamically. Again, you can edit the property in the Expression Editor after you select Format String Expression from the Property dropdown list.

Calculation groups can make use of the following special DAX functions:

- SELECTEDMEASURE Returns the currently used measure; used as a placeholder in calculation item expressions

- SELECTEDMEASURENAME Returns the name of the currently used measure; can be useful in case you want to apply different calculations to different measures, depending on the measure names

- SELECTEDMEASUREFORMATSTRING Returns the format string of the currently used measure; can be useful when you want to dynamically change the format string of measures

- ISSELECTEDMEASURE Logical function that checks whether the currently used measure is contained in a list of measures you specify

For example, you can create a calculation item with the following expression to calculate the month-to-date value of the currently selected measure:

```
CALCULATE(
    SELECTEDMEASURE(),
    DATESMTD('Date'[Date])
)
```

Note that you're not forced to use the SELECTEDMEASURE function in calculation items; for instance, the following expression will substitute the currently used measure with the Total Quantity measure, regardless of the measure used:

```
[Total Quantity]
```

After you create one or more calculation items in your calculation group, you'll need to save changes to your model by selecting **Save** in the upper-left corner or by pressing **Ctrl+S**. You may also need to refresh the calculation group table in Power BI Desktop.

To use a calculation group, you need to add the visible calculation group column to a slicer or filter and select a calculation item. By default, the visible column's name will be Name, which you can change in Tabular Editor 2 or Power BI Desktop; the Ordinal column contains the Ordinal property values of each calculation item.

You can also use calculation groups in DAX. The following example applies the logic of the MTD calculation item from the calculation group called Time Intelligence:

```
Quantity MTD =
CALCULATE(
    [Total Quantity],
    'Time Intelligence'[Period] = "MTD"
)
```

Note that you can use calculation groups only with measures; therefore, the following measure will not apply the MTD calculation item logic:

```
Quantity MTD Wrong =
CALCULATE(
    SUM(Sale[Quantity]),
    'Time Intelligence'[Period] = "MTD"
)
```

Calculation groups can be especially useful when you need to apply the same filters consistently, particularly when filters come from different tables and creating a column to filter is difficult.

Dynamic strings

In situations where you only want to change the formatting of a measure without creating a calculation group, you can use dynamic strings. There are several ways to set a dynamic format string for a measure.

For example, in Power BI Desktop you can:

1. Select a measure.

2. Set its **Format** property to **Dynamic**.

3. Edit the format string expression in the DAX formula bar.

Or, in Tabular Editor 2 you can:

1. Select a measure.

2. In its properties, under **Options**, edit **Format String Expression**.

Unlike custom format strings, dynamic strings need to be enclosed in double quotation marks, because they're DAX expressions. Furthermore, you can use the SELECTEDMEASURE function in a format string expression, which will refer to the measure value. For example, you can use the following format string expression to format numbers above 1,000 with the K suffix:

```
VAR CurrentValue = SELECTEDMEASURE()
RETURN
    IF(
        CurrentValue < 1000,
        "#,0",
        "#,0,.0 K"
    )
```

Field parameters

In some cases, you may want to let viewers of your Power BI reports switch between fields by using slicers. For example, if your Bar chart shows sales by region by default, the report consumers may want to view sales by product category or month by making a slicer selection. User-driven field selection can be achieved by using field parameters. To create a field parameter, select **Modeling** > **New parameter** > **Fields**, and you'll see the options like in Figure 3-46.

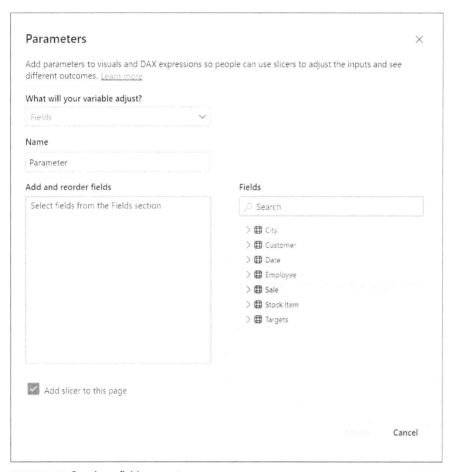

FIGURE 3-46 Creating a field parameter

You can then add fields to the list on the left. You can choose both columns and measures. If needed, you can rename a field just for the field parameter by double-clicking it.

After you finish and select **Create**, Power BI will create a new table in your data model, which is a calculated table with one visible column, similar to the one below:

```
Metric = {
    ("Sales", NAMEOF('Sale'[Total Revenue Excluding Tax]), 0),
    ("Profit", NAMEOF('Sale'[Total Profit]), 1),
    ("Quantity", NAMEOF('Sale'[Total Quantity]), 2)
}
```

To edit a field parameter after creating it, you'll need to edit its calculated table DAX formula.

By default, a slicer with the field parameter names will be added to the page, which you can use to switch between different values. You can also use the field parameter column in a visual to display the selected field value.

If you ever need to switch between field values and field names, you can right-click the field parameter column in a field well and select **Show values of selected field** or **Show selected field**, respectively.

> *IMPORTANT* **FIELD PARAMETERS IN MICROSOFT EXCEL**
>
> Field parameters work properly in Power BI visuals only. Field parameters cannot be used in Excel to switch between different fields.

Design and build a large-format semantic model

In the Power BI service, you can enable large semantic model storage format, which brings the following benefits:

- Semantic models can grow beyond 10 GB in size.
- There is a default segment size of 8 million rows.
- Write operations are faster when using the XML for Analysis (XMLA) endpoint.

> *NOTE* **PUBLISHING SEMANTIC MODELS LARGER THAN 10 GB**
>
> Even with the large semantic model storage format configured, you still won't be able to publish semantic models larger than 10 GB from Power BI Desktop to the Power BI service. To allow semantic models to grow beyond that size, you'll need to leverage incremental refresh.

You can enable large semantic model storage format for each semantic model individually, or you can set it as default in a Premium workspace.

For a specific semantic model:

1. Go to the semantic model settings.
2. Expand **Large semantic model storage format**.
3. Set the toggle to **On** and select **Apply** (Figure 3-47).

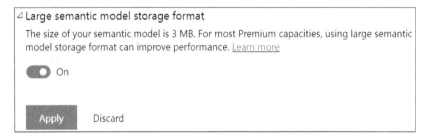

FIGURE 3-47 Large semantic model storage format in semantic model settings

To set large semantic model storage format as default in a Premium workspace:

1. Go to the workspace settings.
2. Go to the **Premium** section.
3. Under **Semantic model storage format**, select **Large semantic model storage format** (Figure 3-48).
4. Select **Apply**.

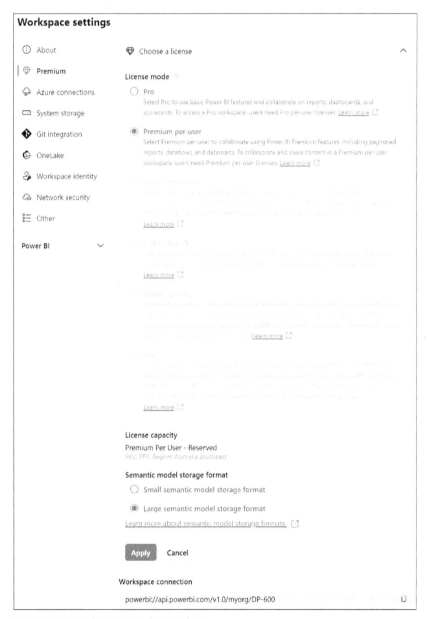

FIGURE 3-48 Workspace Premium settings

Note that with the large semantic model storage format, downloading the .pbix file from the Power BI service may not work.

Design and build composite models that include aggregations

By using composite models, you can optimize the performance of data sources that use the DirectQuery mode by using aggregations. For instance, if you're using DirectQuery, with a fact table containing data for each customer, and you report on values for all customers combined, you can create an aggregation at the total customers level. If you need to report data on individual customers, you can still use the original table, and Power BI will automatically determine whether it should use the aggregation or the original table.

> **NOTE REPRODUCING THE STEPS**
>
> Working in DirectQuery mode requires a database, so there's no corresponding companion file. Setting up a database is not tested on the exam; if you have access to a database, the steps to create and manage aggregations are going to be similar as described in this section.

An aggregation table can be a table created in a variety of ways:

- Imported M query
- Calculated table in DAX
- Another table in DirectQuery mode

Once you have a suitable table, you can turn it into an aggregation table as described next. The aggregation table should contain at least some of the same keys and columns you want to aggregate, and it does not have to come from the same source as the detail table.

For example, suppose you're using the Sales table in DirectQuery mode and you have an aggregation table called SalesAllCustomers, which is the same as Sale, except it doesn't have detailed information on each customer. Managing aggregations involves the following steps:

1. Right-click any table in the **Data** pane.
2. Select **Manage aggregations**.
3. In the **Aggregation table** dropdown, select **SalesAllCustomers**. You'll see the options presented like in Figure 3-49.

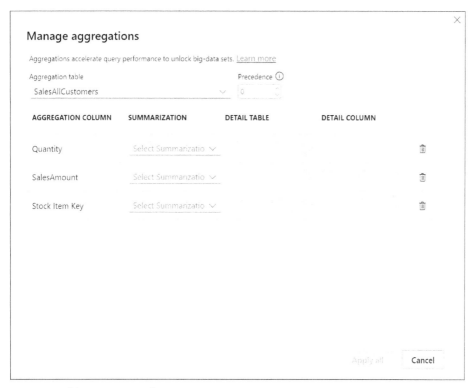

FIGURE 3-49 Manage aggregations

4. For each column, select the appropriate summarization and the corresponding detail table and column, if relevant:

- **Count**   Can be used for count only, not distinct count
- **GroupBy**   Is used for relationship keys
- **Max**   Corresponds to the maximum value
- **Min**   Corresponds to the minimum value
- **Sum**   Corresponds to sum
- **Count table rows**   Counts rows in a table

5. Once you make all selections, select **Apply all**, and Power BI will hide the aggregation table.

Queries that can be resolved by using the aggregation table will use the aggregation table. In case the aggregation is insufficient—in the example that involved reporting values for individual customers—the detail table will be used automatically.

You can use multiple aggregation tables if needed; in this case, tables with higher precedence will be used first.

Implement dynamic row-level security and object-level security

A common business requirement is to secure data so that different users who view the same report can see different subsets of data. In Power BI, this can be accomplished with the feature called *row-level security (RLS)*.

Row-level security restricts data by filtering it at the row level, depending on the rules defined for each user. To configure RLS, you first need to create and define each role in Power BI Desktop, and then assign individual users or Active Directory security groups to the roles in the Power BI service.

> **NOTE** **ROW-LEVEL SECURITY AND LIVE CONNECTIONS**
>
> Defining roles in Power BI works only for imported data and DirectQuery. When you connect live to a Power BI semantic model or an Analysis Services data model, Power BI will rely on row-level security configured in the source, and you cannot override it by creating roles in Power BI Desktop.

Creating roles in Power BI Desktop

To see the list of roles configured in a semantic model in Power BI Desktop, select **Manage roles** from the **Modeling** ribbon in the **Report** view. To create a new role, select **New** in the **Roles** section. You'll then be prompted to specify table filters (Figure 3-50).

FIGURE 3-50 Manage security roles

When you create a role, you have the option to change the default name to a new one. It's important to give roles user-friendly names because you'll see them in the Power BI service, and you need to be able to assign users to the correct roles.

If you select the **ellipsis** next to a role, you'll be presented with the following options:

- **Rename** Use this option to rename the currently selected role; you can also rename a role by double-clicking its name.
- **Duplicate** This option creates a copy of the currently selected role.
- **Delete** This option deletes the currently selected role.

For each role, you can define a DAX expression to filter each table. When row-level security is configured, these expressions will be evaluated against each row of the relevant table, and only those rows for which the expressions are evaluated as true will be visible.

To create a filter, select a table in the **Select tables** section, then select **Add**. You can configure a filter by using the user interface, or you can switch to DAX editor and enter your own expression.

For example, in the Wide World Importers data model that you've been working with, you can create the following roles:

1. Create a new role, and rename it to **Southeast**.
2. Select **City** > **Add**.
3. Select **Sales Territory** instead of City in the dropdown.
4. Enter **Southeast** next to **equals**.
5. Duplicate the **Southeast** role, and rename it to **Plains**.
6. Change the filter in the **Plains** role to **Plains**.
7. Select **Save** > **Close**.

> *NOTE* **HIDING ALL ROWS**
>
> If you want to hide all rows in a table, switch to the DAX editor and enter **FALSE** as the expression. Because `false` is never going to be `true` for any row, no rows will be shown in this case.

Later in the chapter, you'll have a chance to test the roles in Power BI Desktop and the Power BI service.

Dynamic row-level security

The roles you've created so far have been static, which means that all users within a role will see the same data. If you have several rules that specify how you should secure your data, this approach may mean you have to create a number of roles as well as update the data model every time a new role should be introduced or an old one removed.

There is an alternative approach, called *dynamic row-level security*, which allows you to show different data to different users within the same role.

NOTE **DYNAMIC ROW-LEVEL SECURITY**

Because dynamic row-level security can use a single role, this approach is preferable in large-scale implementations of Power BI where there are many users who need to see different data.

For this approach, your data model must contain the usernames of people who should have access to the relevant rows of data. You'll also need to pass the active username as a filter condition. Power BI has two functions that allow you to get the username of the current user:

- USERNAME   This function returns the domain and login of the user in the domain\login format.

- USERPRINCIPALNAME   Depending on how the Active Directory was set up, this function usually returns the email address of the user.

NOTE   **USING** USERNAME **AND** USERPRINCIPALNAME

If your computer is not part of an Active Directory domain, both functions will return the same result—domain\login. Once you publish your semantic model to the Power BI service, both functions will return the email address of the user.

These functions can be used only in measures or table filter DAX expressions; if you try to use either of them in a calculated column or a calculated table, you'll get an error.

To see how dynamic row-level security works in the Wide World Importers data model, first create a new security role:

1. Select **Manage roles** on the **Modeling** ribbon.
2. Create a new security role, and call it **Dynamic RLS**.
3. For the **Dynamic RLS** role, specify the following expression in DAX editor for the **Employee** table:

   ```
   [Email] = USERPRINCIPALNAME()
   ```
4. Select **Save** > **Close**.

Now you can test the new role:

1. Select **View as** on the **Modeling** ribbon.
2. Select both **Other user** and **Dynamic RLS**.
3. Enter **jack.potter@wideworldimporters.com** in the **Other user** box.
4. Select **OK**.
5. Go to the **Table** view.
6. Select the **Employee** table.

Note that the Employee table is now filtered to just Jack Potter's row, as shown in Figure 3-51.

FIGURE 3-51 Employee table viewed as Jack Potter

Although this may be good enough in certain cases, it's a common requirement for managers to see the data of those who report to them. Because Jack is a manager, he should be able to see data of the salespersons who report to him. For that, you can create a new role called **Dynamic RLS (hierarchy)** with the following table filter DAX expression:

```
PATHCONTAINS(
    PATH(
        Employee[Employee Key],
        Employee[Parent Employee Key]
    ),
    LOOKUPVALUE(
        Employee[Employee Key],
        Employee[Email],
        USERPRINCIPALNAME()
    )
)
```

This table filter DAX expression keeps those rows where Jack is part of the hierarchy path, which relies on the Employee table having both the ID and parent ID columns.

After you make this change, the Employee table will show four rows: Jack's row and three rows of the salespersons who report to Jack (Figure 3-52).

Employee Key	Parent Employee Key	Employee	Title	Email
20	19	Jack Potter	Manager	jack.potter@wideworldimporters.com
16	20	Archer Lamble	Salesperson	archer.lamble@wideworldimporters.com
15	20	Taj Shand	Salesperson	taj.shand@wideworldimporters.com
14	20	Lily Code	Salesperson	lily.code@wideworldimporters.com

Now viewing as: Dynamic RLS (hierarchy), jack.potter@wideworldimporters.com

FIGURE 3-52 Employee table viewed as Jack Potter

So far, you've created the roles in Power BI Desktop. Once you publish the report, you'll have to assign users or security groups to roles in Power BI service separately.

Object-level security

In some cases, instead of or in addition to rows, you'll want to secure objects: columns or tables, or both. Hiding columns or tables won't make the objects secure, because anyone who can view a model will be able to view hidden objects. Furthermore, perspectives aren't a security feature, so you can't use a perspective to secure objects. Instead, you can use object-level security, which you can configure in Tabular Editor 2.

For example, suppose want to hide the Targets table from some group of people. Here's how to do it:

1. In Power BI Desktop, create a new role called **Hide Targets**.
2. Launch Tabular Editor 2 as an external tool.
3. In Tabular Editor 2, select the **Targets** table.
4. In table properties, expand the **Object Level Security** section.
5. From the dropdown next to the **Hide Targets** role, select **None**. At this stage, the Targets table properties should look like Figure 3-53.

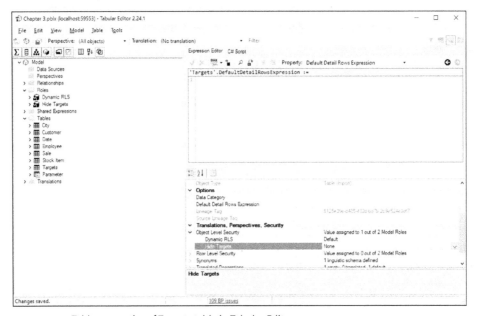

FIGURE 3-53 Table properties of Targets table in Tabular Editor

6. Save changes to the model by pressing **Ctrl+S**.

You can now test the role:

1. In Power BI Desktop **Report** view, select **Modeling** > **View as**.
2. Select the **Hide Targets** role, and select **OK**.

Note that you don't see the Targets table in the Report view anymore, even if it shows hidden objects. Additionally, any visuals that were based on data from the Targets table will show errors.

Also note that measures based on secured columns or tables will be automatically secured as well, so you only need to work on securing columns and tables.

Finally, keep in mind that you cannot combine different roles that use row-level security and object-level security. If you need to secure both rows and objects at the same time, you must create a role that includes security rules for both rows and objects.

Assigning security roles membership

Once you've configured row-level security roles in Power BI Desktop, you can publish your report to the Power BI service and add members to each role. To do so, go to the semantic model security settings by hovering over a semantic model in the list of workspace items and selecting **More options** > **Security**. If you don't have any roles defined in the semantic model, you'll see the message in Figure 3-54.

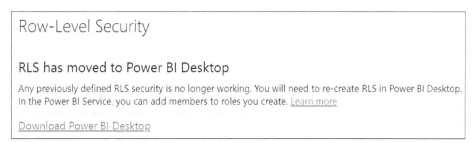

FIGURE 3-54 RLS has moved to Power BI Desktop message

If you've created RLS roles defined in the semantic model, you'll see a page like the one shown in Figure 3-55.

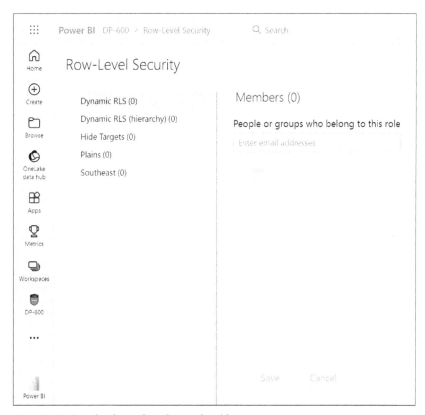

FIGURE 3-55 Row-level security role membership

On the left side of the Row-Level Security page, you can see a list of all roles in the semantic model. The numbers in brackets show how many members each role has. On the right, you can view, add, and remove members for a selected role.

To add a member to a role, first select a role on the left, and then enter email addresses or security groups in the **People or groups who belong to this role** field. After you enter new members, select **Add** > **Save**. The changes will be applied immediately.

To remove a member from a role, select the X next to the member and then select **Save**.

When you use row-level security in Power BI, you can use an email address for each user. Although this solution works, it can be hard to maintain. For example, consider that you have several semantic models that use RLS based on the same rules and it's viewed mostly by the same users. If a new user joins your company and you need to give them access to those semantic models, you will have to update the row-level security settings for each semantic model.

In cases like this, you can assign security groups as members of row-level security roles. When a new user joins the company, you will have to add them to the security group only once. The same principles apply to sharing content in Power BI.

> **NEED MORE REVIEW?** **CREATING SECURITY GROUPS**
>
> Instructions on how to create security groups are outside the scope of this book. For more details, see "Create a group in the Microsoft 365 admin center" *at docs.microsoft.com/en-us/microsoft-365/admin/create-groups/create-groups.*

Validate row-level security and object-level security

When creating roles, you can verify that they work as expected, both in Power BI Desktop and the Power BI service.

Viewing as roles in Power BI Desktop

In Power BI Desktop, you can check what the users with specific roles will see even before you publish your report to the Power BI service and assign users to roles. For this, once you have at least one role defined, select **View as** on the **Modeling** ribbon in the **Report** view. You'll then see the **View as roles** window (Figure 3-56).

Note that you can view as several roles simultaneously. This is because you can allocate a single user or a security group to multiple roles in the Power BI service; in this case, the security rules of the roles will complement each other. For example, if you select both the **Plains** and the **Southeast** roles, you'll see data for both territories. For this reason, you should always have clear names for your RLS roles.

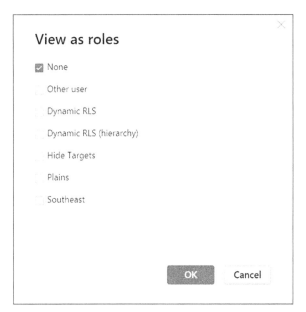

FIGURE 3-56 View as roles

EXAM TIP

You should know the effect of combining multiple security roles for a single user based on the description of security filters of each role.

When viewing data as roles, you'll see the bar at the top shown in Figure 3-57.

FIGURE 3-57 Now viewing as

IMPORTANT **APPLICATION OF ROW-LEVEL SECURITY**

The filters applied by row-level security are applied only at query time and not at processing time. The implication of this is that the filters won't change the values of calculated columns and calculated tables.

Another option in the **View as roles** window is **Other user**. With this option, you can test dynamic row-level security, which is covered next.

Viewing as roles in the Power BI service

As you saw with the **View as** feature in Power BI Desktop, you can test roles in the Power BI service. For this, you need to hover over a role on the Row-Level Security page and select **More options** (the ellipsis) > **Test as role**. You will then see the way a report appears to the members of the role. If needed, you can test a combination of roles or view as a specific user by selecting **Now viewing as** in the blue bar at the top and selecting the desired parameters. Once you are satisfied with how the roles work, you can select **Back to Row-Level Security**.

> ***IMPORTANT*** **ROW-LEVEL SECURITY AND WORKSPACE ROLES**
>
> Row-level security does not work on users who have the Contributor, Member, or Admin role in the workspace in which the semantic model resides. Those who have edit rights will always see the whole semantic model regardless of the security settings, even though the **Test as role feature** may show a filtered semantic model.

Skill 3.2: Optimize enterprise-scale semantic models

Data models in the enterprise environment occasionally grow sufficiently large to affect the report performance, and sometimes users may complain about the poor experience they have. There can be many reasons for poor performance, and this section explores several ways in which you can optimize your data models.

> **This skill covers how to:**
> - Implement performance improvements in queries and report visuals
> - Improve DAX performance by using DAX Studio
> - Optimize a semantic model by using Tabular Editor 2
> - Implement incremental refresh

Implement performance improvements in queries and report visuals

Sometimes you may notice that the report performance is not optimal. Power BI Desktop has a feature called **Performance Analyzer**, which you can use to trace the slow-performing visuals and to see the DAX queries behind them.

To turn on Performance Analyzer, go to the **Report** view and select **Optimize** > **Performance analyzer**. This opens the Performance analyzer pane (Figure 3-58).

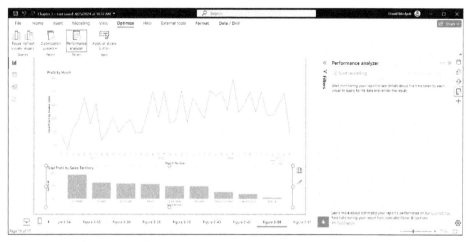

FIGURE 3-58 Performance Analyzer

Performance Analyzer works by recording traces, and it then shows you how long each visual took to render. To start recording traces, select **Start recording**. After that, you need to perform some actions, such as applying filters, that will recalculate the visuals, or you can select **Refresh visuals** to refresh the visuals as they are. You'll then see the rendering duration for each visual.

To identify the slowest visuals, you can sort visuals in the Performance Analyzer by selecting the arrow next to **Duration (ms)**.

Each visual that contains data has a DAX query behind it, which you can copy by expanding the line of the visual in the Performance Analyzer and selecting **Copy query**. You can analyze the query further in DAX Studio, for example. Alternatively, you can select **Run in DAX Query View** to work on the query within Power BI Desktop.

To clear the Performance analyzer pane, select **Clear**. To export all traces, select **Export**. Once you're done recording traces, select **Stop**.

Improve DAX performance by using DAX Studio

DAX Studio can be helpful when you are trying to analyze the performance of measures and queries. If you select **Query Plan** before running a query, you will see the physical and logical query plans. If you select **Server Timings**, you'll see how much time was spent in the formula and storage engine, the number of storage engine queries, and the degree of parallelism, as shown in Figure 3-59.

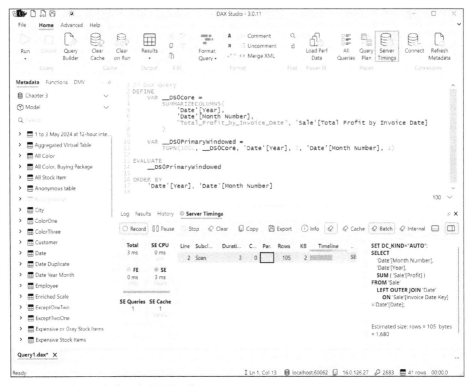

FIGURE 3-59 Server Timings in DAX Studio

As mentioned in "Skill 3.1: Design and build semantic models," it can be useful to clear the cache before running your queries to ensure that the performance differences aren't due to cached results.

Optimize a semantic model by using Tabular Editor 2

Best Practice Analyzer (**BPA**) in Tabular Editor 2 allows you to optimize your model by checking your model for adherence to the rules you add. You can access BPA by selecting **Tools** > **Best Practice Analyzer**. BPA can check your model for adherence to the rules you add. Before you can use BPA, you have to add BPA rules by selecting **Tools** > **Manage BPA Rules** > **Add**. If you don't want to create your own rules, you can load them from a file or URL. For example, the following URL contains some BPA rules developed in Microsoft: *raw.githubusercontent.com/microsoft/Analysis-Services/master/BestPracticeRules/BPARules.json*.

Once you add rules and open Best Practice Analyzer, you should see a list of rule violations (Figure 3-60).

To fix some rule violations, you can right-click a line and select **Apply fix**; other times you may need to apply a fix manually.

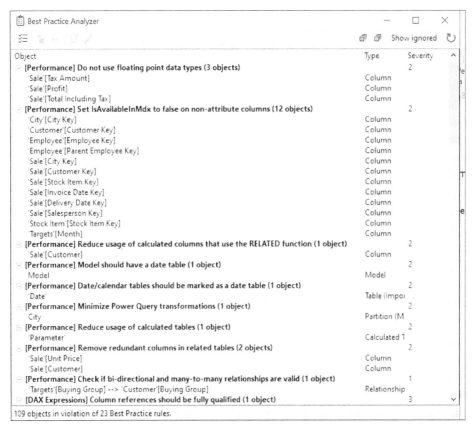

FIGURE 3-60 Best Practice Analyzer

Implement incremental refresh

Power BI allows you to work with semantic models that are hundreds of gigabytes in size even after Power BI automatically compresses data. However, when you refresh large semantic models, you may run into the following issues:

- **Speed**   Semantic model refreshes may take a very long time, preventing you from displaying the information in a timely manner.

- **Resource usage**   Transferring and transforming large amounts of data may use up precious RAM, CPU, and network bandwidth.

- **Reliability**   Long-running queries to data sources may time out or fail, resulting in semantic model refresh failures.

By using incremental refresh, you can address all these issues at once: You'll only refresh a subset of data, resulting in quicker, more reliable refreshes with lower resource consumption.

While you can set a different incremental refresh policy for each table in your semantic model, to set an incremental refresh policy, you'll need to filter a table based on dates. Therefore, usually you'll configure incremental refresh for fact tables that hold time-series data—for example, sales records.

For incremental refresh to work in Power BI service, you need to configure the former in Power BI Desktop, which involves the following steps:

1. Create the `RangeStart` and `RangeEnd` parameters.

2. Filter by using the `RangeStart` and `RangeEnd` parameters.

3. Define incremental refresh policies.

Creating the RangeStart and RangeEnd parameters

The first step in configuring incremental refresh in Power BI Desktop is to create the `RangeStart` and `RangeEnd` parameters that will be used to filter dates. These parameter names are reserved and case-sensitive—other parameter names won't work properly for incremental refresh. You create the parameters in Power Query Editor in the following way:

1. In Power Query Editor, select **Manage parameters** > **New parameter**.

2. Configure the `RangeStart` parameter as follows:

   - Name: **RangeStart**.

   - Type: **Date/Time**.

   - Current value: **01/01/2024**. Power Query may change the input format of this value later, depending on your system settings.

3. Above the list of parameters, select **New** and create the `RangeEnd` parameter as follows:

   - Name: **RangeEnd**

   - Type: **Date/Time**

   - Current value: **31/12/2024**, or **12/31/2024** if your system uses the MDY date format. At this stage, the parameters should look like those shown in Figure 3-61.

4. Select **OK**.

The choice of the current values matters only in Power BI Desktop because parameter values will be automatically overridden in Power BI service.

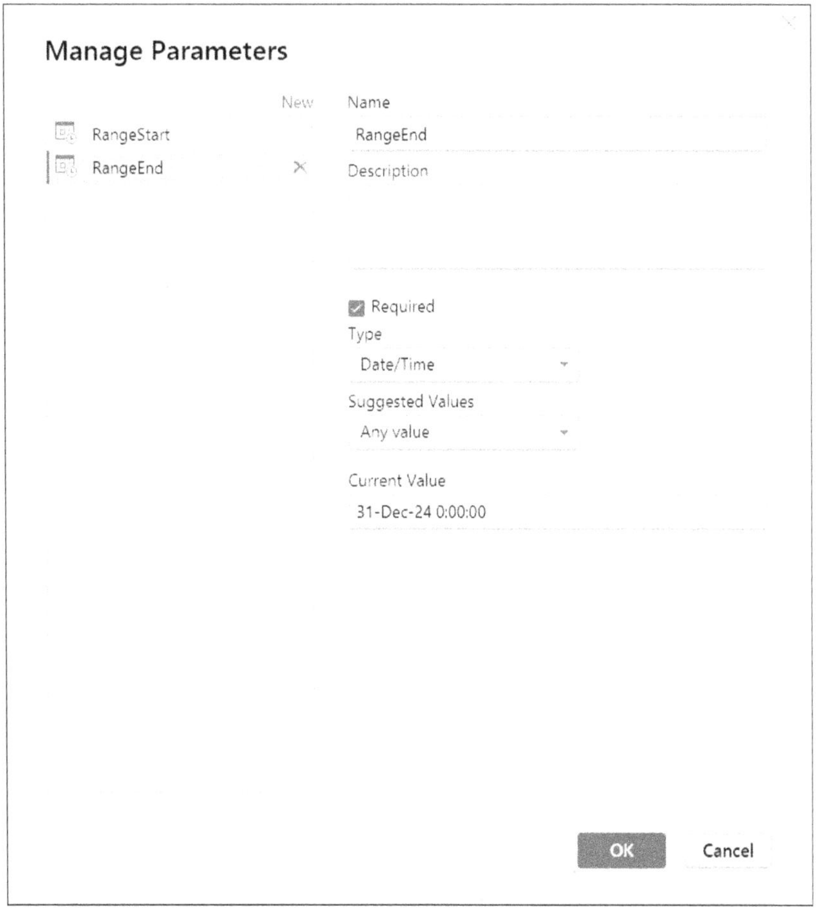

FIGURE 3-61 RangeStart and RangeEnd parameters

Filtering by using the RangeStart and RangeEnd parameters

The RangeStart and RangeEnd parameters are needed to filter based on dates. For example, suppose you have a table called Sale that has a Date/Time column called OrderDate, and you want to incrementally refresh the latest sales records based on OrderDate. In this case, you can apply the filters by implementing the following steps:

1. In Power Query Editor, select the **Sale** table from the list of queries.

2. Select the **filter** button on the **OrderDate** column header and select **Date/time filters** > **Custom filter**.

3. For the first condition, select

   - **is after or equal to** from the first dropdown
   - **Parameter** from the second dropdown
   - **RangeStart** from the third dropdown list

4. For the second condition, select
   - **is before** from the first dropdown
   - **Parameter** from the second dropdown
   - **RangeEnd** from the third dropdown

5. Ensure the logic between the conditions is set to **And**. At this stage, the filter conditions should match the ones shown in Figure 3-62.

FIGURE 3-62 Filter conditions

6. Select **OK**.

7. Close Power Query Editor by selecting **Close & Apply**.

While you can also use **is after** and **is before or equal to** as filter conditions, it's important that one of the conditions is a strict inequality, while the other one is not strict. In other words, if you set one condition to be **is after or equal to** and the other to **is before or equal to**, then you'll run into issues, because the edge values will be allocated to different partitions.

> **NOTE FILTERING DATES**
>
> Even though the RangeStart and RangeEnd parameters must be of type Date/Time, the column you filter can be a different type. For example, it's common for data warehouses to store dates as integers, such as 20240523 for May 23, 2024. In this case, you can employ a custom function to convert the parameter values to the required data type, and then you can use the Power Query Advanced Editor to filter the table by using the converted values.

Defining incremental refresh policies

With the RangeStart and RangeEnd parameters now filtering the table for which you want to apply an incremental refresh—in this example, Sale—you can now define an incremental refresh policy in the following way:

1. In the **Data** pane of Power BI Desktop, right-click the table you want to refresh incrementally.

2. Select **Incremental refresh**.

3. Ensure the correct table is selected in the **Table** dropdown and switch the **Incrementally refresh this table** toggle so it's on.

4. Select the periods for which you want to store and refresh data. Note that you can select different periods for storing and refreshing data. For the example, store the last 10 years of data and refresh the last 15 days of data. At this stage, your incremental refresh settings should look as shown in Figure 3-63.

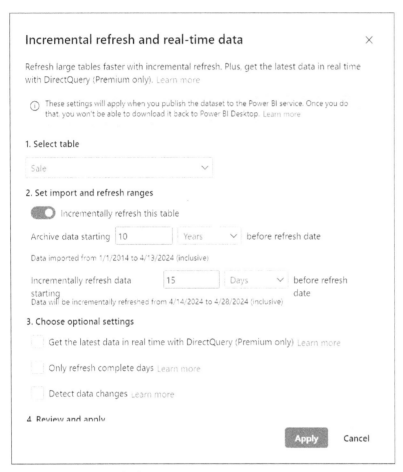

FIGURE 3-63 Incremental refresh

5. Select **Apply**.

When defining an incremental refresh policy, you can also use the following options:

- **Detect data changes**   To make incremental refreshes even more efficient, Power BI can check the maximum value of a Date/Time column you specify, and data will be refreshed only if the value changes. This column should not be the same column that you filter by using the RangeStart and RangeEnd parameters.

- **Only refresh complete periods** You can use this setting to exclude incomplete periods from refreshes. In some cases, reporting incomplete periods does not make business sense. For example, if scheduled refresh takes place at 6 a.m. in the morning and there's some data for the day, then displaying the current day's figures may be misleading to report users. Excluding incomplete periods may be appropriate in this case.

- **Get the latest data in real time with DirectQuery** You can partition tables in such a way that the latest data is in DirectQuery mode, while the old data is imported.

You can define a different incremental refresh policy for each table in your data model while still using the same RangeStart and RangeEnd parameters.

Once you publish your semantic model to Power BI service, the data will be refreshed incrementally. The first refresh may take longer to refresh the whole semantic model, but subsequent refreshes will benefit from incremental refresh and will be faster.

Query folding

Incremental refresh is only effective when query folding occurs—that is, when filtering by dates results in the data source returning a reduced set of data. If query folding does not occur, then filtering happens after Power BI retrieves all data, making incremental refresh policies useless. When you define an incremental refresh policy, Power BI Desktop will try to verify whether query folding occurs. If it's unable to confirm query folding, then you'll see a message as shown in Figure 3-64.

 Unable to confirm if the M query can be folded. It is not recommended to use incremental refresh with non-foldable queries. Learn more

FIGURE 3-64 Query folding warning

Note that query folding may still occur, though you'll need to confirm it yourself by using query diagnostics.

EXAM TIP

You should know what's required for incremental refresh to work successfully.

Chapter summary

- You may want to use DirectQuery when data frequently changes and you need to report the latest data. Another reason to use DirectQuery is when there's too much data to import into a model. Alternatively, if there's too much data to import, you can use the DirectLake mode.

- Power BI Desktop supports various external tools, such as DAX Studio and Tabular Editor. You can use DAX Studio to write DAX queries and troubleshoot query performance, and you can use Tabular Editor to develop your model and apply best practice rules.

- Instead of using snowflake data models, you should strive to use star schemas. You can denormalize in Power Query if needed.

- You can implement many-to-many relationships by using bridge tables or by creating direct many-to-many relationships.

- DAX is a functional language that you can use to create measures, calculated columns, calculated tables, and calculation groups. You can also write queries in DAX that start with EVALUATE.

- Calculation groups are special tables in Power BI that allow you to write less DAX and apply the same calculations to any selected measure. You can create calculation groups in Tabular Editor. When you only need to change format strings, you can use dynamic format strings. If you need to switch between fields, you can do so by using field parameters.

- Large semantic model storage format is a feature in the Power BI service that may improve the semantic model read and write operation performance.

- Composite models allow you to combine DirectQuery and imported data. You can define aggregations to improve the user experience in some cases.

- In Power BI, you can secure data in two ways. Row-level security will show specific rows to different groups of people, and object-level security will hide some columns or tables from some groups of people. You can define roles in Power BI Desktop and assign members in the Power BI service.

- You can validate row- and object-level security in Power BI Desktop and the Power BI service by viewing as roles.

- Performance Analyzer in Power BI Desktop allows you to analyze the performance of visuals. Once you know which visuals are the most problematic, you can copy the underlying query for further analysis.

- In DAX Studio, you can analyze the query performance by seeing how much time is spent in formula and storage engines. You can make changes to your formulas, clear the cache, and see if your changes made any difference to performance.

- The Best Practice Analyzer (BPA) feature of Tabular Editor allows you to check whether your data model adheres to a set of rules. You can define rules yourself or use someone else's rules.

- When working with large semantic models, you can configure incremental refresh to refresh only the latest data while storing the old data. Incremental refresh policies are defined in Power BI Desktop and then applied automatically in the Power BI service. To define an incremental refresh policy for a table, you need to use RangeStart and RangeEnd Date/Time parameters to filter the table you want to refresh incrementally, and then set the periods for which you want to store and refresh data.

Thought experiment

In this thought experiment, demonstrate your skills and knowledge of the topics covered in this chapter. You can find the answers in the section that follows.

You are a Fabric analytics engineer responsible for designing, building, and optimizing semantic models. Some users complain about the performance of some reports, including the speed and accuracy of data.

Based on background information and business requirements, answer the following questions:

1. You need to optimize a specific measure. Which tool should you use?

   A. Query diagnostics in Power Query

   B. Performance Analyzer

   C. DAX Studio

   D. Tabular Editor

2. Your report uses a dataset in DirectQuery mode. Some users complain that their basic reports take a long time to load. How can you improve performance?

   A. Configure incremental refresh.

   B. Build a composite model and configure an aggregation table.

   C. Remove some columns from the dataset.

3. You created a Bar graph with Color on the axis and Quantity on the values. The visual is shown in Figure 3-65.

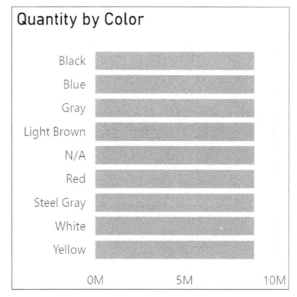

FIGURE 3-65 Bar graph showing Quantity by Color

Upon further checking, you find out that black stock items sold 1.1 million units. How can you fix the graph? The solution should use minimal effort and consider that you may want to analyze sales by metrics other than Quantity.

A. Create the following measure:

```
Total Quantity =
CALCULATE (
    SUM ( Sale[Quantity] ),
    TREATAS ( VALUES ( 'Stock Item'[Stock Item Key] ), Sale[Stock Item Key] )
)
```

B. Create an active physical relationship between Sale and Stock Item.

C. Create the following measure:

```
Total Quantity =
CALCULATE (
    SUM ( Sale[Quantity] ),
    INTERSECT( Sale, 'Stock Item' )
)
```

4. You want to create a line chart showing Quantity by the invoice date. You notice that there is a relationship between the Date from the Date table and the Invoice Date Key from the Sale table, but the relationship is inactive. All other visuals in your report will be analyzing values by delivery date. How should you approach this problem?

A. Create the following measure:

```
Quantity by Invoice Date =
CALCULATE (
    SUM ( Sale[Quantity] ),
    USERELATIONSHIP ( 'Date'[Date], Sale[Invoice Date Key] )
)
```

B. Delete the relationship based on the delivery date and activate the relationship based on the invoice date.

C. Activate the relationship based on invoice date, keeping the other relationship as is.

D. Use the TREATAS function.

5. You work on a dataset that sources its data from Azure SQL Database. The main fact table contains daily sales data for the last five years. To make the dataset refresh more efficiently, you configure incremental refresh for the table by filtering the sales data column. Upon checking the refresh history in the Power BI service, you notice that the refresh always takes approximately the same amount of time, suggesting that incremental refresh doesn't happen. What could be the reason?

A. Azure SQL Database doesn't support incremental refresh.

B. One of the transformation steps breaks query folding before date filtering happens.

C. The Date/Time range parameters are called RangeFrom and RangeTo.

D. The storage mode is set to Import.

Thought experiment answers

1. The answer is **C**. In DAX Studio, you can see the query plan as well as server timings when executing DAX queries that include the measure you want to optimize. DAX is used after you load data, and query diagnostics are a Power Query feature, so option A is wrong. Neither Performance Analyzer nor Tabular Editor can provide a detailed breakdown of why a measure is slow, so options B and D are also wrong.

2. The answer is **B**. Aggregate tables can be used to answer queries that don't need a lot of details. You cannot configure incremental refresh in DirectQuery mode, so option A is wrong. Option C is incorrect because the dataset uses DirectQuery, and removing columns won't affect the performance of the visuals that are already in the report.

3. The answer is **B**. Creating a physical relationship is the least arduous solution and will let you avoid creating virtual relationships like in answer A. While the measure from option A will solve the problem of incorrect values, you will need to write a similar measure for each different metric you want to analyze. The measure formula from option C will not work because Sale and Stock item have a different number of columns. Option D involves too much effort and only solves the problem at hand; if you want to analyze quantity by individual stock items, this approach will fail.

4. The answer is **A**. Because this is going to be a one-off visual, creating a measure that activates the relationship at query time solves the problem and involves the least effort. If you delete the relationship based on delivery date, as option B suggests, other visuals that use the Date table will display the wrong values. Following option C is not possible because no more than one relationship can be active at a time. Using TREATAS as suggested in option D will result in the wrong figures.

5. The answer is **B**. For incremental refresh to work, query folding must take place. Otherwise data is filtered after it's loaded, and the refresh time will be the same as without incremental refresh. Option A is incorrect because Azure SQL databases do support incremental refresh. Option C is incorrect because the Date/Time parameters used for incremental refresh must be called RangeStart and RangeEnd—other names won't work. Option D is incorrect because incremental refresh is designed for imported data, not other storage modes.

CHAPTER 4

Explore and analyze data

Data is meant to help you find the path at the end of which you seek the truth. The truth is to shed light on what happened, why it happened, what can happen next, and how to prevent it or achieve a potential outcome. To find that, however, you must have the ability to go through the data, analyze it, and formulate hypotheses, which are then the subject of investigation.

Skills covered in this chapter:

- Skill 4.1: Perform exploratory analytics
- Skill 4.2: Query data by using SQL

Skill 4.1: Perform exploratory analytics

Exploratory analytics focuses on a statistical summary of data, discovering patterns, outliers, and trends. Whether visualizing distributions or identifying correlations, exploratory analytics sets the stage for deeper understanding. This is also necessary before transforming data to their final form and for analyzing results to extract all insights that can help users in their work and decisions.

> **This skill covers how to:**
> - Implement descriptive and diagnostic analytics
> - Integrate prescriptive and predictive analytics into a visual or report
> - Profile data

Implement descriptive and diagnostic analytics

Descriptive analytics summarizes historical data to provide insights into what has happened. It answers such questions as "What happened?" and "What are the key trends?" Within this type of analysis, three types of output are very often used:

- **Summary statistics** Calculating mean, median, mode, variance, and other statistical measures

- **Data visualization**   Creating charts, graphs, and dashboards to represent data patterns
- **Reports**   Generating periodic reports to highlight performance metrics

These outputs help users get the necessary answers in different areas and phases of data processing. *Summary statistics* can be obtained from the data during its processing or even earlier when the data audit and familiarization with it occurs. They can also be obtained even after the data is ready for use. For example, you can create a basic statistical summary in PySpark Notebook using the `describe()` function (Figure 4-1). If you use the function without an input parameter, it creates statistics for all input columns. If you define specific columns as input parameters, `describe()` will calculate statistics calculated only for those columns.

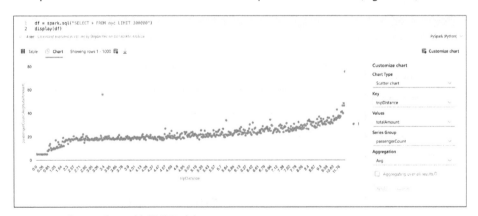

FIGURE 4-1 Executed `describe()`

Data visualization output is more digestible for many users because they can better and independently imagine what the individual values mean in the context of other columns. Within notebooks, you can use the native visualization options provided by the `display()` function. First, select the **Chart** tab, choose a graph from the **Chart Type** menu of graphs, and then place the desired columns from the loaded preview DataFrame (Figure 4-2).

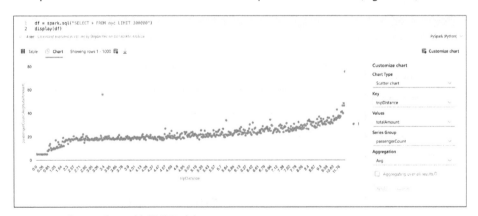

FIGURE 4-2 Scatter chart with NYC Taxi data

By default, these graphs are created based on the first 1,000 rows only. If you need a graph based on all values, turn on the **Aggregating over all results** option. Alternatively, you can use a library, such as **Seaborn**, **Matplotlib**, or **Plotly**, for rendering graphs.

NEED MORE REVIEW? **SEABORN**

For details about Seaborn, please visit *seaborn.pydata.org*.

The output within a Microsoft Fabric report directly targets using the **report** item, which displays data from the semantic model. If you don't want to leave the notebook environment, however, you can use a **powerbiclient** library. This library can render an existing report in the notebook environment but also supports using the QuickVisualize() function, which creates a Power BI report from an existing DataFrame (Figure 4-3).

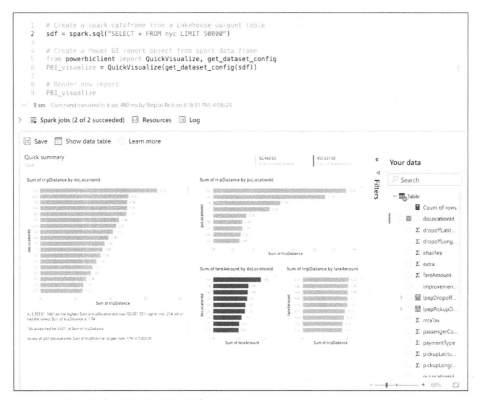

FIGURE 4-3 Result of QuickVisualize() function

You can edit the generated report, examine it, and add additional data for visualizations.

NEED MORE REVIEW? **VISUALIZATION IN NOTEBOOKS**

For details about visualization options in notebooks, please visit *learn.microsoft.com/fabric/data-engineering/notebook-visualization*.

Diagnostic analytics aims to understand why something happened by examining causal relationships. It answers questions like:

- Why did it happen?
- What caused a specific outcome?
- What were the key factors that influenced it?
- What correlations or relationships exist?

To do so, it is often necessary to focus on details in connection with the given results to find the source or cause. If the value of sales in 2020 fell by 70,000 units, for example, it could be because of the arrival of COVID-19 or because customers simply no longer needed the product. It is, therefore, necessary to look not only at the *internal* factors in the data, but sometimes also at the *external* factors. If the input factor and a factor that can be influenced are identified, then this discovery can help to prevent the given behavior in the future or to obtain similar or even better results, depending on the desired outcome. It can also be a space for improving existing processes and increasing efficiency in multiple areas.

Diagnostic analytics often compares two practices, strategies, campaigns, and approaches, examining which worked, which didn't, and why. Hypotheses are also used, which analysts then try to confirm or disprove using data. For example, you might define the hypothesis "We will increase sales of discounted goods by placing a pop-up window on the e-shop page that will encourage visitors to buy things at discounts and help them get to them." Analysts then can start comparing the state before the creation of that window and after this window was implemented, as well as monitoring the click-through rate through the window. Even the fact that visitors see but do not click the window can affect them, and in short, they will visit the discounted goods. Another procedure used is the correlation between individual data (see the "Profile data" section for details).

A large number of techniques can be used as part of diagnostic analytics, such as:

- Regression analysis
- Anomaly detection
- Correlation analysis
- Cohort analysis
- Time series analysis

It's up to you and the scenario you're trying to diagnose as to how you approach it. For example, you could carry out diagnostics in notebooks by compiling code for cohort analysis and subsequent visualization using heat map visualization, while a colleague might prefer to perform diagnostics and create visuals within **Power BI reports**. There the **Line chart visual** allows you to perform anomaly detection using **Find anomalies** (Figure 4-4), which can be turned on within the **Analytics** pane. (You'll see this later in Figures 4-43 and 4-44.)

NEED MORE REVIEW? **ANOMALY DETECTION IN POWER BI VISUALS**

For details about anomaly detection in Power BI visuals, please visit *learn.microsoft.com/ power-bi/visuals/power-bi-visualization-anomaly-detection*.

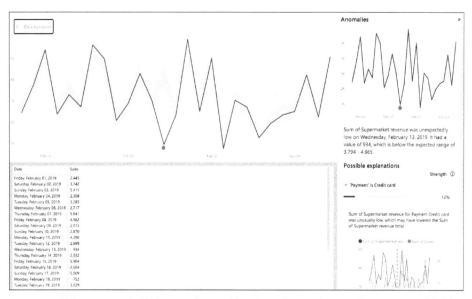

FIGURE 4-4 When you apply Find anomalies to a Line chart, detected anomalies appear as clickable marks in the chart.

One of the most well-known diagnostic visuals within Power BI is the **Decomposition tree and Key influencer visual**, which helps you analyze data, rank the factors that matter, and display them. It has two data views:

- **Key influencers** view shows the top contributors to the selected metric value (Figure 4-5).

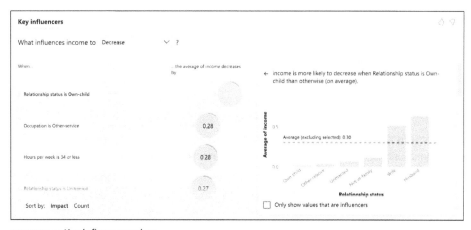

FIGURE 4-5 Key influencers view

- **Top segments** view shows the segments contributing to the selected metric value (Figure 4-6).

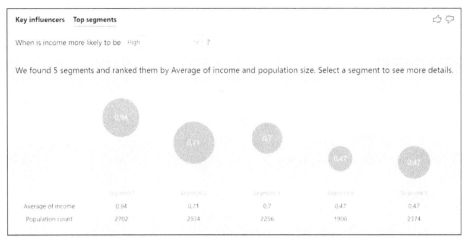

FIGURE 4-6 Top segments

Integrate prescriptive and predictive analytics into a visual or report

Predictive analytics enables organizations to foresee potential outcomes and steer business decisions with invaluable insights. It combines statistical algorithms, data analysis, and machine learning to build accurate models predicting future outcomes. Prescriptive analytics doesn't just focus on predicting the future but also on recommending actions to achieve specific goals. Its key questions are "What will happen?" and "What do we do now?"

The results of predictive analytics are highly dependent on specific factors:

- **Data quality and availability**   Incomplete or impure data will easily affect prediction results, so it is essential to perform this type of analysis on fully prepared data only.

- **Data and model obsolescence**   New technologies advance, and old ones become obsolete. The same is true of predictive models and their data. It is essential to validate the purpose for which the model was created and whether there have been any changes; therefore, there is no need to retrain it on new data.

- **Relearning the model**   The model was created and subsequently learned on sufficiently similar data, and it incorrectly evaluates new data.

- **Interpretability**   More complex models can be more complicated to explain, and the reasons for their results cannot be determined. Less complex models can usually be interpreted more simply but may not always provide the most accurate results.

- **Experience and availability of tools**   The creation of a functioning and used model depends on experience and tools, but mainly the understanding of the author of the given issue.

Within Microsoft Fabric, you can use Data Science items, such as ML models or experiments, in which you use MLflow.

NEED MORE REVIEW? **MLFLOW**

For details about MLflow, please visit *mlflow.org*.

However, you also have the option to create predictions by using the MLflow PREDICT function within notebooks or already existing ML models. The results of these predictions can be stored in lakehouses for further processing or presentation of the output data.

NEED MORE REVIEW? **PREDICT**

For details about scalable function PREDICT, please visit *learn.microsoft.com/en-us/fabric/ data-science/model-scoring-predict*.

In the same way, you can compile your experiment within the notebook you want to use and present. The **Sklearn**, **PyTorch**, and **Prophet** libraries will provide tools and techniques for predictive analytics, such as:

- Decision tree
- Data mining
- Regression analysis
- Clustering

Another option for compiling the information is to work directly within **Power BI reports** or the **Explore** item. Scatter plots and Line charts are frequently used for prediction, and both graphs enable you to add a Trend line within the framework of dynamic reference lines in the **Analytics** pane. The *Trend line* represents a simple indication of whether the data indicate an increasing or decreasing tendency and is usually dotted or dashed to help viewers better orient themselves between represented data and analytical or support lines (Figure 4-7).

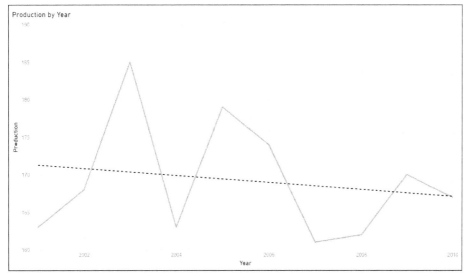

FIGURE 4-7 Trend line in a Line chart

Compared to the Scatter plot, the Line chart allows you to use **Forecasting**, which provides an automatically generated prediction based on the data within the visual. This analysis function will expand the visual by the set number of X-axis points, or if there is a date column on the X-axis, then Year, Quarter, Month, Days, Hours, Minutes, and Seconds can be selected. To do this, the extension displays the predicted value in a new line, the *Forecast line*, and an upper and lower limit to determine the confidence interval. You can set confidence from 75% to 99%, determining the interval in which the resulting value with this degree of probability will move. Figure 4-8 shows a preview of the Forecast line and confidence interval, which can appear as a filled polygon or just lines.

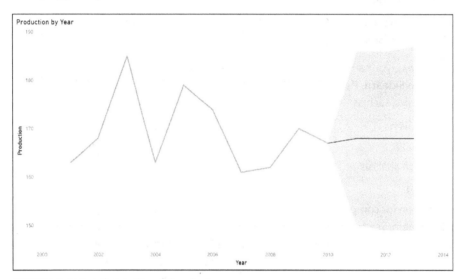

FIGURE 4-8 Forecasting option of Line chart

Individual analysis lines within the graphs are added to the visual as another EVALUATE within the DAX query. The more dynamic reference lines are used, the more instances of EVALUATE must be applied, as shown in Figure 4-9.

```
1   DEFINE
2       VAR __DS0Core =
3           SUMMARIZECOLUMNS('Sales'[Date], "v__Revenue", 'Measure'[# Revenue])
4
5       VAR __DS0IntersectionCount = CALCULATE(COUNTROWS(__DS0Core))
6
7       VAR __DS0BodyBinnedSample =
8           SAMPLEAXISWITHLOCALMINMAX(3500, __DS0Core, 'Sales'[Date], [v__Revenue], 350, , ALPHABETICAL, ASC, 10500C, 60)
9
10  EVALUATE
11      ROW(
12          "DS0IntersectionCount", __DS0IntersectionCount
13      )
14
15  EVALUATE
16      GROUPBY(__DS0Core, "Averagev__Revenue", AVERAGEX(CURRENTGROUP(), [v__Revenue]))
17
18  EVALUATE
19      __DS0BodyBinnedSample
```

FIGURE 4-9 Example DAX code executed by Line chart with Average line and Forecast line

Two dynamic reference lines are used in this example:

- **Forecast** The SAMPLEAXISWITHLOCALMINMAX() function creates the content for __DSOBody-BinnedSample, which is evaluated to create the Forecast line. This name can be different in case of more lines.

- **Average** The GROUPBY() function calculates this line and the values for it.

NEED MORE REVIEW? **ANALYTICS PANE AND DYNAMIC REFERENCE LINES**

For details about the Analytics pane and dynamic reference lines, please visit *learn.microsoft.com/power-bi/transform-model/desktop-analytics-pane*.

Once you know what the future might look like, you and your colleagues must identify the steps you can take to get there. Prescriptive analytics can help businesses understand the best steps to achieve a desired goal, consider the likelihood of worst-case outcomes, and manage uncertainty. Using Power BI, in combination with visuals that can be used for diagnostic analytics, you can identify what influences that potential future and possible results. By identifying these inputs, you can, for example, prepare what-if scenarios to simulate various changes or developments within the data to help you identify which steps to take next.

What-if scenarios can take a various forms. The usable data for these analyses can be prepared in advance (especially for categorical values), and the individual choices can be incorporated into DAX calculations. In the same way, use the option **New parameter** > **Numeric range** in Power BI Desktop on the **Modeling** tab. After selecting this option, a new window will appear (Figure 4-10).

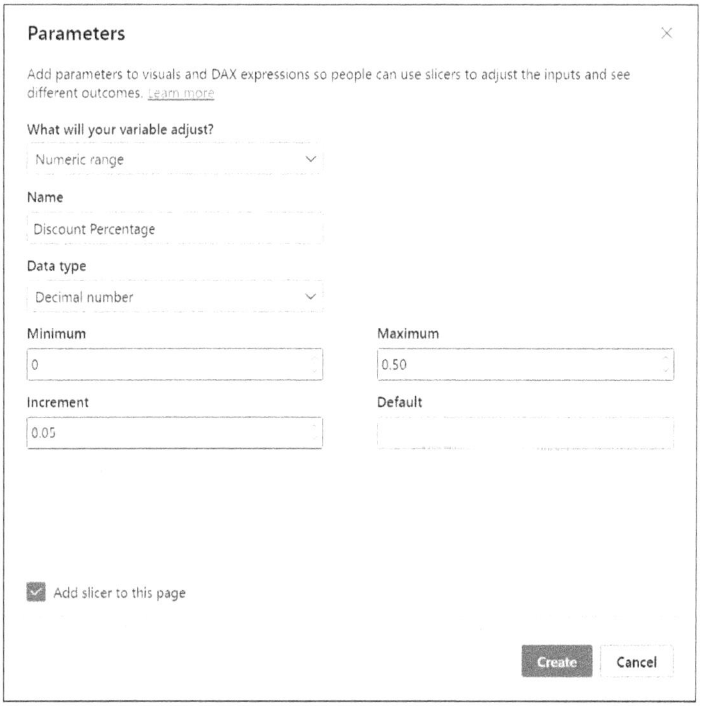

FIGURE 4-10 Numeric what-if parameter

You can then insert your parameter into your calculations as a global modifier of the entire calculation based on the identified scenario and need. This parameter must be capable of creating multiple values, which it creates using the DAX function GENERATESERIES(). If it creates more than 1,000 values, these values will be evenly sampled when used.

Profile data

The *data profiling process* focuses on data analysis from a descriptive level and is intended to help you and your colleagues understand how the data is structured and how to maintain its quality. This process is crucial for data warehousing, business intelligence, and big data projects, as it evaluates incoming data based on such factors as accuracy, consistency (see the "Implement a data cleansing process" in Chapter 2, "Prepare and serve data"), and timeliness. Thanks to this, it is possible to identify whether there are values in the data that can lead to wrong or misleading results. Similarly, data profiling helps to identify missing data in individual columns.

The outputs of data profiling may vary depending on the data examined and the requirements that have been defined. The output obtained from data profiling must be beneficial for further data processing and cleaning. For that reason, the outputs are usually the following:

- **Data statistics** Summary statistics for each column, including mean, median, minimum, maximum, and standard deviation
- **Data distribution** Understanding the distribution of values within columns (for example, histograms, frequency counts)
- **Data completeness** Identifying missing values and assessing their impact on data quality
- **Data pattern** Detecting patterns, anomalies, and outliers
- **Data relationships** Analyzing relationships between columns (such as correlations)

These outputs help to get a comprehensive picture of the data under investigation. But not all of them are always used. Statistics, distribution, and completeness can sometimes be enough for the user.

Microsoft Fabric enables data profiling to be done in multiple places so that you can choose the tool closest to you that is best understood. Each tool has its advantages and disadvantages, of course. For example, within the framework of PySpark Notebook, you can get all the answers you need in one environment and even with a visual form—but you have to understand the language in question. Within Power Query, you can get almost all the answers, but to view them in graphical form, you have to use, for example, **Report** or the **Explore** function. Similarly, you can use SQL to prepare queries that can provide similar outputs.

> **NOTE** **SAMPLE DATASET**
>
> For the following examples, the sample data in the default lakehouse is from the NYC Taxi – Green dataset. To deploy a dataset, use the Copy Data activity in Pipeline, selecting **Copy Data > Source > Sample dataset**.

Data statistics

When performing profiling using notebooks, you can use any library you need, and the functions prepared for these analyses can also serve you. For investigating *data statistics*, you could try such functions as:

- `dtypes()` Returns all column names and their data types as a list (Figure 4-11). The resulting DataFrame can be stored in a new variable for more transformations.

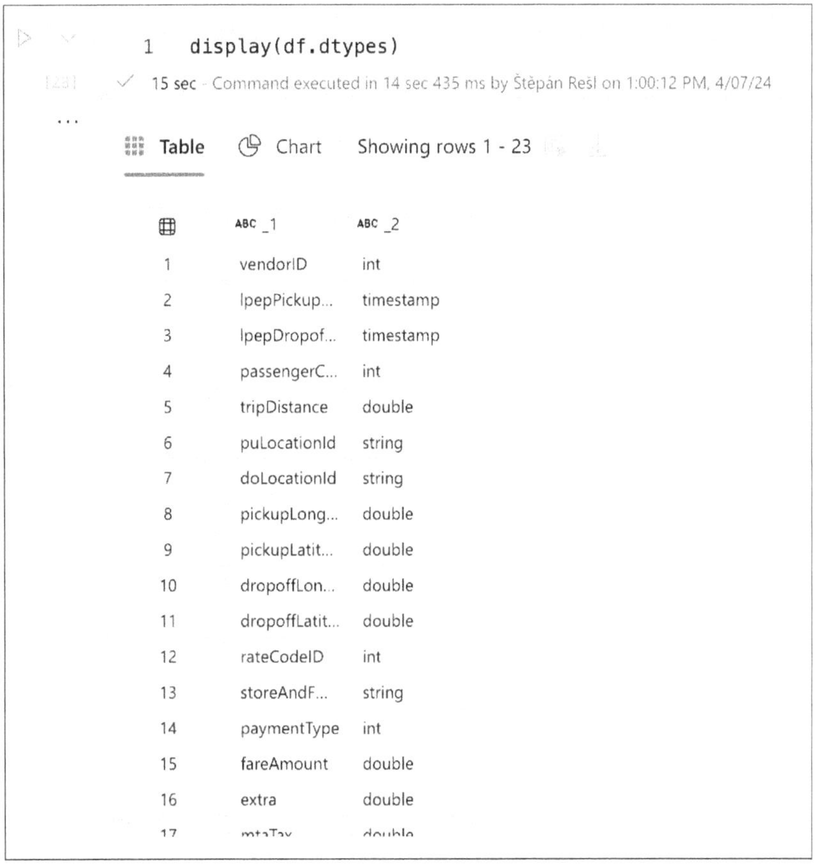

	ABC _1	ABC _2
1	vendorID	int
2	lpepPickup...	timestamp
3	lpepDropof...	timestamp
4	passengerC...	int
5	tripDistance	double
6	puLocationId	string
7	doLocationId	string
8	pickupLong...	double
9	pickupLatit...	double
10	dropoffLon...	double
11	dropoffLatit...	double
12	rateCodeID	int
13	storeAndF...	string
14	paymentType	int
15	fareAmount	double
16	extra	double
17	mtaTax	double

FIGURE 4-11 Returned data types of all columns in an original DataFrame as a new DataFrame

- `summary()` Computes specified statistics for numeric and string columns. If no statistics are given, it computes count, mean, stddev, min, approximate quartiles (percentiles at 25%, 50%, and 75%), and max. For a summary preview, see Figure 4-12.

These two functions provide a basic statistical overview of the data. In particular, `summary()` allows you to determine whether any column is an outlier within its data compared to others or contains extremes and errors with a high degree of probability. Figure 4-13 provides a summary of the DataFrame.

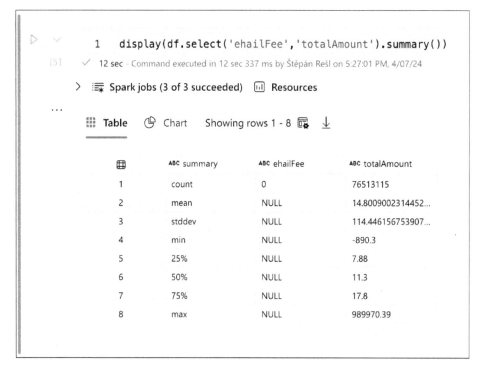

```
1  display(df.summary())
```
Command executed in 5 min 5 sec 163 ms by Štěpán Rešl on 12:43:58 PM, 4/07/24   PySpark (Python)

Table   Chart   Showing rows 1 - 8   ↓

	ABC summary	ABC vendorID	ABC passengerCount	ABC tripDistance	ABC puLocationId	ABC doLocationId	ABC pickupLon
1	count	76513115	76513115	76513115	31213508	31213508	45299607
2	mean	1.7957817035680745	1.3779691756112662	2.905867790639101	111.90426599919496	129.0887732324095	-73.81625
3	stddev	0.4031292422516117	1.059323547364562	3.2277740291321297	75.30006041381317	77.071326746807	2.9625361
4	min	1	0	0.0	1	1	-122.3996
5	25%	2	1	1.05	49.0	61.0	-73.95878
6	50%	2	1	1.9	82.0	129.0	-73.94460
7	75%	2	1	3.62	166.0	193.0	-73.91581
8	max	2	9	8005.88	99	99	73.937637

FIGURE 4-12 Return of summary() function

```
1  display(df.select('ehailFee','totalAmount').summary())
```
12 sec - Command executed in 12 sec 337 ms by Štěpán Rešl on 5:27:01 PM, 4/07/24

> ⥥ Spark jobs (3 of 3 succeeded)   Resources

...

Table   Chart   Showing rows 1 - 8   ↓

	ABC summary	ABC ehailFee	ABC totalAmount
1	count	0	76513115
2	mean	NULL	14.8009002314452...
3	stddev	NULL	114.446156753907...
4	min	NULL	-890.3
5	25%	NULL	7.88
6	50%	NULL	11.3
7	75%	NULL	17.8
8	max	NULL	989970.39

FIGURE 4-13 Specified summary for two columns

It follows from the figure that the ehailFee column does not contain any value because the number of values in it is equal to 0, and all statistical operations returned a null value. On the contrary, the totalAmount column contains 76,513,115 values, and their median or 50% percentile is equal to 11.3. The standard deviation states how far the individual values are spread around their arithmetic mean on average, and in this example, the dispersion is quite large, which is possible but might raise a question in your mind. When you consider the maximum value in the context of the other values, you can be assured that the ehailFee column contains some outliers and possibly extremes. Check such data to determine whether the suspect values could be possible. For example, a very long taxi ride would have a very high fee, but a 989,970.39 fee for a .18 ride would not be justified—especially when you see in the next row that a longer distance is paired with a lower fee (Figure 4-14)! Likewise, a minimum value of −890.3 is suspect; the passenger must have paid the taxi driver a fee, which would be a positive number. You will, therefore, need to either remove these values from the data or solve a repair or replacement and find out how they came about.

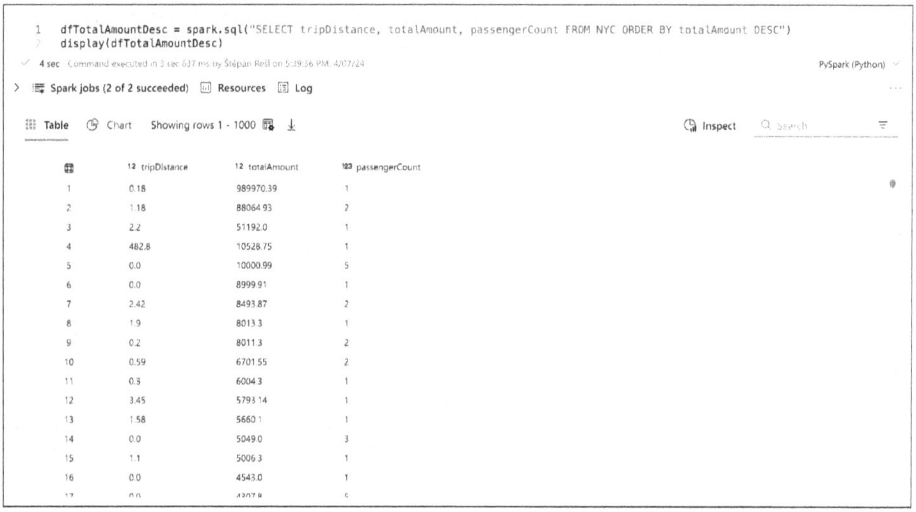

FIGURE 4-14 Showing data extracted with specific Order from the source

You can perform a similar examination Power Query using the `Table.Profile()` and `Table.Schema()` functions. `Table.Schema()` returns the embedded table's schema, providing an overview of the columns and their data types. Within a lakehouse, however, the `Table.Profile()` function can cause a potential error if a column has data with the `datetime` data type in it. From the point of view of the SQL endpoint, this is stored as `datetime2`. The `Table.Profile()` function tries to query the data source, and then tries to convert this data type to `float`. To avoid this error, you must also use the `Table.StopFolding()` function (Figure 4-15), which causes all the data to be loaded into Power Query before profiling is performed on it. This approach may not always be desirable because of its high resource demands; therefore, determine in advance how much data is needed for profiling or use this approach on a minor data source only. The `Table.Profile()` function executes its profiling function based on this data type of columns. Only Count and NullCount are executed on type ANY/GENERAL.

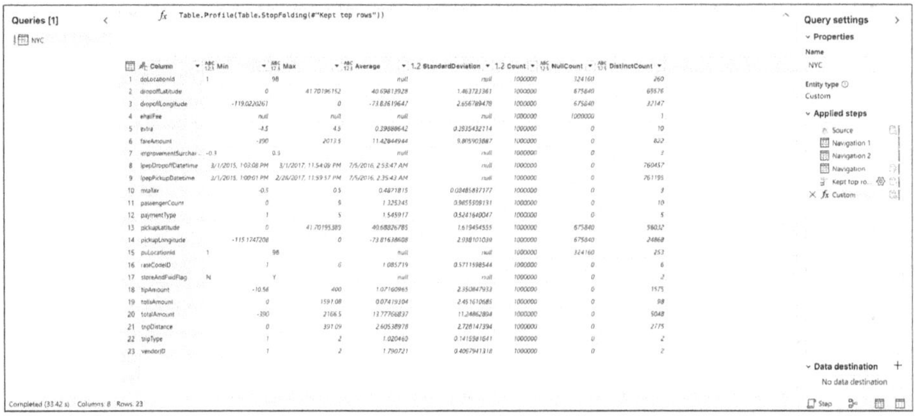

FIGURE 4-15 `Table.Profile()` in Power Query with applied `Table.StopFolding()`

Data distribution

You and your colleagues can also investigate *data distribution*. The notebook offers a relatively large set of options to do so. Your choice depends on the size of the DataFrame that you want to examine or whether you need to work with the data as a whole. Visual form, such as a Histogram or Box and Whisker chart, mainly shows data distribution in a given column. You can display either of these visuals immediately after using the `display()` function because the rendered UI provides the **Chart** option. With it, you can choose a specific type of chart and set what you want to see in it according to the rendered data frame. A fundamental view is created based on the first 1,000 rows in the DataFrame, but you can increase this setting up to 10,000. Some graphs also support the **Aggregating overall results** option, as you can see in the right part of Figure 4-16 in the **Customize chart** section.

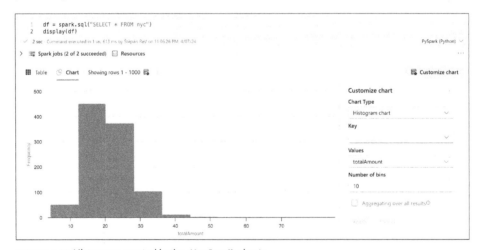

FIGURE 4-16 Histogram created in the `display()` charts

You might need to create this for all columns, however, to obtain a complete data view. Another option is to use the `Inspect` function, provided by the `display()` function from the

Table environment. The Inspect function is based purely on the preview set of the first 1,000 lines with the option to set up to 10,000 lines. The advantage of this view is that it is created automatically for all columns, so you can review the results without the necessity of defining these histograms for every column separately. At the same time above rendered charts, you receive basic information about the completeness of the data (Missing, Unique, Invalid), as previewed in Figure 4-17.

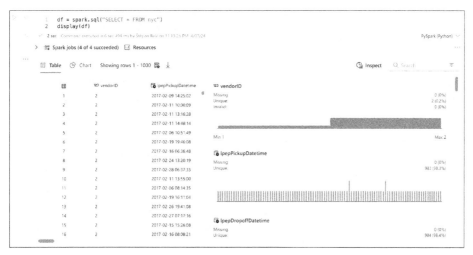

FIGURE 4-17 The Inspect() function and its results

A third option to try is **Data Wrangler**. After it loads the data into itself, it starts rendering column statistics under the column's name. Data Wrangler can use pandas or PySpark DataFrames. PySpark frames convert the columns into pandas and show pandas codes in the preview. Then, if it is possible to translate it into PySpark, the code is deployed into the notebook as a PySpark code. The default distribution of values represents the first 5,000 rows, or you can choose a custom sample size (Figure 4-18).

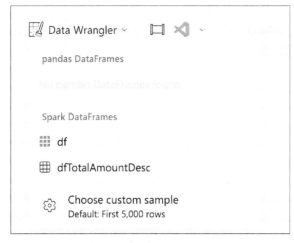

FIGURE 4-18 DataFrame selection

If you select one of the columns, you can see its statistics (Figure 4-19).

Summary	totalAmount	⌄
Data type		float64
Rows		5.000
Distinct values		106
Missing values		0
⌄ Statistics		
Mean		12.98271
Standard deviation		5.63863240431385
Minimum		4.3
25th percentile		9.8
Median		11.8
75th percentile		15.3
Maximum		75.3
⌄ Advanced Statistics		
Kurtosis		6.626827154692587
Skew		1.736401850927787

FIGURE 4-19 Column summary in Data Wrangler

You can create and display graphs using a large number of libraries, as well. One such example is the **MatplotLib** library, which provides you with **Histograms, Box plots, Violin plots,** and other graphs to use in data distribution research. Figure 4-20 shows a preview of the histogram and its required code.

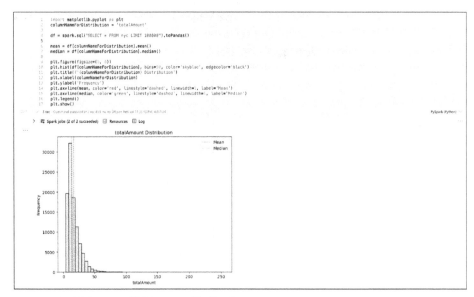

FIGURE 4-20 Histogram with Mean and Median line

Again, with this method you would have to individually examine each column (Figure 4-21). Alternatively, you could modify the code to display a histogram for each nonempty column in the DataFrame.

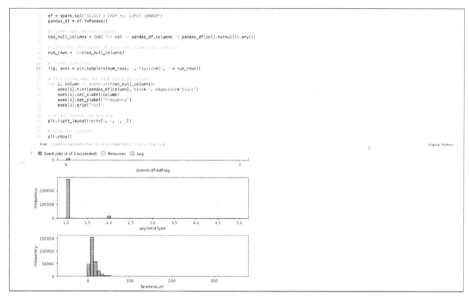

FIGURE 4-21 Multicolumn histogram

NEED MORE REVIEW? **MATPLOTLIB**

For details about MatplotLib, please visit *matplotlib.org*.

Within Power Query, you can take advantage of similar features as found in Data Wrangler, such as Column Value distribution. First, however, you must turn this on by selecting **View tab** > **Data view** > **Show column value distribution** (Figure 4-22).

Data completeness

Data completeness is another beneficial quantity that helps identify the state of the data being examined. Getting completeness-related answers within Power Query is straightforward because the result of the `Table.Profile()` function contains both `Count` and `NullCount`. So, getting an overview of whether the data is complete in all columns is straightforward if they are indeed null values. They will not be included in NullCount here if they are blank string values. It is necessary to slightly expand this function thanks to the second input parameter, which allows you to define your own rules for profiling as you can see in Figure 4-23.

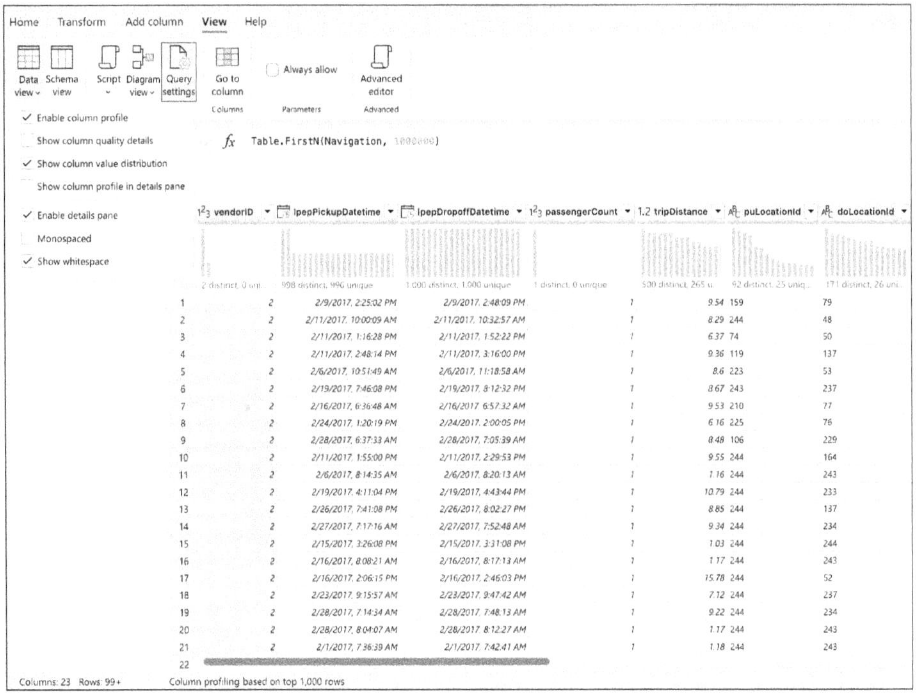

FIGURE 4-22 Column distribution in Power Query and Power Query Online

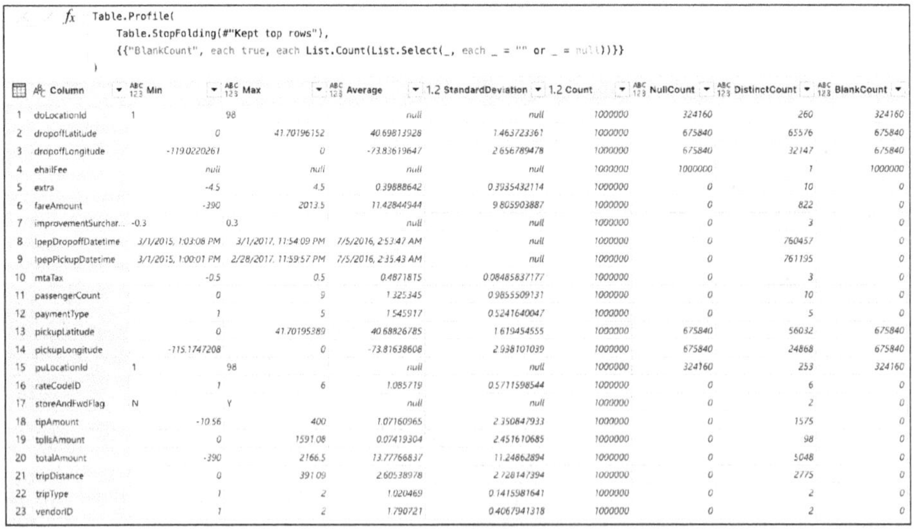

```
Table.Profile(
    Table.StopFolding(#"Kept top rows"),
    {{"BlankCount", each true, each List.Count(List.Select(_, each _ = "" or _ = null))}}
)
```

	Column	Min	Max	Average	StandardDeviation	Count	NullCount	DistinctCount	BlankCount
1	doLocationId	1	98	null	null	1000000	324160	260	324160
2	dropoffLatitude	0	41.70196152	40.69813928	1.463723361	1000000	675840	65576	675840
3	dropoffLongitude	-119.0220261	0	-73.83619647	2.656789478	1000000	675840	32147	675840
4	ehailFee	null	null	null	null	1000000	1000000	1	1000000
5	extra	-4.5	4.5	0.39888642	0.3935432114	1000000	0	10	0
6	fareAmount	-390	2013.5	11.42844944	9.805903887	1000000	0	822	0
7	improvementSurchar...	-0.3	0.3	null	null	1000000	0	3	0
8	lpepDropoffDatetime	3/1/2015, 1:03:08 PM	3/1/2017, 11:54:09 PM	7/5/2016, 2:53:47 AM	null	1000000	0	760457	0
9	lpepPickupDatetime	3/1/2015, 1:00:01 PM	2/28/2017, 11:59:57 PM	7/5/2016, 2:35:43 AM	null	1000000	0	761195	0
10	mtaTax	-0.5	0.5	0.4871815	0.08485837177	1000000	0	3	0
11	passengerCount	0	9	1.325345	0.9855509131	1000000	0	10	0
12	paymentType	1	5	1.545917	0.5241640047	1000000	0	5	0
13	pickupLatitude	0	41.70195389	40.68826785	1.619454555	1000000	675840	56032	675840
14	pickupLongitude	-115.1747208	0	-73.81638608	2.938101039	1000000	675840	24868	675840
15	puLocationId	1	98	null	null	1000000	324160	253	324160
16	rateCodeID	1	6	1.085719	0.5711598544	1000000	0	6	0
17	storeAndFwdFlag	N	Y	null	null	1000000	0	2	0
18	tipAmount	-10.56	400	1.07160965	2.350847933	1000000	0	1575	0
19	tollsAmount	0	1591.08	0.07419304	2.451610685	1000000	0	98	0
20	totalAmount	-390	2166.5	13.77766837	11.24862894	1000000	0	5048	0
21	tripDistance	0	391.09	2.60538978	2.728147394	1000000	0	2775	0
22	tripType	1	2	1.020469	0.1415981641	1000000	0	2	0
23	vendorID	1	2	1.790721	0.4067941318	1000000	0	2	0

FIGURE 4-23 Extended `Table.Profile()` function with additional parameter

Within the notebook, you can use either the `Inspect()` option within the `display()` function or Data Wrangler, which writes Missing and Distinct counts under the column name.

A third option is to use the `isnull()` calculation that can be done within the pandas frame. This function returns TRUE or FALSE, assuming the value is empty. You must summarize them to see which column contains empty values (Figure 4-24).

```
1    dfPandas = spark.sql("SELECT * FROM nyc LIMIT 10000000").toPandas()
2    dfPandas.isnull().sum()
```

✓ 1 min 8 sec Apache Spark session ready in 10 sec 250 ms. Command executed in 57 sec 691 ms by Štěpán Rešl on 12:36:48 AM, 4/08/24

> ≣ Spark jobs (6 of 6 succeeded)   Resources   Log

```
vendorID                    0
lpepPickupDatetime          0
lpepDropoffDatetime         0
passengerCount              0
tripDistance                0
puLocationId          7074548
doLocationId          7074548
pickupLongitude       2925452
pickupLatitude        2925452
dropoffLongitude      2925452
dropoffLatitude       2925452
rateCodeID                  0
storeAndFwdFlag             0
paymentType                 0
fareAmount                  0
extra                       0
mtaTax                      0
improvementSurcharge   602559
tipAmount                   0
tollsAmount                 0
ehailFee             10000000
totalAmount                 0
tripType               602570
dtype: int64
```

FIGURE 4-24 A pandas solution to receive a count of blank rows in columns

In addition to this option, you can use the extension parameter of the `display()` function, which supports the display of tables and graphs. If the function is extended by the `summary=True` parameter, it will display the individual columns of the DataFrame, their data types, and the number of unique and missing values. In addition, when a column is selected, it also shows a basic overview of individual columns (Figure 4-25).

FIGURE 4-25 The `display()` function using the parameter `summary=True`

Data pattern

Within the *data pattern* aspect of data profiling, the Box plot is a great helper because it shows outliers and extremes. Outliers are values 1.5 times greater than the 75% percentile or 1.5 times less than the 25% percentile. Extremes are values three times greater or less than the mentioned percentiles. In Figure 4-26 the extremes are exceptionally far from other data, so it is tough to read the rest of the Box plot.

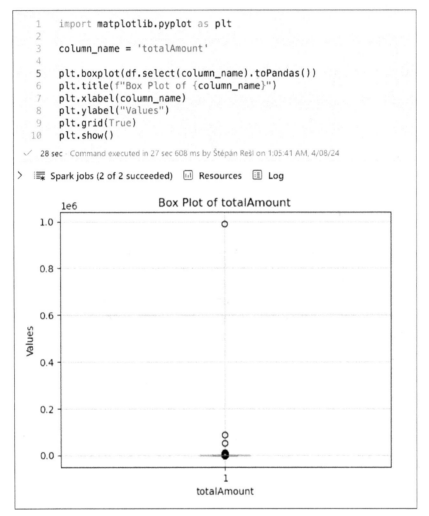

```
1   import matplotlib.pyplot as plt
2
3   column_name = 'totalAmount'
4
5   plt.boxplot(df.select(column_name).toPandas())
6   plt.title(f"Box Plot of {column_name}")
7   plt.xlabel(column_name)
8   plt.ylabel("Values")
9   plt.grid(True)
10  plt.show()
```

✓ 28 sec · Command executed in 27 sec 608 ms by Štěpán Rešl on 1:05:41 AM, 4/08/24

> ▦ Spark jobs (2 of 2 succeeded) ⅢⅠ Resources ▤ Log

FIGURE 4-26 Box plot with very high extreme

This view helps you identify whether such data is in your DataFrame. If so, you can let them list and possibly remove them.

Data relationships

The last part of data profiling is *data relationships*. Here, the correlation between individual columns is sought. For this, you can use the pandas function `corr()`. This function computes the pairwise correlation of columns, excluding NA/null values, and supports Pearson, Kendall, and Spearman's correlation methods. The results of this function can be displayed directly or subsequently using a heat map to make it easier for you to read the output. With this function, the closer the number is to 1, the higher the correlation between the given columns, while –1 indicates a perfect negative linear correlation. As one variable increases, the other variable decreases. A value of 0 indicates no linear correlation. The two variables do not have a relationship with each other, as you can see in Figure 4-27.

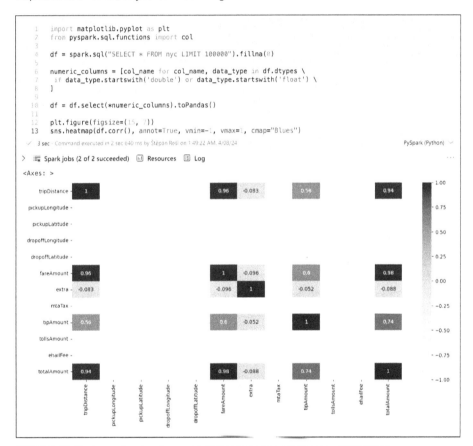

FIGURE 4-27 Heat map for showing a correlation between columns in a DataFrame

Skill 4.2: Query data by using SQL

Lakehouses and warehouses allow access to their data through their SQL endpoints. However, you can decide whether to query the data directly using SQL or visual queries. You can perform the query using whichever form is the most pleasant for you.

This skill covers how to:

■ Query a lakehouse in Fabric using SQL queries or the visual query editor

■ Query a warehouse in Fabric using SQL queries or the visual query editor

■ Connect to and query datasets using the XMLA endpoint

Query a lakehouse in Fabric using SQL queries or the visual query editor

The ability to run queries against data in Lakehouse Explorer is primarily aimed at analytical queries on data that is not yet in its final form for reporting. Through these queries, you can examine what is in the data, determine whether it can be connected, prepare reports for subsequent use, and quickly find answers to your current questions.

SQL queries

Data that resides within the Lakehouse framework in the Tables folder is accessible within the lakehouse SQL analytic endpoint. You can access the data by connecting to the SQL analytic endpoint using Azure Data Studio or SQL Management Studio, or by performing T-SQL queries directly in the lakehouse environment using SQL or visual queries.

Some queries might require data from more than one lakehouse and can combine data from multiple lakehouses in the same workspace simultaneously. All lakehouses and warehouses in a workspace can get data from each other because the workspace acts as a server, and items are stored in separate databases inside this server.

SQL queries created directly in SQL analytic endpoint behave similarly to PySpark Notebook queries. However, constantly creating new shortcuts to ensure answers is optional, because you can just ask directly for the available data.

To query the default lakehouse and its data without further specifications, use the syntax:

… FROM <nameOfTable> …

If you need data from another lakehouse, then use the syntax:

… FROM <lakehouseName>.<schemaName>.<nameOfTable> …

Figure 4-28 shows a sample query and its results.

> **NOTE SAMPLE DATASETS**
>
> For the following examples, the sample data in the default lakehouse are from the Public dataset. Data in the NYC lakehouse are from the sample NYC Taxi – Green dataset.
> To deploy either dataset, use the Copy Data activity in Pipeline, selecting **Copy Data** > **Source** > **Sample dataset**.

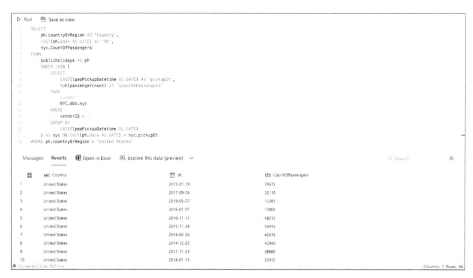

FIGURE 4-28 Querying data from a lakehouse

Figure 4-29 demonstrates a query written to simultaneously use data from multiple lakehouses. Note the use of GROUP BY to cluster an external table and connect the results to the table from the default environment.

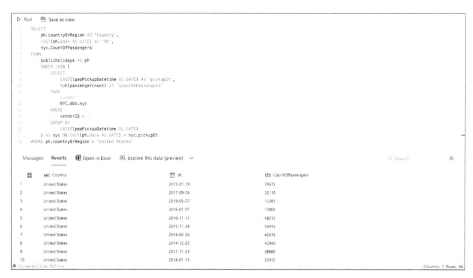

FIGURE 4-29 Multi-lakehouse query

If Figure 4-29's code were transferred to another lakehouse, such as the NYC lakehouse, it wouldn't run because the default tables would be different and the publicholidays table would most likely not be among them. Therefore, defining the source for each table in your queries is a good idea. In the example code, for instance, you could simply specify `pbh.dbo.publicholi-days` instead of `publicholidays`. So, if there were a lakehouse named pbh and the given table, the query would run this query. Lakehouse can also query data stored within warehouses in the same way.

NEED MORE REVIEW? **GROUP BY**

For details about GROUP BY, please visit *learn.microsoft.com/sql/t-sql/queries/select-group-by-transact-sql?view=fabric*.

Within the SQL query editor, many commonly used options, such as subqueries or Common Table Expression (CTE), are possible and are defined using the WITH clause. Thanks to this function, you can, for example, rank individual countries very straightforwardly based on how many public holidays exist in the given countries and how much time is paid within them, as shown in Figure 4-30.

FIGURE 4-30 Common Table Expression

Within Lakehouse Explorer, the output from such a query can be used within SELECT and CREATE VIEW. SQL's CREATE TABLE is unavailable; see the discussion in the "Enrich data by adding new columns or tables" section of Chapter 2, "Prepare and serve data."

NEED MORE REVIEW? **WITH <COMMON_TABLE_EXPRESSION>**

For details about WITH, please visit *learn.microsoft.com/sql/t-sql/queries/with-common-table-expression-transact-sql?view=fabric*.

Visual query editor

In addition to creating queries using T-SQL, you can use the **visual query editor**. Initially, it is empty and waits for at least one table to be inserted (Figure 4-31).

FIGURE 4-31 Default canvas of the visual query editor

The visual query editor uses **Power Query Online** with a slightly modified display that provides operations that can be translated into the native language of the given data source through query folding. The individual operations that you perform in the visual query editor will be translated into T-SQL, which you then can view and possibly copy for further use. Individual operations or steps from the Power Query perspective are not presented using the usual **Query Settings** on the right side of the screen. They are primarily aimed at using **Diagram view** (Figure 4-32). You can insert multiple tables into the diagram, so they then can be used as part of Merge or Append operations.

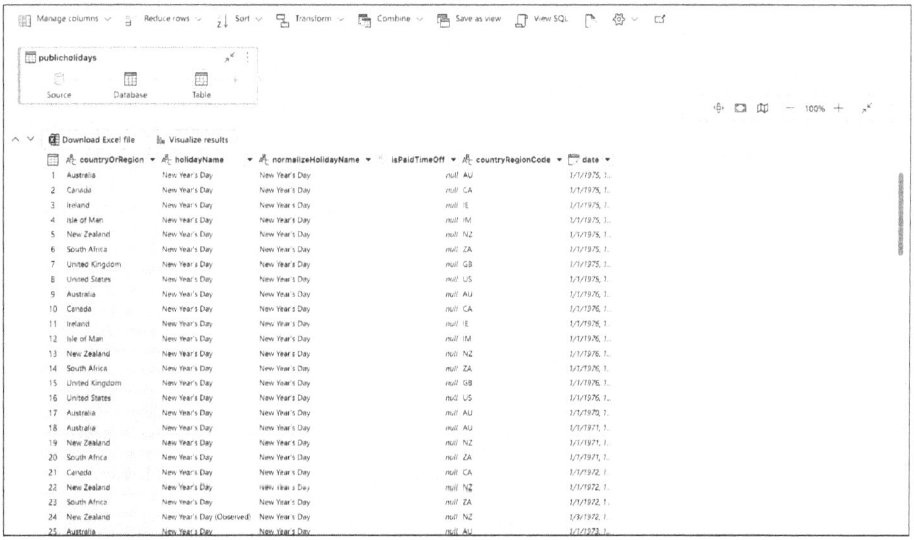

![Preview of data after every transformation]

FIGURE 4-32 Preview of data after every transformation

In addition to the basic operations provided by the toolbar of buttons above the diagram, you can use expected behaviors in Power Query. In other words, you can perform operations directly within the UI columns, such as removing columns in Manage columns and so on.

Click a column's data type to change it, for example, or double-click a column's name to change that. Selecting the arrow next to a column's name expands a menu of choices for filtering the content. Each operation you choose appears in the diagram above the data (Figure 4-33). The diagram's icons work similarly to steps: You can click an icon to return to that step and then view its results, change the step, or add a new step after it.

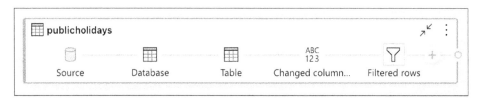

FIGURE 4-33 Diagram of transformations

To preview the T-SQL code your diagrammed query translates into, select the **View SQL** button (either above the diagram or by first selecting the **ellipsis** icon next to the name of the desired visual query). Figure 4-34 shows the result for Figure 4-33's query.

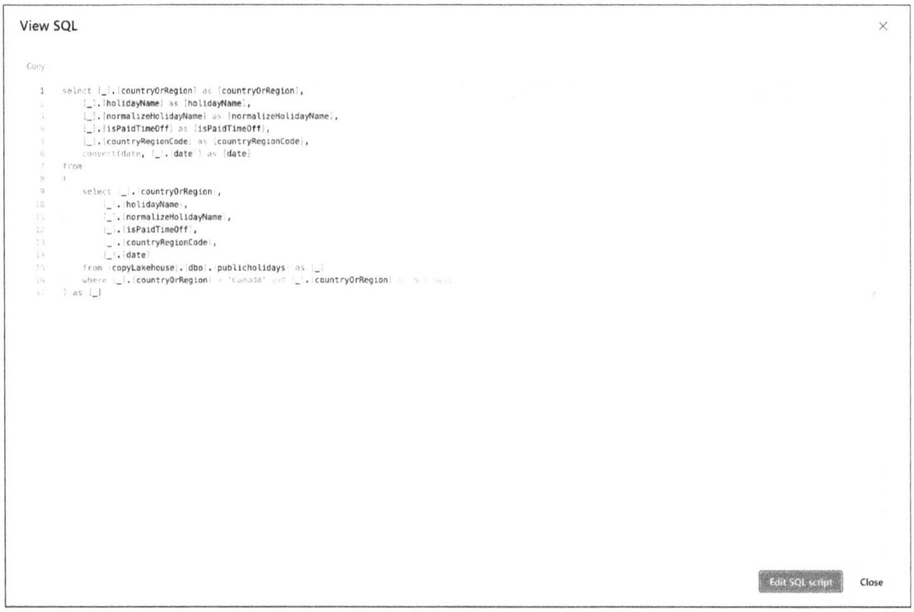

FIGURE 4-34 SQL preview of transformations created in the visual query editor for Figure 4-33

The SQL preview allows you to check and edit the created code. When you edit the SQL script, a new SQL view containing the newly edited code will be created.

A handy feature of the visual query editor is that you can turn on the fundamental overview options that Power Query typically provides:

- Column Quality
- Value Distribution

- Column Profile
- Column Profile in the Details pane

With these, you can quickly overview your data to determine whether it is in order and confirm the most recent operation did not cause a problem (Figure 4-35). Keep in mind, however, that all data profiling is based on the first 1,000 rows only. If you need more, then the best option is to use the `Table.Profile()` function.

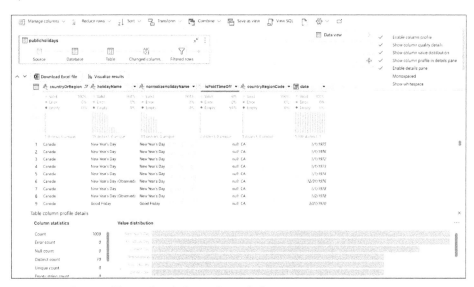

FIGURE 4-35 Data profiling options in Power Query Online

If you need more operations, you can open the entire Power Query Online environment by selecting the **query level context menu** (the three veritical dots) in the diagram's top-right corner. Be aware, however, that some of the operations are not translatable into T-SQL. Although you'll be able to see their results in Power Query, the creation of the SQL script will stop and None will be returned, as shown in Figure 4-36.

FIGURE 4-36 Returned SQL code for non-folded visual query

Because it is a full-fledged Power Query Online experience, you can connect several data types, including those outside of lakehouse, for analysis or subsequent export to a **PQT** (**Power Query template**) file that can be used within **DataFlows Gen2**, **Excel**, or **Dataflows** within **Dataverse**.

If the you were to connect data that is not ordinarily connectable or perform an operation that cannot be translated, after returning to the visual query editor, you would be notified that the newly connected data source cannot be loaded because it has missing or invalid accesses (even if it worked in the complete Power Query experience). In the case of an invalid operation, you'll be informed that the given table or query is not supported within the SQL analytics endpoint (Figure 4-37).

FIGURE 4-37 Errors returned by the visual query editor

Query a warehouse in Fabric using SQL queries or the visual query editor

Querying data within warehouses is possible via SQL and the visual query editor, just like with lakehouses. Unlike lakehouses, however, warehouses give T-SQL users complete control over the data. For example, you can create new tables using T-SQL. In addition, warehouses support INSERT, UPDATE, and DELETE queries and **row-level security (RLS), column-level security (CLS), object-level security (OLS)**, and **dynamic data masking** within their data when all queries made to the warehouse are possibly affected by these rules.

In contrast to lakehouses, warehouses do not support the *creation* of shortcuts, which limits them in terms of not duplicating data already in OneLake. However, you can query data stored within other warehouses or lakehouses. Assuming that a given lakehouse has a shortcut and both it and the warehouse are in the same workspace, the warehouse can query that shortcut and use the data from it. In addition to querying data from other data items within the workspace, the warehouse can perform INSERT, UPDATE, and DELETE operations in that data. You can prepare queries for colleagues, which Warehouse Explorer provides as data-mediated views from another repository or as full-fledged tables into which the warehouse transfers data using INSERT INTO. To clear the data from the warehouse table so it is ready for the full load of new data from the lakehouse, use syntax like this:

```
DELETE FROM <warehouseName>.<schemaName>.<warehouseTableName>;
INSERT INTO <warehouseName>.<schemaName>.<warehouseTableName>
SELECT * FROM <lakehouseName>.<schemaName>.<lakehouseTableName>
```

Because TRUNCATE is not supported, the snippet uses DELETE. Remember that * is used so that all columns will be loaded. So, if someone changes the columns in Lakehouse Explorer but still needs to change the schema in Warehouse Explorer, the users can get into an error. To avoid this, define the columns to be used. You can use the above code as a stored procedure and run it using a pipeline.

Of course, this entry is valid only after the table has been created within the warehouse. If it doesn't exist yet, it needs to be created. The CREATE TABLE … AS … procedure is useful here, because it enables you to create tables based on another query. In this way, it is possible to query, for example, a lakehouse from a warehouse and create a table from the obtained values. This procedure can help you greatly if you know that the current state of the obtained data is precisely what you need for the newly created table, as in Figure 4-38.

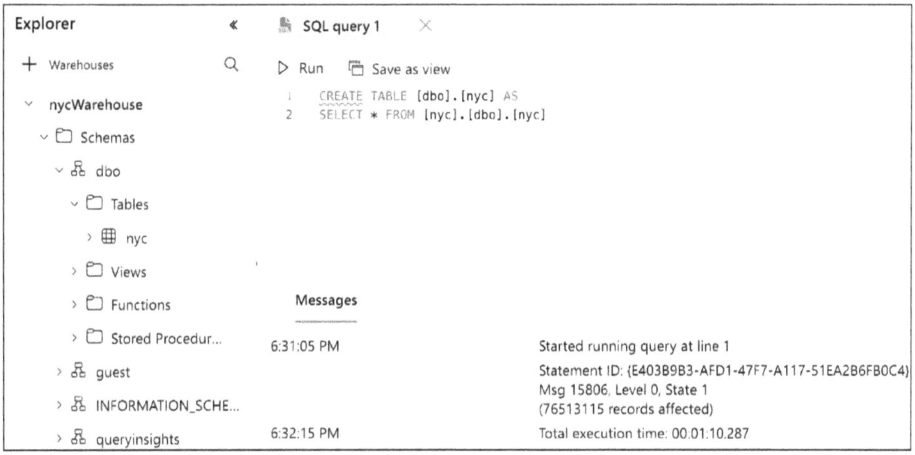

FIGURE 4-38 The CREATE TABLE … AS … procedure

The code creates the table, and then immediately transfers the data in the SELECT query. The warehouse allows you to use the usual options, such as those within **SQL Management Studio**. These options, shown in Figure 4-39, allow you to ask a quick query on the top 100 rows of the table, create a script that creates, drops, and then re-creates it, and so on.

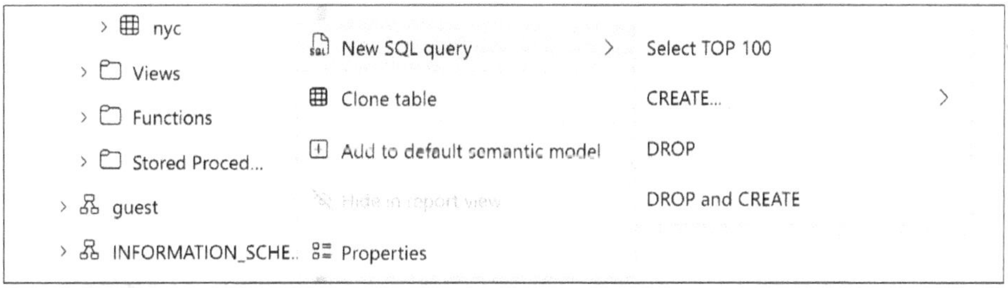

FIGURE 4-39 Option in New SQL Query

Even though Warehouse Explorer supports CREATE, DROP, DELETE, and so on, you will often find applications for conditional queries within its queries. Conditional queries test whether a specific object exists or contains a specific value, and then perform different actions depending on what it determines. The conditional query in Figure 4-40, for example, checks if the People table exists. If it does, the query deletes it and then re-creates it. If the table does not exist, the query will just create it.

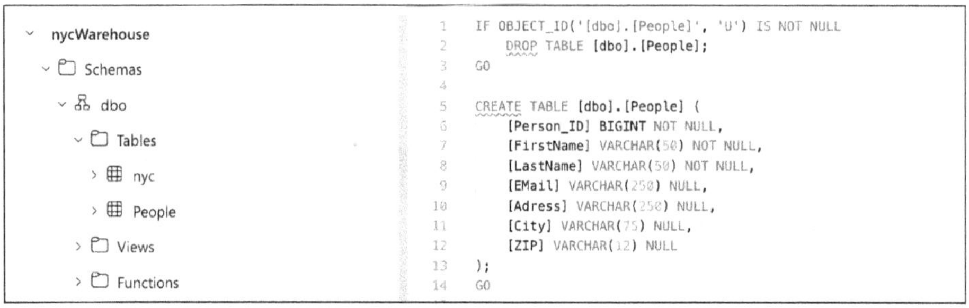

```
1   IF OBJECT_ID('[dbo].[People]', 'U') IS NOT NULL
2       DROP TABLE [dbo].[People];
3   GO
4
5   CREATE TABLE [dbo].[People] (
6       [Person_ID] BIGINT NOT NULL,
7       [FirstName] VARCHAR(50) NOT NULL,
8       [LastName] VARCHAR(50) NOT NULL,
9       [EMail] VARCHAR(250) NULL,
10      [Adress] VARCHAR(250) NULL,
11      [City] VARCHAR(75) NULL,
12      [ZIP] VARCHAR(12) NULL
13  );
14  GO
```

FIGURE 4-40 Example of a conditional query

NEED MORE REVIEW?   **T-SQL SURFACE AREA LIMITATIONS**

For details about T-SQL surface area limitations, please visit *learn.microsoft.com/fabric/data-warehouse/tsql-surface-area#limitations*.

Visual query editor options in Warehouse Explorer have one significant addition compared to those in Lakehouse Explorer. The difference is that Warehouse Explorer supports saving the prepared data as a view and a table. Note the **Save as table** button on the left in Figure 4-41.

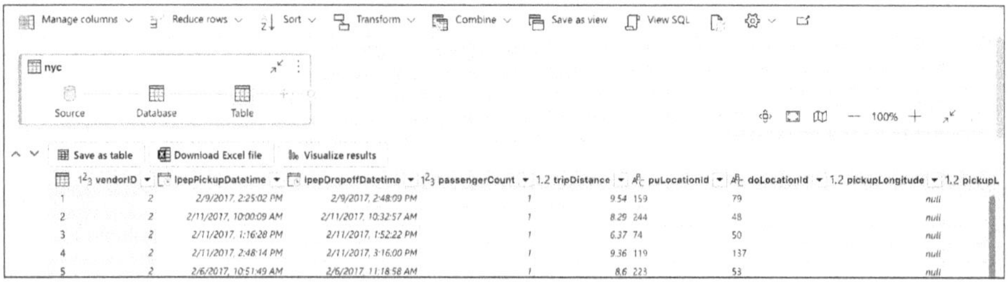

FIGURE 4-41 Visual query editor in the warehouse interface

NEED MORE REVIEW?   **QUERY INSIGHTS**

For details about query insights, please visit *learn.microsoft.com/fabric/data-warehouse/query-insights*.

Connect to and query datasets by using the XMLA endpoint

You can connect to a Power BI semantic model backed by a Premium capacity by using the XMLA endpoint. You can use a Power BI semantic model as a semantic layer and use tools other than Power BI to query your datasets by using the XMLA endpoint. For example, you can use DAX Studio, SQL Server Management Studio (SSMS), Tabular Editor, or ALM Toolkit to connect to a Power BI semantic model.

NOTE **POWER BI PREMIUM CAPACITIES**

In this section, "Premium capacity" loosely refers to datasets in Embedded, Fabric, Premium, and Premium Per User workspaces. You can also connect to datamarts in the same way.

Connect to a dataset

To connect to a Power BI semantic model, use the connection string from the workspace or dataset settings. For example, if your workspace is called Dev Workspace, you can use the following connection string in place of the server address:

`powerbi://api.powerbi.com/v1.0/myorg/Dev%20Workspace`

In case you want to connect to a different tenant where you're a guest, you can replace *myorg* with the domain of the tenant, such as *contoso.com*.

There are several tools you can use to connect to a Power BI semantic model, one of which is DAX Studio, covered in Chapter 3, "Implement and manage semantic models." You can connect to a Power BI semantic model in DAX Studio by performing the following steps:

1. Open DAX Studio.
2. Select **Home** > **Connect**. Figure 4-42 shows the Connect options. If you connected to a workspace before, the **Tabular Server** field may be pre-filled.

FIGURE 4-42 DAX Studio Connect options

3. In **Tabular Server**, enter the workspace connection string.
4. Select **Connect**, and sign in to your account.

Figure 4-43 shows DAX Studio once you connect to a workspace.

You can see the workspace you're connected to at the bottom of the screen. Note how in the **Metadata** pane on the left, you can select the dataset in the workspace if there are multiple datasets. If you wanted to connect to a specific dataset in the first place, you could specify the Initial Catalog option in the Connect Advanced Options.

FIGURE 4-43 DAX Studio connected to a Power BI workspace

Query a dataset

Once you connect to a dataset from a querying tool such a DAX Studio, you can query it. Although DAX is usually used to create calculations, such as measures and calculated columns, you can also write queries by using DAX. DAX queries must return tables, and they differ from calculated tables in the syntax: You'll need to use EVALUATE in front of a table expression. For example, the following DAX query returns a list of state provinces:

```
EVALUATE
VALUES(City[State Province])
```

After you write the query, select **Run** in DAX Studio. Figure 4-44 shows the result of the query.

FIGURE 4-44 DAX Studio showing a list of state provinces

EVALUATE is the only required statement in a DAX query. A DAX query can include multiple EVALUATE statements, and they'll return separate result sets. You can add optional keywords to your DAX queries, as shown next.

DEFINE

In the DEFINE section, you can specify query-level variables, measures, columns, and tables. The following query defines a query-level measure called Total Profit and a query-level column called Country Letter and uses them to show the profit by the first letter of a country:

```
DEFINE
    MEASURE 'Sample'[Total Profit] = SUM('Sample'[Profit])
    COLUMN 'Sample'[Country Letter] = LEFT('Sample'[Country], 1)
EVALUATE
SUMMARIZECOLUMNS(
    'Sample'[Country Letter],
    "Profit", [Total Profit]
)
```

Note that you can override the existing measures by using query-level measures for the duration of the query, but you cannot override the existing columns or tables by using query-level columns or tables. Query-level measures don't affect model measures outside of the query.

When you define a variable in the DEFINE section, there's no need to use RETURN:

```
DEFINE
    MEASURE 'Sample'[Total Profit] = SUM('Sample'[Profit])
    COLUMN 'Sample'[Country Letter] = LEFT('Sample'[Country], 1)
    VAR CountryProfit =
        SUMMARIZECOLUMNS(
        'Sample'[Country Letter],
        "Profit", [Total Profit]
    )
EVALUATE
    CountryProfit
```

While you can have multiple EVALUATE statements in a DAX query, you can only have one DEFINE statement.

ORDER BY

ORDER BY sorts the result table by the specified columns or DAX expressions evaluated in the row context of the result table. In case of columns, they must be part of the result table. The default order is ascending; you can specify ASC or DESC for ascending or descending order, respectively. For example, the following query returns a list of countries sorted in descending order:

```
EVALUATE
VALUES('Sample'[Country])
ORDER BY
'Sample'[Country] DESC
```

Each ORDER BY clause corresponds to its own EVALUATE statement.

START AT

START AT skips all values before the values you specify, the order of which corresponds to the order of columns in the ORDER BY section. You can enter fewer values than there are columns in ORDER BY. For example, the following query returns the list of countries in descending order and their profit, skipping all countries before Mexico:

```
EVALUATE
SUMMARIZECOLUMNS(
    'Sample'[Country],
    "Profit", SUM('Sample'[Profit])
)
ORDER BY
'Sample'[Country] DESC
START AT "Mexico"
```

The values you specify in START AT can be values or parameters. As with ORDER BY, each EVALUATE statement has its own ORDER BY and START AT clauses.

PARAMETERS

If you want to parameterize a query, you can prefix a parameter name with the @ character and use it in a query. For example, the following query filters the list of countries with profit over the user-specified amount:

```
EVALUATE
FILTER(
    SUMMARIZECOLUMNS(
        'Sample'[Country],
        "Profit", SUM('Sample'[Profit])
    ),
    [Profit] > @TargetProfit
)
```

When you run this query in DAX Studio, you'll be prompted to enter the parameter value and select its data type, as shown in Figure 4-45.

FIGURE 4-45 DAX Studio Query Parameters dialog box

Depending on how you run your parameterized queries, you may need to explicitly change the data type of the parameter in the query, as sometimes a parameter may be typed as text. The following query will type the parameter as a number even if it's originally typed as text:

```
EVALUATE
FILTER(
    SUMMARIZECOLUMNS(
        'Sample'[Country],
        "Profit", SUM('Sample'[Profit])
    ),
    [Profit] > CONVERT(@TargetProfit, DOUBLE)
)
```

Parameterized queries can be especially useful with paginated reports in Power BI.

Chapter summary

- Quick summary statistics about DataFrame users can be obtained using the `describe()` function.

- The `display()` function can also render charts based on limited rows, but this limit can be extended, or you can decide to show all the data.

- The **powerbiclient** library contains the function `QuickVisualize`, which can auto-generate Power BI reports from a DataFrame.

- A Line chart in Power BI has an option called **Find Anomalies** that helps you find anomalies in data. If an anomaly is detected, it is presented as a clickable mark in the chart. After you click this mark, the slide window shows a potential explanation of the anomaly.

- The Key Influencer visual is another Power BI chart for diagnostic analytics that can help you identify correlations between your data.

- ML models in Microsoft Fabric use MLflow.

- Already pre-trained models can be called in notebooks by function PREDICT.

- Power BI provides Trend lines and Forecast lines in the Analytics pane that can help you understand how your data will change in the future. Trend lines can be used in Scatter plots and Line charts, while forecasting is available in Line charts only.

- Dynamic reference lines used in a visual are executed as separate EVALUATES.

- What-if parameters can be used for prescriptive analytics but must be assigned to calculations.

- Data statistics can be `types()` and `summary()` in the case of a PySpark, and in the case of a Power Query, they can be `Table.Profile()` and `Table.Schema()`. `Table.Profile()` can be extended with another parameter to add additional profiling rules.

- Histograms, Box plots, and Violin charts are commonly used for data distribution. Many libraries, like **Matplotlib** or native charts in the `display()` function, can create them.

- Lakehouses and warehouses support SQL queries that use CTE or across database queries.
- The visual query editor folds all its steps into SQL, which is directly executed against a lakehouse or warehouse. You can open the full Power Query Online experience and perform transformations or use functions that are not foldable. In that case, you will not be able to use the visual query editor for creating views or tables.
- The table in a warehouse can be created as a CREATE TABLE … AS ….
- Warehouses support row-level security, column-level security, object-level security, and dynamic data masking.
- You can connect to Power BI datasets by using the XMLA endpoint. To query a dataset, you can write queries in DAX.

Thought experiment

In this thought experiment, demonstrate your skills and knowledge of the topics covered in this chapter. The answers are in the section that follows.

You are a Fabric analytics engineer responsible for performing exploratory analytics and querying data by using SQL. Management tasked you with uncovering some insights from the corporate data, which can be done in a Fabric notebook. Based on background information and business requirements, answer the following questions:

1. What will the Return function display when it contains summary=True as a second parameter?

   A. The results are the same as they are without this parameter.

   B. Error.

   C. Individual columns, their data types, and the number of unique and missing values.

   D. The same results are found in the function summary().

2. What patterns are needed to receive data from different lakehouse tables in the same workspace?

   A. FROM <lakehouseName>.<schemaName>.<nameOfTable>

   B. FROM <schemaName>.<nameOfTable>

   C. FROM <lakehouseName>.<nameOfTable>

   D. FROM <nameOfTable>

3. What display() capability shows data distribution in preview data for all columns?

   A. Inspect

   B. Table

   C. Chart

   D. Distribution

4. What library can render already prebuilt Power BI reports in notebook?

   A. sempty

   B. reportrender

   C. powerbiclient

   D. powerbireports

Thought experiment answers

1. The answer is **C**. `summary=True` is a secondary parameter for the `display()` function, and it displays a table of columns with their data types and the number of unique and missing values. If the user selects any column, it will also show the summary statistics of a column.

2. The answer is **A**. To receive data from a different lakehouse or warehouse in the same workspace, it is necessary to provide the name of an item, a scheme where you want to get the table, and the table name.

3. The answer is **A**. Inspect can be turned on from Table view, which shows data distribution for all columns. It also shows missing, unique, and invalid values in particular columns.

4. The answer is **C**. The **powerbiclient** library contains the `Report()` function, which can render an existing report in a workspace. This library also contains the function `QuickVisualize()`, which can create an automatic report from a DataFrame.

CHAPTER 5

Exam DP-600: Implementing Analytics Solutions Using Microsoft Fabric updates

The purpose of this chapter

For Chapters 1 through 4, the content should remain relevant throughout the life of this edition. For this chapter, we will update the content over time. Even after you purchase the book, you'll be able to access a PDF file online with the most up-to-date version of this chapter.

Why do we need to update this chapter after the publication of this book?

- To add more technical content to the book before the next edition is published. This updated PDF chapter will include additional technology content.

- To communicate detail about the next version of the exam, to tell you about our publishing plans for that version, and to help you understand what that means to you.

- To provide an accurate mapping of the current exam objectives to the existing chapter content. Although exam objectives evolve and products are renamed, most of the content in this book will remain accurate and relevant. The online chapter will cover the content of any new objectives, as well as provide explanatory notes on how the new objectives map to the current text.

After the initial publication of this book, Microsoft Press will provide supplemental updates as digital downloads for minor exam updates. If an exam has major changes or accumulates enough minor changes, we will then announce a new edition. We will do our best to provide any updates to you free of charge before we release a new edition. However, if the updates are significant enough in between editions, we may release the updates as a low-priced standalone e-book.

If we do produce a free updated version of this chapter, you can access it on the book's product page. Simply visit *MicrosoftPressStore.com/ERDP600/downloads* to view and download the updated material.

About possible exam updates

Microsoft reviews exam content periodically to ensure that it aligns with the technology and job role associated with the exam. This includes, but is not limited to, incorporating functionality and features related to technology changes, changing skills needed for success within a job role, and revisions to product names. Microsoft updates the exam details page to notify candidates when changes occur. If you have registered this book and an update occurs to this chapter, you will be notified by Microsoft Press about the availability of this updated chapter.

Impact on you and your study plan

Microsoft's information helps you plan, but it also means that the exam might change before you pass the current exam. That impacts you, affecting how we deliver this book to you. This chapter gives us a way to communicate in detail about those changes as they occur. But you should keep an eye on other spaces as well.

For those other information sources to watch, bookmark and check these sites for news:

Microsoft Learn: Check the main source for up-to-date information: *microsoft.com/learn*. Make sure to sign up for automatic notifications at that page.

Microsoft Press: Find information about products, offers, discounts, and free downloads: *microsoftpressstore.com*. Make sure to register your purchased products.

As changes arise, we will update this chapter with more details about the exam and book content. At that point, we will publish an updated version of this chapter, listing our content plans. That detail will likely include the following:

- Content removed, so if you plan to take the new exam version, you can ignore this content when studying.
- New content planned per new exam topics, so you know what's coming.

The remainder of the chapter shows the new content that may change over time.

News and commentary about the exam objective updates

The current official Microsoft Study Guide for the DP-600 Implementing Analytics Solutions Using Microsoft Fabric exam is located at *learn.microsoft.com/en-us/credentials/certifications/resources/study-guides/dp-600*. This page has the most recent version of the exam objective domain.

This statement was last updated in May 2024, before the publication of *Exam Ref DP-600 Implementing Analytics Solutions Using Microsoft Fabric*.

This version of this chapter has no news to share about the next exam release.

Updated technical content

The current version of this chapter has no additional technical content.

Objective mapping

This *Exam Ref* is based on the topics and technologies covered on the exam but is not structured based on the specific order of topics in the exam objectives. Table 5-1 maps the current version of the exam objectives to the chapter content, allowing you to locate where a specific exam objective item is covered without having to consult the index.

TABLE 5-1 Exam objectives mapped to chapters

Exam Objective	Chapter
Plan, implement, and manage a solution for data analytics	
Plan a data analytics environment	1
■ Identify requirements for a solution, including components, features, performance, and capacity stock-keeping units (SKUs)	
■ Recommend settings in the Fabric admin portal	
■ Choose a data gateway type	
■ Create a custom Power BI report theme	
Implement and manage a data analytics environment	1
■ Implement workspace and item-level access controls for Fabric items	
■ Implement data sharing for workspaces, warehouses, and lakehouses	
■ Manage sensitivity labels in semantic models and lakehouses	
■ Configure Fabric-enabled workspace settings	
■ Manage Fabric capacity	
Manage the analytics development lifecycle	1
■ Implement version control for a workspace	
■ Create and manage a Power BI Desktop project (.pbip)	
■ Plan and implement deployment solutions	
■ Perform impact analysis of downstream dependencies from lakehouses, data warehouses, dataflows, and semantic models	
■ Deploy and manage semantic models by using the XMLA endpoint	
■ Create and update reusable assets, including Power BI template (.pbit) files, Power BI data source (.pbids) files, and shared semantic models	
Prepare and serve data	
Create objects in a lakehouse or warehouse	2
■ Ingest data by using a data pipeline, dataflow, or notebook	
■ Create and manage shortcuts	
■ Implement file partitioning for analytics workloads in a lakehouse	
■ Create views, functions, and stored procedures	
■ Enrich data by adding new columns or tables	

Exam Objective	Chapter
Prepare and serve data	
Copy data	2
■ Choose an appropriate method for copying data from a Fabric data source to a lakehouse or warehouse	
■ Copy data by using a data pipeline, dataflow, or notebook	
■ Add stored procedures, notebooks, and dataflows to a data pipeline	
■ Schedule data pipelines	
■ Schedule dataflows and notebooks	
Transform data	2
■ Implement a data cleansing process	
■ Implement a star schema for a lakehouse or warehouse, including Type 1 and Type 2 slowly changing dimensions	
■ Implement bridge tables for a lakehouse or a warehouse	
■ Denormalize data	
■ Aggregate or de-aggregate data	
■ Merge or join data	
■ Identify and resolve duplicate data, missing data, or null values	
■ Convert data types by using SQL or PySpark	
■ Filter data by M formula language	
Optimize performance	2
■ Identify and resolve data loading performance bottlenecks in dataflows, notebooks, and SQL queries	
■ Implement performance improvements in dataflows, notebooks, and SQL queries	
■ Identify and resolve issues with Delta table file sizes	
Implement and manage semantic models	
Design and build semantic models	3
■ Choose a storage mode, including Direct Lake	
■ Identify use cases for DAX Studio and Tabular Editor 2	
■ Implement a star schema for a semantic model	
■ Implement relationships, such as bridge tables and many-to-many relationships	
■ Write calculations that use DAX variables and functions, such as iterators, table filtering, windowing, and information functions	
■ Implement calculation groups, dynamic strings, and field parameters	
■ Design and build a large format semantic model	
■ Design and build composite models that include aggregations	
■ Implement dynamic row-level security and object-level security	
■ Validate row-level security and object-level security	
Optimize enterprise-scale semantic models	3
■ Implement performance improvements in queries and report visuals	
■ Improve DAX performance by using DAX Studio	
■ Optimize a semantic model by using Tabular Editor 2	
■ Implement incremental refresh	

Exam Objective	Chapter
Explore and analyze data	
Perform exploratory analytics	4
■ Implement descriptive and diagnostic analytics	
■ Integrate prescriptive and predictive analytics into a visual or report	
■ Profile data	
Query data by using SQL	4
■ Query a lakehouse in Fabric by using SQL queries or the visual query editor	
■ Query a warehouse in Fabric by using SQL queries or the visual query editor	
■ Connect to and query datasets by using the XMLA endpoint	

Index

D

DAX, continued

X-Y-Z

Plug into learning at

MicrosoftPressStore.com

The Microsoft Press Store by Pearson offers:

- Free U.S. shipping

- Buy an eBook, get multiple formats – PDF and EPUB – to use on your computer, tablet, and mobile devices

- Print & eBook Best Value Packs

- eBook Deal of the Week – Save up to 60% on featured title

- Newsletter – Be the first to hear about new releases, announcements, special offers, and more

- Register your book – Find companion files, errata, and product updates, plus receive a special coupon* to save on your next purchase

Discounts are applied to the list price of a product. Some products are not eligible to receive additional discounts, so your discount code may not be applied to all items in your cart. Discount codes cannot be applied to products that are already discounted, such as eBook Deal of the Week, eBooks that are part of a book + eBook pack, and products with special discounts applied as part of a promotional offering. Only one coupon can be used per order.

 Pearson

Hear about
it first.

Since 1984, Microsoft Press has helped IT professionals, developers, and home office users advance their technical skills and knowledge with books and learning resources.

Sign up today to deliver exclusive offers directly to your inbox.

- New products and announcements

- Free sample chapters

- Special promotions and discounts

- ... and more!

MicrosoftPressStore.com/newsletters

 Pearson

www.ingramcontent.com/pod-product-compliance
Lightning Source LLC
Chambersburg PA
CBHW080153060326

40689CB00018B/3958